Socratic Rationalism and Political Philosophy

D1545954

Socratic Rationalism and Political Philosophy

An Interpretation of Plato's *Phaedo*

Paul Stern

State University of New York Press

Published by
State University of New York Press, Albany

© 1993 State University of New York

For information, address State University of New York
Press, State University Plaza, Albany, N.Y., 12246

Production by Dana Foote
Marketing by Theresa A. Swierzowski

Library of Congress Cataloging in Publication Data

Stern, Paul, 1953–
    Socratic rationalism and political philosophy : an interpretation
of Plato's Phaedo / Paul Stern.
        p.   cm.
    Includes bibliographical references and index.
    ISBN 0–7914–1573–2 (hard : alk. paper).—ISBN 0–7914–1574–0
(pbk. : alk. paper)
    1. Plato. Phaedo.   2. Immortality (Philosophy)   3. Death.
4. Socrates.   I. Title.
B379.S74   1993
184—dc20   92–32010
                                                            CIP

10 9 8 7 6 5 4 3 2 1

CONTENTS

V. Socrates' Final Teaching

VI. Conclusion

To my parents,
Bernard and Sara Stern

ACKNOWLEDGMENTS

This book began as a dissertation under the guidance of Joseph Cropsey, Nathan Tarcov, and David Bolotin in the Department of Political Science at the University of Chicago. Whatever is worthwhile in the book began from reflections initiated by Joseph Cropsey's inspiring classes on Plato. In those classes, I received a gift beyond measure, nothing less than the foundation for a lifetime of reflection. Nathan Tarcov read the dissertation with his characteristic care and penetration. In so doing, he gave me an understanding of the requisite standard of clarity and precision. It was my good fortune that David Bolotin was a visiting professor at Chicago while I was completing the dissertation. Professor Bolotin generously agreed to serve on the dissertation committee. His enlightening comments and challenging questions have guided the subsequent revisions on the manuscript. A remarkable teacher, Richard Zinman of James Madison College, Michigan State University, introduced me to Platonic political philosophy. I continue to look to him as a standard of teaching and thought.

For their friendship and for the conversations that helped me to understand the *Phaedo* better, I thank John Cook, Don Brand, Paul Franco, and, above all, Leonard Sorenson, whose love of rational inquiry is unparelleled. Jean Yarbrough, Gerald Mara, Mary Ann McGrail, Christopher Colmo and the other reviewers for the State University of New York Press made many useful comments on the manuscript.

I have benefitted from the support of my colleagues, Nick Berry, Gerard Fitzpatrick, and Steve Hood at Ursinus College. I also want to thank my former colleagues at Kenyon College, especially Peter Ahrensdorf, a fellow student of the *Phaedo*.

To my wife, Lisa, I owe an incalculable debt. I would simply not have been able to complete this project were it not for her encouragement, her confidence in me, and her love. My brother, Dr. Edward Stern, was a constant source of support throughout the writing of the manuscript. My first and greatest debt is to my parents to whom I dedicate this book.

Ursinus College has provided generous financial support through its Faculty Development Committee. An earlier version of some of the ideas in chapters 4, 5, and 6 can be found in "Antifoundationalism and Plato's *Phaedo*," *The Review of Politics,* Spring, 1989.

Introduction

The Issues of the *Phaedo*

I undertake this study of the *Phaedo* in order to understand the rationalism of Plato's Socrates. It is a striking feature of the contemporary intellectual situation that a study such as this can be of more than simply historical interest. But the question of the character of Socratic rationalism has been made a vital question by those contemporary thinkers, beginning with Nietzsche, who doubt the availability of objectively valid answers to our deepest questions—who doubt, in other words, that reason can guide life. These thinkers point unambiguously to Socratic rationalism as the source of all rationalism in Western philosophy. In Nietzsche's words, it is Socrates whose influence "down to the present time and even into all future time, has spread over posterity like a shadow that keeps growing in the evening sun."[1] Clearly, if we wish to render an independent judgment of the contemporary rejection of rationalism, we must begin with an understanding of Socratic rationalism. A sketch of Nietzsche's charge against Socrates will enable us to see that the *Phaedo* in particular is a crucial piece of evidence in the contemporary trial of Socrates.

According to Nietzsche, it was Plato's Socrates who first expressed the central assertion of Western philosophy, classical as well as modern. This assertion declares that the whole of nature is intelligible or that we live in a cosmos and not a chaos.[2] Nietzsche refers to this contention as

the profound *illusion* that first saw the light of the world in the person of Socrates: the unshakable faith that thought, using the thread of causality, can penetrate the deepest abysses of being, and that thought is not only capable of knowing being but even of *correcting* it.[3]

The famous Ideas—eternal, unchanging, and incorporeal intelligibles overseen by the Idea of the Good—constitute this metaphysically certain teleological order.[4] Yet, this metaphysical certainty—so the argument goes—was *asserted* rather than proved. The rationalism of Plato's Socrates rests on an arbitrary choice and is therefore, at bottom, irrational.

The evidence for the assertoric character of Socratic doctrine lies especially in the unbridgeable chasm between the intelligible order and the corporeal, contingent world of our experience, the world which was supposed to be explained.[5] Plato's Socrates merely posits the distinction, in Nietzsche's terms, between "the true world" and "the apparent world," the former characterizing the realm of the intelligible and the latter the world in which we live.[6] In revealing Plato's dogmatism, Nietzsche exposes Socratic doctrine as a projection of a new world aimed at providing the "metaphysical comfort" of cosmic support for the human good, support that is uncertain in the world of our experience. For Nietzsche, the view of Plato's Socrates dictates a preference for that which is universal, rational, and unchanging over that which is individual, instinctual, and transient. This preference, in Nietzsche's view, amounts finally to an unfounded preference for wisdom over life.[7] It is a preference that is purportedly revealed most clearly in the words Socrates utters as he dies:

> Concerning life, the wisest men of all ages have judged alike: *it is no good*. Always and everywhere one has heard the same sound from their mouths—a sound full of doubt, full of melancholy, full of weariness of life, full of resistance to life. Even Socrates said, as he died, "To live—that means to be sick a long time: I owe Asclepius the Savior a rooster."[8]

It is in the *Phaedo* that we find the portrayal of that day on which Socrates uttered his last words. And, appropriately, it is in this dialogue that Socrates confronts the issue that is central to Nietzsche's judgment of Socrates, the issue of the relation between wisdom and life. For this reason, then, an understanding of the *Phaedo* can assist us in rendering an independent judgment of the contemporary verdict concerning rationalism.

The most conspicuous aspect of the *Phaedo* would seem to substantiate Nietzsche's judgment of Socrates. Pervading the dialogue are those two doctrines, the doctrine of the Ideas and the doctrine of the Immortality of the Soul which, taken together, seem to confirm that Socrates does indeed prefer the "true world" of the eternal intelligibles to the transient "apparent world." The Ideas are those intelligibles which must be unchanging in order to fulfill the requirements of perfect wisdom. If these objects of knowledge were themselves subject to change, they would stand in need of further explanation with reference to whatever was responsible for their alteration. In order that they be regarded as unchanging, the Ideas must also be thought to be incorporeal, because all that is corporeal is subject to change. Given this unchanging, incorporeal character, the question arises as to how we who are (at least in part) corporeal can communicate with such intelligibles. All that is corporeal impedes the establishment of any such connection so that our apprehension of these eternals must occur independent of sense-perception, of desire, of pleasure, of all that is inseparable from our existence as embodied living beings. Accordingly, it is maintained that we can only hope to attain this perfect or (to use the oft-repeated word of the *Phaedo*) "pure" wisdom when we are free of the body—that is, when we are no longer alive. Here lies the link between the doctrine of the Ideas and the doctrine of the Immortality of the Soul. The immortal—and thus unchanging and eternal—soul is the vehicle by which otherwise transient humans may commune with the unchanging intelligibles.

It is, indeed, difficult to see in these doctrines—doctrines so familiar to us as Socratic—anything other than a preference for wisdom even at the cost of abandoning this world. Yet, as I will argue, this portrayal of Socrates as an otherworldly, life-denying philosopher conflicts with another famous characterization of Socratic thought, a characterization that is also present in the *Phaedo*. I refer to the traditional view that Socrates was the first of the humanizing philosophers.[9] While the *Phaedo* is famous as a locus classicus of Socrates' otherworldliness, it is also in this dialogue that we find Socrates' equally famous recommendation that philosophic inquiry begin with speeches, with what people say about themselves and their world. This recommendation occurs in the intellectual autobiography that Socrates recounts in the waning moments of his life. In this autobiography, Socrates articulates the inadequacies of his predecessors which led him to adopt a new approach to the study of nature, an approach which, again, far from being otherworldly, begins with what humans say about the world. It is this approach that Socrates terms his "second sailing," a designation indicating that his method is a next-best alternative to his original mode of investigation.

One purpose of my study is to show that the true character of Socratic rationalism is to be found in his "second sailing" rather than in the doctrines of the Ideas and the Immortality of the Soul.[10] In fact,

Socrates' alteration of philosophy follows from his recognition of the insuperable difficulties of the view that promises perfect or pure wisdom. More specifically, I will show that Socrates himself realizes the inadequacy of the proofs of immortality, that indeed the several proofs, precisely in their defectiveness, constitute a meditation on those limits that our being embodied, living beings impose on our understanding. Socrates knows full well the obstacles that life poses for the possession of perfect wisdom. Thus, as far as he knows, there exists only an imperfect harmony between the human mind and perfect intelligibility as represented by the Ideas. Nor does he think that we can know that these obstacles are overcome in another existence. Whatever might be said concerning other forms of rationalism, Socratic rationalism does not rest on the dogmatically asserted foundations attributed to it by its critics. To the extent that this is the case, the characterization of Socratic thought by Nietzsche and other antifoundationalist thinkers is more aptly described as a caricature.

But then the question arises, if Socratic rationalism is not based on the Ideas, then on what does Socratic rationalism rest? One possible response to this question, offered by other commentators (who are likewise dubious concerning the link between the Ideas and Socrates' "second sailing") runs as follows. Socrates proposes that we begin rational inquiry with speeches or with opinions. These speeches express the natures or the class-characters of the things we perceive. In this view, the essence of Socratic rationalism lies in the discernment of that which is general, the class-characters, in the particulars we see before us and in the *techne* by which further ascent from these speeches is accomplished—namely, the hypothetical method.

I will argue that this is a true but partial explanation of the character of Socratic rationalism because this explanation does not adequately appreciate the extent to which the relationship between the particular and the general, especially regarding human beings, is problematic. More specifically, the foregoing response fails to confront that question of which Socrates is all too aware on his death day: how can the life of reason be justified in the face of our manifest ignorance evident not only in the limited knowledge contained in our necessarily tentative speeches, but also in the manifest ignorance about ourselves, highlighted most dramatically by oncoming death? In order to confront this question we must focus on the knowledge which leads Socrates to conclude that philosophic investigation ought to begin with an examination of what people say.[11]

The second purpose of my study is precisely to elicit the underlying knowledge that grounds Socratic rationalism. I will argue that Socrates' new approach to nature is grounded not in some comprehensive view of the whole of nature nor in our apprehension of the natures of things.[12] Rather, Socratic rationalism is grounded in knowledge of the human situation, in the self-understanding that Socrates gained through the recognition of the inadequacy of his previous views. Socrates sees that if we lack perfect wisdom, if we must therefore ascend toward such a comprehensive view, self-understanding—knowledge of ourselves and our relation to nature as a whole—becomes crucial. Only in this way can the philosopher acquire that wisdom, *phronesis*, that can substantiate philosophy as a choiceworthy way of life. But furthermore, such self-understanding constitutes that wisdom, *sophia*, that is available to beings such as ourselves. It is this wisdom that provides the ground of Socratic rationalism in the sense of serving as a criterion for knowledge.

The traditional view is therefore correct when it sees in Socrates' alteration of philosophy the origin of political philosophy.[13] For political philosophy is the study of human affairs, a study which, as I will argue, is inseparable from the consideration of humanity's place in the whole. Political philosophy is first taken seriously not only to provide a practical defense of philosophy against the political community but also to provide a ground for the activity of philosophy itself. Political philosophy remains at the heart of philosophic investigation because it provides the best access to the knowledge of nature itself.

Socratic rationalism does not then rest on some implausible or anachronistic cosmology. Nor does it squint at those difficulties which have led contemporary thinkers to abandon rationalism. Beginning as it does in self-understanding, it is especially aware of those aspects of humanity, exemplified by the questions surrounding our mortality, that seem to resist rational scrutiny. Plato's Socrates, I will argue, offers the possibility of a rationalism that denies the existence of an insuperable distinction between life and wisdom. The two purposes of my study, then, lead to the conclusion that Socratic rationalism—political philosophy in its original form—may yet offer a basis for rational inquiry that is both nondogmatic and nonarbitrary.

Mode of Interpretation

I follow the view that every detail in the Platonic dialogues, the form as well as the content, is a product of—and thus illustrative of—Plato's intention. An interpretation of a dialogue must therefore heed not only the arguments but also the ways in which the arguments are defective. It must heed as well the nondiscursive elements of the dialogue such as the setting and the characters of the interlocutors, including that of Socrates.[14] This principle directs the primary effort of interpretation toward explaining the coherency of the dialogue as a whole. Thus, for example, in the face of what are widely agreed to be the *Phaedo*'s defective arguments for immortality, an attempt must be made to explain the positive teaching that Plato means to convey through these particular defects. Moreover, any plausible interpretation must also explain why Plato chooses to convey his understanding through such roundabout means.

I adopt this principle as the safest—that is, the least distorting—of interpretive principles. Other principles of interpretation, such as those that refer to Plato's intellectual development or to his historical context, preclude from the start the most serious consideration of Plato's thought. In order to judge Plato's development, we would have to know better than does Plato the issues with which his work is concerned. But if we already possess such knowledge, then we need hardly turn to Plato for guidance concerning these issues. Moreover, even if our *goal* is simply to understand what Plato thought about these issues, we cannot rely on an interpretive principle—the developmental principle—that assumes that we already have grasped the ultimate character of Platonic thought. Finally, interpreting Plato as a product of his historical context is to adopt in advance Nietzsche's view of one of the most important issues in his quarrel with Plato. The principle I have adopted is itself open to dangers, principally the danger of idiosyncratic and implausible interpretations. But these can be corrected through the marshalling of evidence either to support or to contravene such interpretations. This potential damage is far less costly than an interpretive principle that would deny the ultimate significance of the work from the start.

I want to say one more thing about interpretation that bears specifically on the *Phaedo*. As is clear from what I have said, my interpretation of this dialogue depends on a distinction between two incompatible teachings in the dialogue. I would not characterize this distinction as one between the surface and the depths because the expressions of both teachings are often both on the surface—as exemplified above all in the tension between the otherworldliness of the doctrine of the Immortality of the Soul—and the this-worldliness of Socrates' intellectual autobiography. The latter teaching is less evident, however, in that it requires us to take seriously Socrates' qualifications of his teaching which are explicit but not emphasized. Specifically, we must appreciate the extent to which these qualifications, when taken together, amount to a rejection rather than a mere modification of the main teaching. We shall heed those heterodoxical statements which Socrates states explicitly for all to hear only if we are not deafened by our expectations of what Socrates will say. The distinction to which I am pointing then might best be characterized as a distinction between more and less reflective readings of the dialogue. The plausibility of any reading depends upon the interpreter making as clear as possible the path that runs between the less reflective and the more reflective interpretation. Again, this requires that the interpreter show in each case the *necessity* for traversing this path as well as the reason that Plato has chosen to present his teaching so as to require such interpretation.

Two recent book-length studies of the *Phaedo,* Kenneth Dorter's *Plato's "Phaedo": An Interpretation* and Ronna Burger's *The "Phaedo": A Platonic Labyrinth,* share the same interpretive premises as the present study.[15] These works reflect an unusually acute sensitivity to the dialogue form, and I have learned much from these authors. Yet, as Burger suggests in distinguishing herself from Dorter, agreement on the importance of the dialogue form does not produce a necessarily uniform result; the need for interpretation carries with it the possibility of a variety of such interpretations.[16] I would distinguish my own interpretation from both Dorter and Burger on the basis of the observation made by David Bolotin that they "do not pay . . . sufficient attention to the surface of the dialogue."[17] What Bolotin means by this is that they do not take as seriously as they should Socrates' own expressions of his fears and doubts regarding death. While I think that this criticism applies somewhat more strongly to Dorter than to Burger, my attempt has been to exceed both authors in giving such expressions their full weight.

This leads to a substantive difference between our interpretations. In my view, Socrates sees the status of philosophic activity as much more fundamentally challenged by those uncertainties introduced into human existence by the fact of death. Philosophy is more questionable for Socrates than appears in either Dorter's or Burger's interpretation and thus more in need of a defense. I see Socrates' "second sailing" as indicating that the character of such a defense rests on an understanding of the human situation. Therefore, I also emphasize more than does either Dorter or Burger the traditional view which saw in Socrates' alteration of philosophy the origin of the philosophic treatment of human affairs—the origin of political philosophy.

The Defense of Socrates

Overview

(57a1–70c3)

The opening scene presents a conversation between Echecrates and Phaedo, in which Phaedo relates the story of Socrates' death day. Following this initial conversation, Phaedo's narration brings us into Socrates' cell. The question of the meaning that death holds for the philosopher becomes explicit. Socrates abruptly offers the startling advice that the one who engages worthily in philosophy ought to be willing to die, although it is prohibited that the philosopher take his own life. This strange advice elicits from two young men in attendance, Cebes and Simmias, the demand that Socrates defend his willingness to die in terms of both the prudence and the justice of this disposition.

Socrates rests the most prominent and paradoxical claim of his ensuing defense—that the philosopher prepares for and welcomes rather than fears death—on the character of the philosopher's goal, pure wisdom. The object of such wisdom is eternal, unchanging, and thus incorporeal. It follows that we can only communicate with such wisdom when we are likewise incorporeal. Socrates' definition of death points to the locus of the necessary link between humanity and pure wisdom: death, we are told, is nothing but the separation of body from incorporeal soul. Therefore, in pursuit of the goal of pure wisdom, the philosopher scorns his embodied existence and yearns for death.

In order to show the desirability of the next world, however, Socrates must portray the character of this world in all its defectiveness. Accordingly, running alongside his otherworldly presentation is a characterization of the philosopher's earthly existence. This dual presentation gains in importance when we recognize that Socrates' defense of his willingness to die, his evocation of the rewards awaiting the philosopher in the next world, is explicitly mythic; at the conclusion of his defense, the crucial question of whether the soul does in fact endure after death remains entirely unresolved. Thus, the search for the proof of the immortality of the soul begins. But should this search prove futile, we, as well as the interlocutors, will have to reconsider the alternative posed by Socrates' defense: whether philosophy is defensible if it is not oriented on pure wisdom—that is, whether it is defensible even in the face of those abiding uncertainties and contingencies that Socrates portrays in his characterization of our earthly existence.

This alternative is present from the start of the dialogue in the conversation between Phaedo and Echecrates. It is expressed in the tension between the certain and comprehensive teachings to which Phaedo and Echecrates adhere and those doubts and uncertainties that they cannot help but feel in the face of death.

The Opening Scene

As the dialogue opens, we break into the conversation between Phaedo and Echecrates which has apparently been going on for some time. The conversation occurs a considerable time after the death of Socrates in the city of Phlius. Phaedo, who was present at the momentous event, now movingly recalls for Echecrates the drama of Socrates' death day. We must follow this opening conversation carefully in order to determine why Plato introduces his portrayal of this most solemn event through such a conversation between two such individuals in this particular setting.

Though neither Phaedo nor Echecrates is particularly well known, we do know that Phaedo is the future founder of a philosophical school, and Echecrates is himself the founder of a Pythagorean school of philosophy.[1] In fact, the conversation occurs at Echecrates' school in Phlius, a city associated with the Pythagoreans, the original philosophical sect.[2] A strict discipline seems to prevail at this school, for while there are members of Echecrates' school in attendance, only the master speaks. The students, not willing or not permitted to ask questions, look on in silence.

At the urging of Echecrates, Phaedo begins to depict the scene of Socrates' death as well as the swirl of emotions he felt on that unforgettable day. For his part, Echecrates seems slightly more interested in who was there than in Phaedo's heartfelt description of his feelings as he shared Socrates' last moments. Phaedo responds to Echecrates' interest by listing those present at that philosophic convention. The representatives of many sects attended Socrates in his cell (59b5–c6).[3]

The characters of Phaedo and Echecrates, as well as the circumstances in which Phaedo recounts his story, seem designed to place us in the atmosphere of the philosophic sect. The first impression of philosophy that we receive in this dialogue, whose centerpiece is Socrates' story of his own philosophic career, is that philosophy involves adherence to a group united by a shared understanding. The *Phaedo* as a whole evokes this view of philosophy as sect-like and even dogmatic as it shows Socrates delivering his final word on such famous Socratic doctrines as the Ideas, the Immortality of the Soul, and Recollection, often without the support of arguments. Indeed, early in the dialogue Socrates goes so far as to present what he explicitly labels a *doxa*, a set of beliefs to be held by all "genuine philosophers." Undoubtedly, the *Phaedo*'s reputation as a key source for understanding Socratic thought must derive in part from the doctrinal, not to say dogmatic, character of the dialogue.

The background of Socrates' main interlocutors also contributes to this aspect of the dialogue. Phaedo's narration has Socrates conversing almost entirely with Simmias and Cebes, two young students of Pythagoreanism. They are specifically identified as students of Philolaos, the man who was supposed to have transmitted the written report of Pythagoreanism to Plato.[4] Given this background, the young men would be familiar with those doctrines expressed in the *Phaedo* such as the doctrine of the soul as a harmony, the doctrine of rebirth, and the doctrine of purification, as well as the use of arithmetical examples at crucial points in the argument. The Socratic doctrines of Recollection and the Immortality of the Soul also prove to be very congenial to Simmias and Cebes because of their training, as does the doctrine of the Ideas; both Pythagoreanism and what might be called Socratism embrace the notion that the sensible world requires explanation through reference to nonsensible entities which both *are* more emphatically and which are more knowable than the sensible world.[5] In the *Phaedo,* then, Plato portrays what Aristotle will state—namely, the kinship of Pythagoreanism and Socratism.[6] That affinity is dramatized when Echecrates responds to Phaedo's evocation of his pleasure in remembering Socrates by saying: "You certainly have an audience of the same mind" (58d7–8). More substantively, it is evident when Simmias and Cebes assent easily and eagerly to the Socratic doctrines of the Ideas, the Immortality of the Soul, and Recollection (65d6, 72e3–73a2, 74b1, 92c10–d10).

But what does Plato intend by providing an atmosphere redolent more of pious orthodoxy than of searching inquiry? Some scholars see the *Phaedo* as a tribute to Socrates, that tribute apparently being facilitated by showing Socrates in the midst of those who admire him.[7] But apart from the fact that the one whose admiration would be most worthwhile is absent, it is hard to believe that the acclaimed artistry of Plato would have contrived such feeble means to this end; surely, the stature of Socrates cannot be enhanced by achieving the concurrence of those so ready to concur. More appropriate might have been an engaging account of Socrates' activity of cross-examination which engages us precisely because of the searching character of Socrates' thought, his obstinate refusal to find satisfaction with the certainties that satisfy most people.

Another, more prevalent explanation of the atmosphere of the *Phaedo* is the claim that the dialogue intends to set out in clear and final form the positive doctrine of Socrates.[8] Once again, lending credence to this claim is the fact that the *Phaedo* does present an unusually dogmatic Socrates in which he casts his positions in the most extreme terms. Perhaps in no other dialogue does Socrates separate so starkly the body from the soul or the Ideas from the sensible world.

Yet, this dogmatism is not the whole story of the *Phaedo*. Socrates himself will question crucial components of what might be considered to be his own orthodoxy. And at the conclusion of his last argument, he makes emphatically clear the need for further investigation of the doctrine of the Ideas. Where there exists so much ground for agreement, such questioning must raise a further question about the ground of that agreement. It is critical to see that, given the kinship of Socratism and Pythagoreanism, this means to raise a question about not only Pythagorean but also Socratic orthodoxy. In this light, I suggest that the Pythagorean atmosphere of the dialogue, in providing a surface of unquestioning agreement, makes all the more impressive the questioning of the orthodox view.[9]

The questioning begins early on. Even in the opening scene certain dramatic details suggest reservations with the life of philosophic orthodoxy. Plato quietly passes judgment on the life of the disciple by having Phaedo twice mention that individual, Apollodorus, who embodies all that is objectionable about philosophical discipleship (59a9, 59b6). This sorry man is familiar to us from the *Symposium*, where he is seen to glory in his obsequious and overheated devotion to Socrates.[10] Even those as devoted as Echecrates and Phaedo hold their noses at the mention of his name; Phaedo dismisses him by saying: "You know the man and his manner" (59b1). The rare occurrence of Plato's own name in this context also bears on Plato's judgment of discipleship. Phaedo mentions Plato's own absence from the philosophic convention gathered in Socrates' cell (59b10). It is startling to learn that the reason for Plato's absence is not particularly compelling nor even very clear (59b10). It is certain that one such as Apollodorus would have moved mountains in order to be counted among those in Socrates' cell, whereas Plato goes out of his way to suggest his distance from Socrates.[11]

Present in the opening pages of the *Phaedo,* then, is not only the philosophic sect, a group organized around a certain orthodoxy, but also (albeit less prominently) a questioning of philosophy so conceived. But why should philosophic orthodoxy as such be questionable? We can begin to answer this question as Phaedo and Echecrates address the issue that inevitably pervades this dialogue, the issue of death. Understanding this issue, we can gain greater clarity on the question with which we began: why does Plato choose to begin the dialogue with this setting and with these characters?

Echecrates asks Phaedo why Socrates died when he did, and Phaedo reports the Athenian belief that made necessary the delay in Socrates' execution. The Athenians annually send a ship to Delos in accordance with their vow to Apollo that they would do so if the ship carrying Theseus and the seven pairs of youths to Crete were saved.[12] Phaedo continues:

> Once they've started the mission, it is their law that the city shall be pure during that period, which means that the city shall put no one to death until the ship has reached Delos and returned; and this sometimes takes a long time, when the winds happen to hold them back (58a10–c5).

Phaedo indicates his view of the status of this belief by referring to the real cause as chance (58a6, b8, c3). Echecrates does not stop to comment on Phaedo's answer but, rather, changes the subject. Yet, we must pause to reflect on Phaedo's answer.

Phaedo, it must be remembered, has already heard those extensive discussions of death which he is about to tell Echecrates.[13] But now, when asked about death—specifically, about the death of the one he so admires—Phaedo explains Socrates' death as being a matter of chance. It is troubling to see that this is all he can say about death even after having heard the forthcoming discussion. Now it may well be that we will understand the forthcoming arguments more fully than does Phaedo and therefore ascertain the perfectly rational explanation of the character of death. But we must also consider the possibility that the element of chance in our explanations of death is ineradicable.

It is this troubling possibility that bears on the questionability of orthodoxy as such. For if this possibility should prove to be the case, then we must wonder how much we do understand of ourselves and our situation if the death of even so important a human as Socrates must be attributed, at least in part, to chance. If we cannot fully explain death—when it will come, whether it is the end of our existence (for Phaedo remains uncertain about this too)—how far do we really understand our human existence? With such matters remaining in doubt, we must wonder whether the members of this or that or any philosophic sect possess a certain and comprehensive understanding of the human situation. Perhaps it is in reaction to just such considerations that Echecrates—the member of that sect which claimed to explain all in terms of number, which claimed in other words to possess such a teaching—changes the subject.

But obviously this cannot be the final response to the issue that death raises for philosophy. We cannot legitimately resolve difficulties or uncertainties by ignoring them or defining them away. Admittedly, the temptation to do so is great, especially for one whose way of life testifies to his desire for a certain and comprehensive teaching. But if nothing else, our self-concern, our concern for the ultimate disposition of our lives, makes it difficult to ignore this crucial human question or to paper it over with abstract propositions.[14] In focusing on these adherents of the philosophic sect, Phaedo and Echecrates, Plato dramatizes the conflict between such a certain and comprehensive teaching and that which above all threatens it—namely, our incomplete understanding of ourselves, represented most dramatically by death.

Clearly this conflict between abstract propositions and the individuals who express them—as well as Plato's invitation to reflect on this conflict—exists, at least potentially, in each of his works. For Plato of course writes dialogues or dramas in which distinct characters do and say distinct things, rather than treatises in which only Plato speaks. But this conflict may be at a peak in the *Phaedo*, wherein that most abstract of the philosophical schools—those who held all to be reducible to number—provides the background for the event that most emphasizes the irreducible particularity of each human, death.[15] The literary reputation of the *Phaedo* lends support to this point. Among the Platonic dialogues, only the *Symposium* rivals the *Phaedo* in being considered a literary masterpiece. Commentators who thus celebrate the *Phaedo* call attention to its drama—

the deeds and the motivations for those deeds portrayed therein—rather than its speeches.[16] In fact, it is not unusual to find in a single commentary both praise for the drama and a critique of the arguments.[17]

This tension between the arguments of the *Phaedo* and the deeds it portrays is evident also in the discord between, on the one hand, those motives that lead Phaedo to tell his story, and on the other, the most prominent arguments presented in the dialogue. We hear the story of Socrates' death because Echecrates wants to hear it and Phaedo is eager to tell it. Echecrates makes clear that he is especially pleased to learn the story from Phaedo. In response to Echecrates' question—"Were you there with Socrates yourself?"—Phaedo assures Echecrates that he was an eyewitness: "I was there myself, Echecrates"(57a1–3, a4). Echecrates wishes to know especially about Socrates' death day rather than the many other days that Socrates spent in jail. Although he knows that Socrates spent many days in jail before his death, Echecrates asks only about the last day (58a3–5). He does not ask about the undoubtedly interesting conversations Socrates must have had on previous days. Concerning this last day, Echecrates wishes to know what was done at least as much as what was said (57a5–6, 58c6–8). His questions—for example, his unremitting inquiry as to who was present—seek the circumstances peculiar to the event. He repeatedly urges Phaedo to "tell all" (58d2–3, d8–9). Phaedo, who is always pleased "to remember Socrates," vows to try to tell all—that is, to tell the story, the words and deeds, of this unique individual, Socrates, as he faced this unique event, death (58d4–6, 59c8).

Although such an interest in death and dying is not unusual, it is remarkable in light of those arguments Phaedo has already heard. Specifically, this interest runs athwart the argument that considers humans as reducible to incorporeal souls in order to explain the soul's communion with the incorporeal intelligibles. Such a teaching would be quite congenial to a Pythagorean such as Echecrates, but it is difficult to reconcile this teaching with Phaedo's and Echecrates' intense interest in the death of this particular individual, Socrates, whose story Phaedo is so eager to relate. Why should death be of interest if we know quite well what the posthumous career of the human soul will be? And why should we care about Socrates' deeds if, as humans, we are each reducible to incorporeal soul? Whatever it is about us that is particular or individual, and whatever concerns our action, would ultimately be of little interest in light of our common, incorporeal, and thus indistinguishable nature.[18]

Yet the emphasis on something other than the incorporeal soul is also evident in Phaedo's explanation of his own emotional state as he sat on a stool in Socrates' cell. Phaedo confides that he was affected not only by Socrates' words but also by the manner of the man (58e4). Socrates' manner, his deeds, seem finally to have affected Phaedo more than his words. Phaedo indicates that what pleasure he felt on this day was not due to being occupied with philosophy even though that is what they were engaged in (59a2–3).

Again, concerning the interest in Socrates' death, such a reaction as Phaedo describes is not at all uncommon. We might even call it natural. But this is precisely the point: the tension between the philosophic doctrines and the characteristically human behavior portrayed in the dialogue suggests the inadequacy of these very doctrines. In other words, Phaedo's philosophic training does not seem to reach certain essential human questions. Despite having heard Socrates' speeches concerning immortality, Phaedo continues to express uncertainty as to the disposition of humanity after death. Phaedo can only conjecture that those qualities which Socrates exhibited—fearlessness and nobility—would be rewarded in the afterlife (58e3–59a1). Having heard Socrates' argument, Phaedo is still not sure what human qualities, if any, are favored by the superhuman. Phaedo is still unsure of humanity's place in the whole, and thus he is unsure of something crucial concerning humanity. Accordingly, Plato has Phaedo say that it is precisely his reflection on himself, his being affected by his feelings at Socrates' death— an unusual mixture of pleasure and pain, laughter and tears—that causes him to wonder (59a4–6, 58e1).[19]

The first word of the dialogue, *self*, points to the source of Phaedo's wonder.[20] Although in other dialogues the word *soul* is defined to reflect the complex character of humanity, in the *Phaedo* the most explicit teaching pushes soul in the direction of an incorporeality akin to the eternal intelligibles. Of course, a leading question of the dialogue is precisely what is meant by soul. But it is significant that Plato begins the dialogue with a word that pertains emphatically to humans as embodied intelligences, as individuals.[21]

The lengthy opening scene makes clear that in order to hear the story of Socrates' death, we must depend on one particular individual with his own particular capacities; Phaedo promises to "try" to tell all that occurred that day (58d4–5, 59c8–d1). Moreover, Phaedo must rely on his sense-perception and memory as well as on his reason (58d7–9).[22] Apparently, there is not an 'Idea' of this event accessible to the pure mind alone. Perhaps to make us more acutely aware of the way in which our particularity impinges on our understanding, Plato names the dialogue after Phaedo, the only dialogue in the Platonic corpus named for its narrator.[23] The view of the self, of humans as embodied intelligences, is evident in other aspects of the dialogue. It is as a self that one can ingest poison and undergo fundamental changes; it is as a self that a feeling of pleasure can give rise to a desire to speak; it is as a self that one prefers the report of someone who was there to that of one who was not.[24] It is as selves that we are dependent on all the vicissitudes of chance mentioned in these opening passages, all those preconditions of this conversation which emerge in the opening scene: the chance blowing of the winds involved with the Athenian belief, the chance that Athenians happen to allow conversation in the cell of the convicted. Above all, however, it is as selves that we fear death. Being aware of our existence as individuals and being aware of the finitude of our existence, we fear death and long for assurance that we in fact do endure beyond death, that we are in harmony with that which endures.

But is there available a *logos* of this self that is the source of Phaedo's wonder? Or does there exist an Idea in which the self participates?[25] Can that certainty that Echecrates repeatedly asks of Phaedo be supplied in the case of human beings (57b1, 58d2)? Is the self reducible to body or number, to a certain, unproblematic teaching? In the *Phaedo*, we are given a *muthos* about Socrates rather than a *logos*—a remembrance of Socrates conveying not only his words but also his deeds. Again, is that because a *logos* of the self, of human existence in all its complexity, is not available? If it is not available, must we then conclude that philosophy, which aims at a comprehensive understanding, is futile?

Such questions are raised by the conflict between philosophic doctrine and human existence, between wisdom and life, evident especially in those such as Phaedo and Echecrates, as well as in the two young students of philosophy, Simmias and Cebes. These questions also make evident why Plato might give more prominence to the philosophy of the sect, which at least promises a certain teaching. But the questions that the sect attempts to obscure ultimately surface, driven by the hopes and fears of the individual characters. In raising this issue of the meaning for philosophy of the human experience of the human, the opening scene—the particular conversation of these particular individuals—prepares us for the issue that Socrates now explicitly introduces. He introduces the same issue in its most telling form—the issue of the relationship between philosophy and death.

Socrates' Poetic Defense of Philosophy

The view of humanity implicit in the opening remarks of Phaedo and Echecrates emerges also in Phaedo's initial presentation of Socrates' death day. Socrates addresses his first words to his old acquaintance, Crito. In the dialogue bearing his name, Crito appears as a man whose world is circumscribed by self-concern or, at most, by concerns arising out of self-concern. In the *Crito,* his attempt to persuade Socrates to flee his cell relies on arguments appealing to matters of reputation, wealth, and family. Even those arguments based on friendship have as much to do with Crito's own loss as with Socrates' well-being.[26] In short, Crito seems impervious to concerns that transcend the self. Judging from Crito's activity in the *Phaedo,* it is not at all clear that Socrates' attempt to elevate Crito's gaze to the concerns of community and divinity has been successful. In this dialogue, as in the *Crito,* Crito argues for the basis of self-concern; he argues for the mere prolongation of one's life as good.

Crito's characteristic view finds expression also in Socrates' first words in the dialogue which deal with his own family. It is in Socrates' cell that Xanthippe, his wife, makes the only 'live' appearance by a woman in the Platonic corpus. Socrates' first words in the dialogue are directed at Crito but they concern Xanthippe who, apparently sharing Crito's view, laments Socrates' approaching death. Socrates himself seems not to be immune from the view that mere life is good: Xanthippe appears carrying the aged Socrates' infant son.[27] The existence of his infant son bears witness that Socrates has engendered life beyond what might be considered civic duty and certainly beyond what is compatible with the forthcoming depreciation of terrestrial existence.

Crito's prominence subsides and, having been dismissed by Socrates, Xanthippe is led away. With Xanthippe's exit there occurs the first in a series of dismissals by Socrates.[28] In each of these dismissals, Socrates advises the students of philosophy gathered in his cell to dismiss from their minds aspects of what we now might call the 'real world.' They are told to neglect, for example, the power of the legal authority and the power of the many. They are advised to disdain the usual pleasures of food, drink, and sex. And Socrates dismisses his own family in order to spend much of his remaining time with his philosophically inclined acquaintances. These dismissals give to Socrates' most explicit teaching those characteristics attributed to it by both his old accuser, Aristophanes, and his new accuser, Nietzsche. Socrates' teaching appears to be otherworldly, ascetic, antipolitical, and in general depreciative of human existence.[29] But the view represented by Xanthippe and Crito reverberates throughout the dialogue as a counterpoint to this world-denying character. And, at the end, Xanthippe returns along with Crito and his characteristic advice. Then it will be clear that Crito, like Phaedo, remains unconvinced even by the speeches of the man they both so admire.

Plato does then appreciate the power of the view that mere life itself is desirable. Recognizing this makes more emphatic the need to consider his intention in having Socrates oppose this natural desire. Why should Socrates only suggest the prosaic while proclaiming the perverse? We can go further in answering this question than we have done thus far by considering why Socrates' audience of young students of philosophy might require such a teaching. To do so, we must first trace the path by which Socrates comes to offer a defense of the philosopher's stance toward death.

With Xanthippe being led away, Socrates rubs his leg where the fetters had been. His first speech to those gathered in the cell concerns the "wondrous" relationship between pleasure and its supposed opposite, pain (60b4). For Socrates, as for Phaedo, human existence in its complexity is a cause for wonder. In order to 'explain' this perplexing character of our human existence, Socrates concocts a myth in the manner of Aesop. The myth relates how the god had wanted to reconcile pleasure and pain but, failing this, he fastened their heads together, thus insuring that anybody visited by one is later visited by the other (60b1–c7).

The character of opposites, a theme present in Socrates' first speech, is a theme running throughout the *Phaedo*. The questions raised about our existence both here and in the hereafter are cast in terms of life versus death, body versus soul, corporeal things versus incorporeal Ideas. The *Phaedo* certainly provides support to the view expressed by such thinkers as Nietzsche and Heidegger that the Platonic world is one rent by an irreducible dualism. Moreover, as Socrates' first speech manifests, in the *Phaedo* we are led to believe that these oppositions exist also within human beings. How can we give a unified account of the whole when it is characterized by such divisions? How can we give a unified account of a being as complex as we are? In the face of such perplexity concerning human existence, Socrates refers to a trans-human and, in this case, mythic explanation in the manner of Aesop. But is there no rational explanation available? Questions such as these might have followed Socrates' opening remarks. They will surface later in the dialogue. However, Socrates lets the students of philosophy find their own way (or fail to find their own way, as the case may be) to these questions.

Cebes does not now raise these questions, nor does he even inquire into the substantive theme of Socrates' comments, the nature of pleasure and pain. He focuses on the form of Socrates' opening remarks rather than the content. Something about the form of Socrates' comments must trouble Cebes deeply because he does not follow the lead of the one he so admires. Instead, Cebes swears by Zeus and blurts out his question, a question asked him by several people among whom was Evenus, the sophist and poet. He asks Socrates: "What had you in mind . . . in making them [poems] up after you'd come here, when you'd never made up anything before?" (60d3–4).

What would lead Cebes to focus on Socrates' jail-cell poetizing? Clearly, both Cebes and Simmias have a high regard for Socrates. We have testimony to this effect in the *Crito* where Crito names these two young men as willing to supply the bribes necessary to secure Socrates' escape.[30] Because Socrates has declined the offer, they have undertaken the journey from Thebes to be present in Socrates' final days. Their high regard for Socrates must stem in part from their philosophic interest. But that philosophic interest is at the very least supported by their admiration, not simply for Socrates' arguments but for Socrates as a model of the philosophic life. In short, Socrates is their hero. Yet at this solemn time of his life, Socrates seems cavalier about his devotion to philosophy, apparently abandoning—or at least ignoring—it in favor of poetry. We pay special attention to the last words and deeds of the dying with the thought that at the end of life something about human life as a whole might be revealed. But what Cebes sees when considering Socrates' last days is Socrates' divergence from his lifelong pursuit of philosophy.

What is Cebes to think? Even apart from Socrates' poetizing, he must be wondering whether it is in fact the case that philosophy is the most choiceworthy way of life.[31] Indeed, all those gathered in the cell must be uneasy about this question. They have been visiting Socrates in his cell for quite some time, "gathering at the court-house where the trial was held" prior to entering the cell (59d2–3). Throughout this time, then, they have had a constant and stinging reminder of the questionability of the philosophic way of life from the standpoint of the political community as well as the dangers that can follow therefrom. Cebes and the others must be wondering: is the philosophic life sufficiently choiceworthy as to risk the dangers and dishonor inseparable from that life? In the face of these tormenting doubts, they now learn that their hero, who is about to be martyred on the altar of philosophy, spends his last moments setting the tales of Aesop to verse!

The impertinent questions of Evenus add to Cebes' anxiety. And Cebes is sure that Evenus will ask his taunting questions again (60d5–7). Evenus is certainly the right man to ask Cebes about Socrates' activity. In the *Apology*, Evenus is said to be knowledgeable in virtue both of human being and citizen (20b8–c1). In this regard, he rivals or exceeds Socrates, whose claim to wisdom is much more moderate. This expert on human virtue generously takes time out of his busy schedule to point out to Cebes the discrepancy in his hero's way of life: Socrates' lifelong devotion to philosophy fades in the face of impending death. Socrates might have responded to Cebes' question that he really does not care what Evenus, whom Socrates had mocked in the *Apology,* might think. However, to put it in the words that Cebes uses, Socrates seems to want Cebes to "have an answer" for Evenus when he asks his questions again. Socrates' concern is perhaps less for the sake of his own reputation than for Cebes' sake, that he will be able to defend the philosophic life not primarily to Evenus but, above all, to himself.

Yet, in what follows, Socrates makes the defense of the philosophic life, if anything, more difficult. More specifically, Socrates' explanation of his poetizing makes philosophy even more questionable than it already was. This explanation expresses his uncertainty concerning the impetus for his philosophizing. He reveals that his philosophizing rests on nothing more than a certain interpretation of a recurring dream that had bid him to "make music and work at it" (60e6–7). Throughout his life Socrates had interpreted this dream as encouragement to philosophizing. But now, in the face of death, Socrates allows for an alternate interpretation. In order to be safe, Socrates responds to the dream by practicing what he calls demotic music (60d8–61b1). An explanation of this kind can only exacerbate the anxiety felt by Cebes as a potential philosopher.

Socrates' report of his dream is, I think, a playful way of introducing a very serious doubt concerning the ground of philosophy, a doubt that arises from our uncertainty about the gods and what they may desire from us. My interpretation of the importance of this dream illustrates a significant difference between my general understanding of the *Phaedo* and that held by both Burger and Dorter. Both Burger and Dorter think that the problem raised here concerns the means by which philosophy must deal with the unphilosophic rather than a doubt about philosophy itself.[32] This seems to me to assume what is in question. As becomes clear in what follows, at stake is the solidity of the ground of the philosophic life in the face of the uncertainties raised by our mortality.

Socrates concludes his explanation instructing Cebes to give Evenus the following advice: "Come after me as quickly as he can" (61b8). This advice pulls Simmias into the conversation. He blurts out, "What a thing you're urging Evenus to do, Socrates! I've come across the man often before now; and from what I've seen of him, he'll hardly be at all willing to obey you" (61c2–5). Although he attributes this reaction to Evenus, Simmias himself is clearly aghast. Simmias' attachment to this world rivals that of Evenus who, to repeat, would "hardly be at all willing" to follow Socrates' advice—hence, Simmias' outburst. Socrates coolly retorts that his advice is for one "who wishes to engage worthily in this thing (*prag-*

matos)"—namely, philosophy (61c8–9).[33] Socrates has certainly given Cebes something to say to Evenus about the philosophic life, but it is not at all clear how his advice would aid Cebes if Cebes' desire is to defend the philosophic life to Evenus. For after having portrayed his own cavalier attitude toward philosophy, Socrates adds that philosophy makes perhaps the greatest possible demand on a human: it demands no less than that one prefer death to life.

Socrates has used Cebes' original question as an opportunity to add to the doubts of those in the cell concerning the philosophic life. In this way he makes those in attendance feel more acutely the need for a defense of the philosophic life. Furthermore, in joining genuine philosophic activity to a preference for death over life, Socrates prepares a confrontation between philosophy and the source of the greatest doubt concerning the attainment of its goal, if that goal is understood as a certain and comprehensive view of the whole. For death, as it eludes our understanding, seems an insuperable limit on what we can claim to know. The question of death acts as a solvent of certainty. In what follows, Socrates sharpens this conflict as he focuses the discussion on the following question: what does substantiate the philosophic life in the face of the undeniable uncertainties surrounding the afterlife? Socrates moves the potential philosophers, the philosophic disciples, and the hangers-on gathered in his cell closer to a confrontation with the question of the existence, if any, of a rational defense of the philosophical life.

Socrates now attaches an addendum to his advice to Evenus: "Perhaps, though, he won't do violence to himself; they say it's against divinity" (61c9–10). In their responses to Socrates' addendum, we can begin to see the respective characters of his two main interlocutors. For his part, Cebes points out the problem that this addendum raises: how can suicide be forbidden, yet it's the case that the philosopher would be willing to follow the dying? (61d3–5). In response to Socrates' question as to whether he and Simmias had heard about these matters from Philolaus, Cebes replies: "No, nothing certain, Socrates" (61d8). Cebes' express desire is for certainty. But surprisingly, Cebes focuses his desire for certainty on the prohibition against suicide. The direction of Cebes' interest points to a distinction between the characters of Cebes and Simmias that emerges through the course of the dialogue. Unlike Simmias, Cebes seems—initially at least—to be bothered less by having to abandon life than by being prevented from achieving the certainty that he identifies with the goal of philosophy. Given Cebes' leading desire, he automatically puts himself in the place of the philosopher whose desire is thwarted. He is less concerned that the fulfillment of this desire may require death. In his desire for comprehensive certainty, Cebes comes closer to a world-denying posture than does anyone else in the dialogue. As we will soon see, he is clearly distinguished in this regard from the disposition of Simmias.

Socrates responds to Cebes' inquiry by describing the problematic situation of the philosopher and affirming the ban on suicide:

> Perhaps, it will seem a matter of wonder to you if this alone of all things is absolute and it never happens as other things do sometimes and for some people that it is better for a man to be dead than alive and for those for whom it is better to be dead, perhaps it seems a matter of wonder to you if for these men it is not pious to do good to themselves but they must await another benefactor (62a1–7).[34]

Socrates has described a situation in which it is doubtful that there are any absolutes, but if there is one it may be that it's never better for anyone to be dead rather than alive. Yet, if even this is not absolute—and thus for some it *is* better to be dead than alive—it is a matter of wonder if such people are prohibited from achieving this good through their own efforts.

In response to this description, Cebes chuckles and utters an expletive in his native dialect, perhaps in the way that we revert to slang in the face of unfathomable or troubling truths about the ways of the world (62a8–9). Socrates recognizes that it may appear unreasonable that the philosopher, who according to Socrates ought to hasten into death, should be thus prohibited. He offers two possible explanations of this situation in order to clarify the prohibition. The explanations share the view that we are subordinate to beings higher than us—namely, the gods. The first of these doctrines, which Socrates calls a mystery doctrine, characterizes our lives as lived in a prison from which we must not escape. This Socrates calls a lofty idea and one not easy to penetrate. He extracts a somewhat milder account from this first one: gods care for us and we are their possessions. As such, we should not remove ourselves from their care without permission (62b1–9).

By mollifying the first mythic explanation, Socrates introduces to Cebes the possibility that the situation of the philosopher is not quite so desperate as first appears: there is, perhaps, a ruling intelligence. In this way, Socrates deflects the world-denying Cebes from thoughts of suicide to the prior question which he so readily passed over—namely, why should one want to die? Socrates has put the issue in terms of what is reasonable and thus brings Cebes to judge the issue in terms of the desires of the type of individual he so admires, the wise man. His success is seen by the fact that Cebes himself now articulates the reason why the wise man would not wish to die: the wise man should least of all desire to leave the tutelage of gods who are, as such, undoubtedly wiser than the wisest of men (62c9–e7). Although Cebes' initial reaction to the prohibition against suicide revealed him as one who is inclined to put the desire for certainty even above the desire for this life, he now argues on the premise that life is, in fact, good. After Cebes presents his view of the question, Socrates shows pleasure and praises him for his dogged pursuit of the argument (62e8–63a1). At least part of Socrates' pleasure might also be at the effectiveness of his own rhetoric in moderating Cebes' otherworldliness.

No such moderating is required in Simmias' case. While Cebes' other arguments do not touch Simmias, the idea that Socrates is abandoning the world—and especially his acquaintances—captures Simmias' attention. Specifically, Simmias applies to himself what Cebes had said about Socrates leaving his wise masters. Socrates is abandoning the gods but—more to the point—he's leaving "us" (63a8). Whereas Cebes finds Socrates in a contradiction and considers his action imprudent, Simmias charges Socrates with injustice. Simmias' language reflects this concern. Referring to Socrates' hope that the good will fare better than the wicked after death, Simmias asks Socrates whether he means "to go off keeping this thought to yourself or would you share it with us too? We have a common claim on this good as well" (63a4–9).

Socrates does not praise Simmias' ability to follow arguments. Rather, he takes what Simmias is saying as an accusation and proposes that he deliver a defense, one more convincing than that delivered to the Athenians. Socrates states:

> Now then, with you for my jury I want to give my defense, and show with what good reason a man who has truly spent his life in philosophy feels confident when about to die, and is hopeful that, when he has died, he will win very great benefits in the other world (63e8–64a3).

Socrates' startling advice to Evenus, then, has the result of raising the urgent need for a defense of the philosophic life. Specifically, through the linkage of philosophy and death, it has caused the young men to wonder whether the philosophic life, or any life for that matter, has cosmic or divine support—surely an appropriate topic of reflection for these potential philosophers. The topic is also appropriate to the present circumstances. The question of humanity's situation in the whole properly arises in the context of the *Phaedo,* the context of Socrates' imminent death. Throughout our lives, we may wish to know or to be assured that we are living in accordance with whatever order transcends us, but it is especially in the face of death that this desire becomes acute. We desire assurance that, contrary to appearances, this transient human existence does indeed share in some permanent order that favors our particular way of life.

For the one who wishes to know how things really are, such assurance would seem to require a demonstrable proof as its basis. Such a one could hardly be satisfied with, for example, the story the Athenians tell themselves concerning Theseus' slaying of the minotaur in order to reassure themselves that they have some control over death. Yet it is easy to understand the motives that incline us to hold such beliefs. For who has not felt the attraction of such stories in response to our desires for certainty, for justice, or for consolation in the face of lost loved ones—or simply to respond to the simple and powerful desire to endure as oneself? Each of these, separately and in combination with one another, lead us to accept accounts of the next world that may answer our desires but which we do not know to be true. Precisely because of this almost irresistible attraction, the potential philosopher must strive unwaveringly to resist the temptation to be satisfied with unfounded accounts of the next world. He must do this if he wants to be one who knows for himself—that is, if he wishes to fulfill his potential.

Given that this is the case, it is startling to discover that Socrates' defense of the philosophic life is itself avowedly mythic. Its mythic character can be confirmed by a brief consideration of some of the details of Socrates' presentation.

Socrates does not offer a simply rational account of the situation in which the philosopher finds himself. In speaking of this situation, Socrates calls what he is doing "mythologizing," speaking "only from hearsay" (61e2, 61d9). It is clear that he uses the word *mythologizing* in a precise manner—that is, in its distinction from reasoning. Plato makes this evident by having Socrates correct Cebes when he refers to Aesop's stories as *logoi.* In this context, Plato has Socrates go out of his way to show that he is aware of the distinction between myths and *logoi* (compare 60d1 and 61b4). In addition, Socrates begins his defense in a haze of uncertainty. When he relates that after his death he expects to join the company of good men, Socrates immediately adds that this is a contention he would not "affirm with absolute conviction" (63c1–2).[35] And concerning whether he will enter the presence of gods who are good masters, he says: "Be assured that *if there's anything* I should affirm on such matters, it is that"(63c3–4, emphasis added). Socrates, who is not famous for bowing to tradition, finally relies for his assurance on "what we've long been told" (63c6). His entire claim about the next world is cast as a hypothetical. Accordingly, Socrates repeatedly insists that his goal is persuasion (63b4, 69e3–4). And as he makes clear in the *Phaedrus*, persuasion is accomplished by what is likely, a characterization he twice applies to his forthcoming speech (63e9, 69d9).[36] Socrates does not say that either his goal or his standard is truth.

Apparently, Socrates' unwonted poetizing is not limited to setting other men's tales to verse. Socrates' mythologizing includes, and indeed rests upon, his doctrine of the Ideas.[37] This doctrine will itself partake of a mythic character, for although the intelligibles are not equivalent to the good and wise gods who are supposed to rule our terrestrial existence, they are not simply distinguishable from "other gods" who exist in the next world (63b6–7). Socrates' myth concerns the rule of reason in the whole of nature, and in light of this rule it lays down a way of life for these students of philosophy. The notion that reason rules does not rest upon reasoned arguments, however, but rather upon a belief in the existence of an otherworldly realm wherein the defects of this world, especially the defects related to intelligibility, are rectified. This realm awaits the one who has practiced philosophy aright on earth. On this understanding, then, the terrestrial activity of philosophy is not a good in itself but is rather a means to this otherworldly reward.

On the basis of the foregoing description, it is evident that Socrates contrives what deserves to be called a religion. It is a religion for philosophers, complete with a dogma and purificatory rites.[38] But to utter this phrase, 'religion for philosophers,' is to realize the paradox at hand. Philosophy is that endeavor that aims to provide a rational account of the whole of nature. To regard philosophy as itself resting on nonrational grounds must, therefore, be to strike at its every heart.[39] Philosophy based on belief, like philosophy based on a dream, is not philosophy at all. Socrates' poetic defense of philosophy thus raises the question as to whether Nietzsche is not right in maintaining that Socrates' deathbed poetizing reveals Socrates' doubt that reason is ultimately adequate to guide life.[40] According to this reading, Socrates' death-row poetry is tragic poetry. It is the only kind of poetry appropriate to the absurd condition of the human situation, a condition that only becomes apparent to Socrates when faced with his own imminent death. Also pertinent to this claim is, I think, the great prominence in the *Phaedo* of Apollo, that god whose oracle depreciated human wisdom, for Socrates has made vivid the question of what we truly can claim to know about ourselves.[41]

The poetic character of Socrates' defense has raised this troubling question: if Nietzsche's characterization of the dying Socrates is inaccurate, if Socrates does not finally lose confidence in reason, why does he not share the source of his confidence with those gathered in his cell? An answer to this question may lie in the possibility, admittedly paradoxical, that Socrates sees a need to speak, rhetorically even or especially to those who sympathize with him.[42] We are used to the Platonic notion that reason must accommodate itself to unreason in the speeches the philosopher makes to the city; as Socrates indicates in the *Apology*, to say publicly what is true concerning justice inevitably results in the destruction of the truth-teller.[43] But does this need for unreason, for dissembling speeches, also include the speeches the mature philosopher makes to the partisans of philosophy and to potential philosophers? A brief comparison of Socrates' present audience and his audience in the *Apology* serves to sharpen the point.

In the *Apology*, Socrates defends himself before judges who are his fellow citizens. He defends himself against the two charges of impiety and corruption of the youth. Plato indicates that the former is the more serious charge and that it can be traced to the charges of atheism made against Socrates by Aristophanes in the *Clouds*.[44] In the *Phaedo*, however, Socrates has as his judges a group consisting in part of foreigners, each of whom is at least favorably disposed toward, if not a student of, philosophy. In addition, having received a capital sentence, Socrates is beyond any punishment the city might exact from him. One might think that he is, in a sense, a philosopher beyond the need to dissemble. In this, his partially self-imposed defense, given indoors before his philosophical friends, we might have expected Socrates to have been somewhat more candid concerning the teaching attributed to him by Aristophanes.[45] Yet not only does Socrates not deny the existence of the gods, he does not even raise their existence as a question. He does speak of his familiar doctrines, but only in the aforementioned amalgam of myth and philosophy. Socrates voluntarily imposes on the free speech of philosophical friends the constraints of the courtroom.

Apparently, then, Socrates considers philosophy to require nonrational means in its presentation even to its partisans. That it should suggests that not only is the existence of the individual philosopher in the political community problematic but that philosophy itself is problematic.

As we have seen, the problematic character of philosophy is present at the very start of the dialogue. The degree to which the questions surrounding death elude certain philosophic doctrine is evident in the ex-

change between Phaedo and Echecrates. We have seen in Socrates' explanation of his novel poetizing an expression of uncertainty as to what the
superior powers desire from us. This uncertainty cannot help but have an
absolutely serious meaning in light of his impending death. As Socrates
acknowledges in the *Apology,* death raises the question of the limits of human knowing precisely by tempting us to forget such limits, to claim to
know what we in truth do not know.[46] But in the face of such limits, lacking any certain knowledge of what, if anything, awaits us after death, the
philosophic life itself becomes questionable. It becomes questionable with
regard to its possibility and with regard to its desirability. For the one
leading such a life, above all, would want to *know* whether the goodness of
the philosophic life can be defended, whether it truly satisfies a human
desire. He or she would want to know whether it is more choiceworthy
than competing ways of life. Is the philosophic life the right way of life,
the way of life sanctioned by that which transcends individual humans, or
is the verdict against Socrates by Athens but a foretaste of the unending
punishment to be visited upon the philosopher in the next world?[47] The
answers to these questions depend on whether philosophy is possible—
that is, whether through reason alone we have access to knowledge of ourselves and our world sufficient to respond to these questions. Without
this knowledge, it seems that the philosophic life rests on belief or faith.
As such, it is indistinguishable from any other way of life. Or rather, it is
more contemptible; its pretensions to knowledge in this light are at the
very least boastful but at worst subversive in making dubious the arguments of authoritative piety without making available an alternative basis
for moral and political life.

    In the presentation to follow, Socrates does pose the question of the
ground of the philosophic life. But the most manifest aspect of his teaching responds to desires other than the desire to know. It responds to
Cebes' desire for the certainty, or perfect wisdom, that will allow him to
make prudent decisions, and it responds to Simmias' desire for justice, for
getting his due.[48] Socrates posits rather than proves the existence of the
guaranteed path to perfect wisdom; he asserts that it can be earned by a
proper way of life in this world and that the one so living gains perfect
wisdom after death. His defense involves a depreciation of life. For it sees
the great impediment to comprehensive wisdom as lying in corporeality,
and life is inseparable from body. The manifest character of the defense is
illustrated nicely by still another of Socrates' dismissals. Immediately prior
to Socrates' offering his defense, he recognizes Crito, and Crito reports
the poisoner's warning that through talking too much people get overheated and this affects the action of the poison (63d5–e2). This activity of

the soul, thought and speech, has an affect on the body. Socrates tells Crito to tell the poisoner, "never mind" (63e3). Again, the most manifest aspect of the subsequent teaching considers the affect of our corporeality on us as something that we can dismiss as we journey to another, better world.

But the ultimate purpose of Socrates' defense is not to console the bereaved, to reassure the doubters, or to hearten the fearful. Socrates' defense is characteristically just; he gives to each individual what each most needs, and this includes the potential philosophers who may hear his words firsthand or in a later retelling. Socrates does respond to the desire to know. In this mythic presentation, Socrates does not simply obscure the problems that make his mythic presentation necessary.[49] He presents the next world as the remedy for the defects of terrestrial human existence, and in so doing, he does not avoid presenting those defects, those limitations on human existence, that make the next world desirable. In this way, Socrates' defense brings these potential philosophers face-to-face with the difficult alternative that characterizes the issue of the philosopher's situation in the whole. Either they must have proof that we do somehow survive in the next world or, failing this, they must face these defects and ask how philosophy is possible in the face of the limits on our understanding.

Appreciating the difficulties involved in such an alternative, we can begin to appreciate why Socrates should provide a mythic presentation *especially* to this audience. Socrates' religion for philosophers can serve to support the idea that reason can and should govern, not only in the world, but within each individual. He can maintain that the governance of passion by reason earns as its reward the goal of the philosopher—pure wisdom. In this manner, Socrates' defense conveys a benefit to the extent that it is beneficial that reason strive to rule passion. Moreover, the philosopher can derive benefit from those who become partisans of reason. While the sect may not represent the highest form of philosophy, the philosopher may receive aid from the partisans of philosophy as Socrates surely did. And as Plato makes evident in the *Phaedo,* the sect may provide the vehicle for the transmission of philosophic understandings.

Socrates' religion for philosophers thus allows those who can be satisfied with such a presentation to avoid the troubling issues surrounding the question of the trans-human support for the philosophic life. Yet it also provides the appropriate introduction to these same issues. For in order to consider the question of the ground of the philosophic life free from any prejudices, one must set aside for a moment those desires that incline us to perceive certainty where none yet exists. It would require a willingness to place the desire to know how things truly are—however this might be—above our most cherished hopes for ourselves. As we will see, the issue of the philosopher's stance toward death is the most severe test of this willingness.

Whether any of those in Socrates' cell are ready to meet this challenge is not yet clear; the drama of the *Phaedo* involves precisely the manner in which Simmias and Cebes comport themselves in the face of this challenge. It is clear, however, that Socrates cannot meet the challenge for anyone else. At most, he can provide the path to it, a path strewn with comforting answers as obstacles in the way of a direct confrontation with the central issue. Only those whose desire to know prevents them from remaining satisfied with the inadequate answers along the path will find their way to this choice.[50] For this reason, Socrates' defense also serves as an appropriate—and just—introduction to the question of the ground of the philosophic life.

In sum, Socrates' defense permits the potential philosopher to face the issues necessary for him to face if he is to fulfill that potential. The mythic character of Socrates' defense—especially given the present audience—is an index of the difficulties and dangers involved in facing these issues. In considering his defense, then, we must bear in mind the reasons behind the need for dissembling before his present audience. Specifically, as we investigate Socrates' otherworldly presentation that follows, we will grasp his complete teaching only if we, like Socrates, keep our feet planted on the ground (61c10–d2).

Philosophy as Preparation for Death

At both the beginning and end of his present defense, Socrates invites comparison between this defense and the one delivered to the Athenians (63b5–6, 69e3–5). He suggests that there is a kinship between his private and his public defenses and that that kinship lies in the fact that the distinction between the philosopher and the many derives from their contrary postures toward death. But this claim seems curious. What is the possible political bearing of the seemingly private concern of how one faces death? For many of us, the link between politics and death sounds strange because we live in political communities that abjure consideration of the next world.[51] But this link is more intelligible for those communities that aim to provide a comprehensive guide for human life, as did Athens.

The issues of politics and death are in fact joined in the figure of Theseus, the founder of Athens, whose deeds Athens celebrates prior to

Socrates' execution. In her work, *On Revolution,* Hannah Arendt helps us to understand the links between Theseus, politics, and death. Arendt first quotes what she calls "the famous and frightening lines" of Sophocles' *Oedipus at Colonus:*

> Not to be born prevails over all meaning uttered in words; by far the second-best for life, once it has appeared, is to go as swiftly as possible whence it came.

She then draws the connection to Theseus and politics:

> There he [Sophocles] also let us know, through the mouth of Theseus, the legendary founder of Athens and hence her spokesman, what it was that enabled ordinary men, young and old to bear life's burden: it was the polis, the space of men's free deeds and living words, which could endow life with splendor.[52]

Politics, the life in and of the city, presented itself as the best possible remedy for the transiency of all human existence, the transiency that is the source of the tragic character of human life expressed in the lines of the chorus.[53] The transiency of individual human life could be remedied to some extent by earning immortal glory through participation in the enduring political community in the manner of Theseus, the founder of Athens, who is celebrated as one who "fought as few men have with danger and with death."[54]

In the *Apology,* Socrates presents quite a different view of the proper disposition toward death, a view that does not involve investing one's city and one's deeds with splendor out of a fear of oblivion. To quote the *Apology:*

> For to fear death, men, is in fact nothing other than to seem to be wise, but not to be so. For it is to seem to know what one does not know: no one knows whether death does not even happen to be the greatest of all goods for the human being.[55]

Socrates' "human wisdom," his resistance to thinking that he knows what he does not know, is expressed most clearly in his reluctance to succumb to the fear of death, a fear that presumes knowlege of what awaits us after death. This moderately skeptical stance raises the ire of his fellow citizens to the point of bringing about Socrates' execution. Socrates' human wisdom denies what all good citizens 'know'—namely, the orthodox teaching of their political community concerning the things rewarded and punished by the gods and concerning the afterlife. Such wisdom potentially undermines the belief that the gods are looking after our good both here and in the hereafter, that as individuals and as a community we have divine support for life in this world and in the next, and that therefore all that we care for—self, family, community—has abiding significance. The ire raised by Socrates' stance is directly proportional to the degree that the citizens require assurance in this regard. In response to this anger, Socrates was brought to trial for challenging the guarantors of these fundamental assurances, the gods, and he now awaits execution, having been found guilty of impiety. And although our community does not appeal to divine authority, it is not at all clear that we have dispensed with the personal need to feel that our lives are not merely transient. We can, I think, still appreciate the feelings of the Athenians when we experience the pain engendered by the questioning of our most cherished beliefs in this regard.

It is then appropriate to juxtapose Theseus, the founder of Athens, and Socrates with respect to the proper disposition toward death. This juxtaposition also makes intelligible the link between Socrates' public and private defenses. The different stances toward death go to the root of the difference between the philosopher and the political community. The distinction between the philosopher and all other people lies in the willingness of the former to face death in the way that Socrates does and the willingness of the latter to 'forget' this practice (64a5, 64b8). In drawing the connection to the *Apology,* Socrates reminds us how difficult and rare the philosophic life is, not simply because of its danger owing to the anger it engenders, but because of the requirement that the philosopher 'remember' what most would do almost anything to 'forget.'

In direct opposition to the desire of the many to evade death, Socrates defines philosophy as nothing but "practicing dying and being dead" (64a4–6). Drawing on Socrates' understanding in the *Apology,* we might surmise that this characterization of philosophy pertains precisely to the aforementioned refusal to think one knows what one does not know and to the fact that the unprejudiced examination of those views that respond to our fear of death are the severest test of this refusal. Yet precisely because of this difficulty, Socrates does not explicitly present the notion of philosophy as preparation for death in these terms. He explicates the notion of philosophy as preparation for death in terms of the posthumous reward that awaits what he calls the 'genuine philosopher' rather than in terms of knowing what one does not know (66b2). Being difficult and rare, the philosophic life is not for everyone, certainly not for everyone who calls himself a philosopher. Yet alongside his more explicit presentation, Socrates provides the outlines of the stance toward death evident in his speech in the *Apology*.[56] The difference between the two presentations emerges when we compare Socrates' advice to the "genuine philosophers" with Socrates' own philosophic practice.

In Simmias' response to Socrates' distinction, we see how far he is from facing up to the nearly superhuman demands inherent in the latter view of philosophy. Socrates addresses his speech to both Simmias and Cebes, but the promise that one who has spent his life in philosophy might earn very great benefits in the other world seems to attract Simmias more than Cebes—at least the promise cast in these terms. Accordingly, Simmias becomes Socrates' interlocutor throughout the defense. Simmias seems to believe that he belongs on the side of the philosophers rather than on the side of the many. Yet Simmias' response to Socrates' characterization of philosophy as preparation for death casts doubt on this self-evaluation.

Socrates' characterization elicits laughter from Simmias "even though I wasn't much inclined to laugh" (64a10–b1). Later, in Socrates' defense, Simmias *agrees* that it would be laughable for a philosopher to be resentful at death; however, he does not actually laugh as he does here (67e3). Simmias' laughter is prompted by the view of the many—a view which occurs to him spontaneously—that it

> is very well said of philosophers—and our own countrymen
> would quite agree—that they are, indeed, verging on death,
> and that they, at any rate, are well aware that this is what phi-
> losophers deserve to undergo. (64b2–6)

Evident even in this report of the many's view is that ridicule for the philosopher which could easily become contempt.[57] Simmias' avowedly unintentional laughter suggests that the view of the many strikes a chord with him, if only to the extent that he is not eager to spend his life absorbed by thoughts of death. Socrates denies Simmias' claim that the many truly apprehend the philosopher's stance toward death and says, "Anyway, let's discuss it among ourselves, disregarding them" (64c1–2). But we are left with the suspicion that, as long as Simmias is present, the view of the many will also be present. Not fully understanding the root of the distinction between the philosopher and the many, Simmias thinks it easy to traverse the gulf between the two.

Socrates begins his defense, which has the following arrangement. He first explains the obstacles that the philosopher's embodied existence places in the path to the attainment of perfect wisdom. This then leads to

Socrates' formulation of a *doxa* for genuine philosophers, an unrelenting diatribe against the evils of corporeality. Following the *doxa*, Socrates details what can be done in this life in order to have reasonable hopes for pure wisdom. Let us consider Socrates' defense in detail.

Having advised Simmias to bid farewell to the derisive many, Socrates asks him whether "we believe death is something" (64c2). In the exchange with Simmias, Socrates does not ask the characteristic Socratic question—what is death? The question of the status of death in fact haunts the proceedings and is still in doubt, at least for Socrates, in the final proof of immortality. Here Socrates simply posits a definition of death and asks Simmias whether "it is nothing other than this" (64c4). Socrates puts his points in the form of rhetorical questions, and Simmias finally gives his assent to the last of a series of uninterrupted questions. It is a most unpromising beginning for a serious investigation into the character of death. What follows does not improve on this beginning.

Socrates defines death as the separation of soul from body, "each having come to be separate alone by itself" (64c5–8). With this definition, Socrates assumes the existence of an entity called the soul which may exist independently of an entity called the body. The precise meaning of each of these entities remains uncertain, as does the nature of the whole whose decomposition is death.

At this point, Socrates could have moved directly to the argument that joins the incorporeal soul to the likewise incorporeal intelligibles. Instead, he asks Simmias' agreement to "further points" (64c10). These further points pertain to the earthly existence of the philosopher. But how can this existence matter, since on the basis of Socrates' definition of death all humans willy-nilly achieve the desired state of separation? Moreover, if the soul is absolutely separable from body, how could one's activities when embodied affect the incorporeal soul? Such questions derive from the more fundamental question of how one accounts for human life when one begins from the reduction of the human whole to contradictory opposites.

The requirements of pure wisdom as represented by the incorporeal intelligibles may well demand such a reduction. But Socrates' 'further points' show that he also wishes to speak of life, of the human whole, and in doing so he allows us to consider the tension between human life and the requirements of perfect wisdom. Specifically, Socrates presents the philosopher's life through a consideration of the stance that the 'genuine philosopher' ought to take with respect to the bodily pleasures, the 'bodily senses,' and the objects of knowledge themselves, the intelligibles. He thereby enables us to explore the problematic existence of the earthbound philosopher that makes him yearn for the next world. This yearning is then encapsulated in the *doxa* of the 'genuine philosophers.' My examination of Socrates' treatment of the philosopher's life will reflect the double aspect of Socrates' defense in considering both the promised satisfactions of the next world and the difficulties of the world of our experience. In order to do this, I will first recount Socrates' portrayal of the life of the members of the sect—the 'genuine philosophers' and the *doxa* which they are to believe—as these appear on a first reading without focusing on the complications of the position that Socrates articulates. Subsequently, I will formulate the view of the philosophic life that emerges when we give due weight to the qualifications and contradictions inherent in the presentation. This procedure will enable us to better appreciate each of the alternative views of philosophic endeavor—represented in the two meanings of philosophy as preparation for death—expressed in Socrates' defense.

Socrates secures Simmias' agreement to the contention that the true philosopher separates himself from the bodily pleasures of eating and drinking, sex, and bodily adornment, and that with respect to bodily pleasures in general, the 'genuine philosopher' is said to "disdain them, except insofar as he's absolutely compelled to share in them" (64e1). Simmias readily agrees to this connection between the philosophic life and asceticism, even though it has not been made clear why such a connection should exist.

Turning to the actual gaining of wisdom, it is claimed that here too the body places impediments in the way of our apprehension of wisdom, at least if we attribute the senses to the body as Socrates does. He asks:

> Do sight and hearing afford men any truth, or aren't even the poets always harping on such themes, telling us that we neither hear nor see anything accurately? And yet if these of all the bodily senses are neither accurate nor clear, the others will hardly be so. (65b1–6)

The soul attains its goal, again, only when it flees the body and its senses, this flight being complete only in death.

Socrates applies his teaching on the senses to the object of the philosophical quest. He refers not to what the many think or to what the poets say but to what "we say." When asked whether "we say that there is something just in itself" as well as beautiful and good, Simmias responds with great fervor, saying: "Certainly, we say this, by Zeus" (65d4–6). Socrates then asks, "Now did you ever yet see such things with your eyes?"(65d9).

Simmias emphatically denies that he has, and Socrates proceeds to draw the by-now-familiar conclusion that only if we lose the body and its senses can we hope to attain wisdom.

Socrates' locution for the intelligibles, the X-itself (*autē kath' hautēn*), conveys the notion that these intelligibles are *the* exemplars of the quality they name.[58] But it also conveys the separate status of the intelligibles. As Burnet notes, the use of *auto* in the technical sense is a development of *autos*, 'alone.'[59] And in the *Phaedo*, the use of 'alone' or 'itself' with reference to the intelligibles means 'separated off from any particular instances of the quality'—that is, 'separated off from anything corporeal.' This locution mirrors that used with reference to the soul's coming to be separated, alone, by itself, from the body (c4–8). Socrates' language thus prepares the conclusion that incorporeal, unchanging, pure wisdom can only be ascertained by that which shares its nature—the incorporeal, unchanging, pure soul. From what has been said, then, Socrates derives the conclusion that the only hope for pure wisdom lies in the next world when the soul will also be pure.

At this point, Socrates offers a *doxa* which, according to the master ironist, 'genuine philosophers' ought both to say and to think (65b1–3). It forms the binding credo of the sect of the 'genuine philosophers.' The *doxa* follows directly from all that has been said in that it responds to the genuine obstacles to the philosophic life just presented (66b1). It responds to the portrayal of the earthbound philosopher caught between the ridicule of the many and the futile pursuit of his object. The philosopher must appear ridiculous as he forgoes palpable pleasures for some invisible fantasy. And he must wonder at himself when he realizes the futility of pursuing perfect wisdom by the imperfect means of the embodied human mind.

The *doxa* holds that the body deprives the philosopher of the leisure necessary for his endeavor by such internal impediments as illness, desire, and the need for nourishment. In addition, in one of the few explicit comments on politics in the dialogue, Socrates blames bodily needs as the cause of war, which is certainly antithetical to the leisure required for philosophy. Socrates states:

> It's nothing but the body and its desires that bring wars and factions and fighting; because it's over the gaining of wealth that all wars take place and we are compelled to gain wealth because of the body enslaved as we are to its service. (66c5–d2)[60]

Although it is immediately apparent that war leaves little time for philosophy, Socrates' comments seem to depreciate the whole realm of politics by denying that the greatest acts of a political community partake of anything noble. Apparently, the 'genuine philosophers' are to believe that all activities other than philosophy are focused on the body.

The *doxa* is not limited to considering the affects of the body on the existence of the individual philosopher. It also considers the affects of the body on the activity of philosophy itself. Socrates speaks of the situation in which the philosopher does obtain leisure—that is, when the exigencies of the body are satisfied, and he is able to turn to some investigation. It is in this situation that Socrates finds the body to present the 'worst' of all its evils (66d3–8). But this means that the body causes greater harm when the philosopher is engaged in thought than when it merely prevents such activity at all; the ill effects of body reach to the essence of philosophy. Since the philosopher can, in fact, obtain leisure to think, the conclusion reached here—that wisdom is available only after death, if then—must finally be derived from the effects of body on the activity of philosophy itself rather than on the individual existence of the philosopher (66e4–6).

If we put together the explicit teaching of Socrates' defense thus far, the following view emerges. The intelligibles must be separate from all that is particular and thus corporeal, because that which is corporeal is always subject to change. This must be the case because were the intelligibles subject to change, then they could not be the ultimate explanation; more explanatory would be whatever caused *them* to change. In order to be in communication with such intelligibles, we must in some way be incorporeal ourselves. This cannot occur in this life since, because as long as we are living we remain encumbered by body. Especially as regards our understanding, we must still rely on sense-perception which necessarily involves the movement of body. Only if we are free of the body can we communicate with the intelligibles and, given what was just stated, such freedom can only be obtained after death. These considerations culminate in the view that,

> If we can know nothing purely in the body's company, then
> one of two things must be true: either knowledge is nowhere
> to be gained, or else it is for the dead. (66e4–6)

According to this understanding, the notion of philosophy as preparation for death does reflect a sacrifice of life for the sake of wisdom. To repeat, however, this view comes to us laden with qualifications and beset

by contradictions.[61] When we heed the qualifications and the contradictions of Socrates' presentation—unheeded by Simmias—we see that in
the course of founding the philosophic sect of genuine philosophers,
Socrates suggests the possibility of an alternative view of the philosophic
life.[62] I want now to cover the ground we have just traversed in order to
grasp the outlines of this alternative view.

In beginning his teaching for the genuine philosophers with the recommendation of asceticism, Socrates alerts us to the possibility that this
teaching is not his final word on the philosophic life. For although
Socrates counsels the genuine philosophers to forego the pleasures of
food, drink, sex, and bodily adornment, we have already seen evidence of
Socrates' failure to heed his own advice as regards sex. In other dialogues,
Socrates adorns himself and partakes liberally of drink.[63] Moreover, contrary to the suggestion of this passage, there are pleasures and desires
other than those of the body. Later in the *Phaedo,* Socrates will speak of
the pleasures of learning, and in the *Apology* he refers to his way of life as
one which is "not unpleasant" (114e3–4).[64] In the *doxa* itself, Socrates has
the genuine philosophers speaking of their "desire" for wisdom whose
"lovers" they claim to be (65b6–7, 66e2–3). Apparently, it is not only the
body that desires but also the soul. The view of the philosopher as ascetic
seems to have more in common with the view of the many, who think that
the philosopher "finds nothing of that sort pleasant," than it does with
Socrates' own life (65a5).

Other features of the passage under consideration suggest that the
distinction between body and soul, on which Socrates' recommendation
of asceticism rests, is itself questionable. For example, it is clear that body
as such does not adorn itself, nor for that matter does body as such need
to be fed or to have sex. Only the animated body does this; Socrates' use
of the term *body* is as much an abstraction as his use of *soul.*[65] In addition,
the philosopher is said to separate his soul from body not absolutely, but
only "as far as possible." The separation of body from soul with respect to
pleasures would seem, finally, to be an attitude not an actuality, especially
since among these pleasures are the necessities of eating and drinking.
Similar difficulties are raised by the question that Socrates asks Simmias:
"Do you think in general then that such a man's concern is not for the
body but so far as he can stand aside from it is directed towards the
soul?"(64e4–6). In this question, the philosopher is cast as a third entity
standing apart from the body and directing his concern to the soul.[66] But
what is the relationship between the individual philosopher and the soul?
What is the relationship between his concerned mind and the soul to
which he directs his concern? Questions such as these would have to be

faced if one abandoned the simple body-soul distinction characteristic of Socrates' defense.[67]

Questions also arise with respect to those 'bodily senses' that Socrates had depreciated. Socrates criticizes these as entirely inaccurate. Yet if they were *entirely* inaccurate, how would we judge them to be so? [68] In light of what standard of sense-perception could we make such a judgment? Along these same lines, if all are wholly inaccurate, how can Socrates judge some senses as superior to others, as he does in the present passage (65b5–6)? Simmias also fails to point out that he must use one of these defective senses—hearing—precisely in order to apprehend Socrates' depreciation of the senses. Nor does Simmias challenge Socrates' claim that mathematical reasoning is the whole of wisdom.[69] Such a thought might have been prompted by Socrates' reliance in the context on the wisdom of the poets, masters of the use of imagery, as well as by Socrates' constant use of images.[70] For if we must rely on the use of images, derived as they are from that which is visible, we would have to reconsider whether the senses, characterized here as the 'bodily senses,' do not contribute to understanding in some way. We would also have to consider whether all the entities of which we have images are equally susceptible to mathematical understanding.

The contribution to understanding of the senses is especially important in relation to Socrates' treatment of the intelligible, the X-itself. In the course of securing Simmias' agreement to the claim that these intelligibles are not accessible through the senses, Socrates gives indications as to why they may nevertheless be dependent on the senses, especially the sense of sight. Having asked Simmias whether we say the various intelligibles exist, Socrates offers an unusually expansive description of them. He states:

> And I am talking about them all—about largeness, health, and strength, for example—and, in short, about the Being of all other such things, what each thing actually is. Is it through the body that the truest of them is viewed? (65d12–e2)[71]

To the extent that the intelligibles are heterogeneous, it would seem that they reflect the world as it appears to us, the world of things different in kind. The words that Socrates usually uses to refer to the intelligibles, *idea* or *eidos,* express this connection insofar as these words are derived from the verb *to see.* Socrates goes out of his way to avoid these words in the present context precisely because they recall the relationship of the intelligibles to the sense of sight. But he suggests the existence of this relationship when he says that the intelligibles may be the 'truest' aspect of the

things. This statement in no way entails that the intelligibles are absolutely separable from perception and, indeed, it suggests that perception is
necessary insofar as *some* understanding is conveyed by the perceivable.[72]
Socrates' use of the superlative *truest* suggests precisely that, while the intelligible may be the highest element of understanding, it is not the only
such element.

Were we to ask the questions, then, that Simmias fails to ask, we
would arrive at a much different understanding of the philosophic endeavor than is presented in the *doxa*. First of all, according to this view, the
one pursuing philosophy would wonder at the precise distinction of body
and soul. He would have to consider, without the guidance of the simple
body-soul distinction, what the choiceworthy pleasures and desires might
be. He would also wonder about the role played by perception in our understanding: in what way does the character of our understanding affect
our access to the intelligible?[73] And finally, he would inquire into the precise character of this intelligible: is it incorporeal and unchanging, or is it
somehow related to the perceivable and thus not clearly separable from
the particulars?

These are questions that animated Socrates' own philosophic quest.
Socrates' characteristic activity—the activity which, as we learn in the
Apology, is guided by the awareness of what he does not know—lies closer
to this sort of philosophy than to the beliefs of the 'genuine philosophers.'
Taken together, these questions suggest the need to treat the issue of humanity's place in the whole of nature *as a question*. Clearly, there is a vast
difference between a view of philosophy as oriented upon this question
versus a view of philosophy oriented on pure wisdom. If nothing else, philosophy of the former kind would necessarily involve a searching skepticism in opposition to the promised certitude of the latter. Philosophy of
the former kind would for this same reason be a much more dangerous
and difficult endeavor than philosophy understood as the possession of
perfect wisdom. It would involve not only dangers to the individual philosopher, but also the difficulty of substantiating philosophy in the face of
so much uncertainty.[74] Indeed, simply to begin to face the latter issue requires the overcoming of formidable psychic obstacles.

Given the circumstances of the dialogue, the dangers of the philosophic search are self-evident. It involves an examination of, and therefore
a challenge to, accepted views that bear directly on the matters that touch
humans most deeply. Again, philosophy runs the risk of provoking the
political community, one of the purposes of which is to provide authoritative assurances concerning the issues of what is good and what is just.
Socrates' desire to protect the potential philosophers from such danger ex-

plains finally, I think, the depreciation of politics in his comments on war. The point can best be appreciated if we recall that, in the *Republic*, Socrates participates in a course of argument that suggests the contrary of what he states here. In that dialogue, Plato presents the need for war as an outcome of Glaucon's desire for something more than the subsistence provided in what Glaucon calls the city of pigs. Indeed, war is required for that excess of material goods, for wealth, which makes possible a luxurious life. But wealth also makes possible that leisure which enables some to devote themselves to something beyond what is necessary, to the satisfaction of more than bodily desires.[75] Surely, Socrates could not engage in his activities were there not men with wealth to support him and with leisure to appreciate his activity. Socrates' remarks concerning war are not his final word on war, nor are they his final word on the status of politics. But the view of the *doxa* is safer for potential philosophers to hold. It is safer than encouraging all those present to a direct examination of the community's authoritative basis. Again, such an investigation risks not merely the ridicule but the ire of the political community. For this reason, Socrates allows the 'genuine philosophers' to think of politics as something low and thus not worthy of examination.

More central to the *Phaedo* than the dangers of the Socratic way are what I have called the psychic obstacles to this pursuit. Those who pursue the philosophic life as a search would seem to have to forego many of the pleasures derived from membership in a sect because it is difficult to imagine a philosophic sect arising around a view of philosophy so lacking in doctrines. Specifically, they would have to forego the sense of belonging and of self-definition offered by the sect, the sharing in 'what we believe.' They would also have to be willing to jeopardize the sort of immortality offered by the enduring sect.

Above all, however, they would have to endure the pain of reconsidering the answers to their deepest questions that the sect provides. To elaborate what I suggested earlier, it is the need to overcome this last obstacle that explains what is otherwise very difficult to explain—namely, Socrates' guidance of the argument thus far. It is Socrates who has made the fulfillment of philosophy depend on knowledge of posthumous existence. Socrates has joined the attainment of perfect wisdom to the immortality of the soul. But why should he do this? Why raise the standard of intelligibility to such cosmic heights? One possible outcome of this move is to make more serious the threat of absolute skepticism (or what is later termed 'misology') when such a standard fails to be met. Socrates himself acknowledges this possibility when he concludes the *doxa* with the alternative that "either knowledge is *nowhere to be gained*, or else it is for the dead" (66e6, emphasis added). Such dialogues as the *Republic,* the *Phaedrus,* and the *Symposium* make clear that Socrates has certainly reflected on the demonstrability of the immortality of the soul prior to his death day. And it is entirely possible that Socrates believes that one last attempt at a proof of immortality may yet result in an ironclad demonstration of this doctrine. But it is at least equally possible that Socrates suspects, if he does not know, that the search for such a proof will yield, as it does in the *Phaedo,* a less-than-certain foundation for this doctrine. Given the link between this doctrine and the availability of pure wisdom, such an outcome cannot help but cast doubt on the attainment of that wisdom. Why then does Socrates deliberately risk this outcome?

The rationale behind Socrates' guidance of the argument lies in the possibility that an examination of the doctrine of the immortality of the soul may be the necessary precursor for one who would live the philosophic life understood as an ongoing search. Specifically, such an examination is necessary in order to overcome the psychic obstacles to this alternative view.[76] The one who would live the philosophic life, understood as an ongoing search, would have to question both the precise character of human beings and the precise character of our relationship to the transcendent order, if any such order does in fact exist. To do so requires that one overcome the nearly irresistible desire for certainty regarding these questions. The risk that Socrates is willing to take in this argument is an indication of the hold that this desire has on us. Whether that desire is born of a yearning for absolute wisdom or the longing to get what we think we deserve, we cannot help but want to be assured that we will possess what is truly good. Given the evidence that such satisfaction does not always occur in this world, we look to a realm beyond this world, a realm in which the defects of this world are rectified. Crucial to the desire for our own good, then, is the belief that we will exist somehow in this other realm; herein lies the importance of the doctrine of the immortality of the soul. On the basis of this doctrine, it becomes possible to maintain—our terrestrial experience to the contrary notwithstanding—that there is a harmonious relationship between humanity and the trans-human such that the cosmos participates in bringing about, indeed, is oriented on, human good. But if one is going to examine this relationship seriously one would have to question whether there is such a harmony. Or, to state the foregoing more concretely, one would have to question precisely what the young men want Socrates to prove in his defense: that it is reasonable to hope that the good will be theirs, if not in this world then in the next.

To face this question in all seriousness means to entertain the possibility that there is no reasonable ground for this hope. The more powerful the grip of such hope, the more it threatens to thwart an unprejudiced examination of the human situation. Perhaps only an argument of the kind that Socrates presents in his defense can make possible such an examination. More specifically, the willingness and the capacity of the potential philosopher to set aside such hope can best be tested and enhanced precisely by working through those doctrines, including above all the doctrine of the immortality of the soul, that maintain the existence of cosmic support for our individual good. In this way, the philosopher might surmount the psychic obstacles that lie in the way of at least considering the possibility that philosophy should be understood as an ongoing search rather than as oriented on pure wisdom.

When Socrates designates the goal of philosophy as pure wisdom, with its supporting doctrines, he gives to some the comfort of a certain and comprehensive teaching. He describes a way around the obstacles that earthly existence presents to such a teaching. As Martha Nussbaum has written, the notion of purity, dominant in the *Phaedo,* has as its "primary, ongoing, central meaning" the sense of 'clearing up' or 'clarification'— that is, of the removal of some obstacle", a sense that Plato widens to include matters of cognition.[77] But as we have seen in the double aspect of Socrates' defense, by focusing on purity, Socrates also makes more vivid the character and configuration of these obstacles. For those who are impressed by these obstacles, and who see the inadequacy of the arguments for the doctrines that support the attainment of pure wisdom, Socrates increases the danger of misology, the hatred of reason. This risky procedure would be hard to justify were it not the case that only in this way can the potential philosopher face the question of humanity's place in the whole free of prejudice. How far either Simmias or Cebes pursue that issue, how far either of them succeed in following the Socratic way rather than the way of the sect remains to be seen.[78] The last portion of Socrates' defense tests their resolve by offering an easy answer to their hopes.

At the end of the *doxa,* Socrates explains how we must act in this world if we are to have hope of gaining wisdom in the next. We should consort with the body as little as possible so that after death "we shall probably be in like company" (67a7–8). Socrates refers to philosophy as the preparation for the next world, calling this preparation *katharsis.* Specifically, Socrates maintains that "there's plenty of hope for one who arrives where I'm going that there if anywhere he will adequately possess the object that's been our great concern in the life gone by"(67b8–10). In this way, Socrates begins to speak of what his defense has not yet addressed—namely, the grounds for hope.

Yet as Socrates undertakes the final section of his defense, the location of the hope shifts from the next world to this world. The earthly practice of purification comes to be identified with death itself:

> Then doesn't purification turn out to be just what's been men-
> tioned for some while in our discussion—the parting of the
> soul from the body as far as possible, and the habituating of it
> to assemble and gather itself together, away from every part of
> the body alone by itself, and to live, so far as it can, both in the
> present and in the hereafter, released from the body, as from
> fetters? (67c5–d2)

Socrates says that this practice applies both "in the present and in the hereafter." Within a few pages, this practice of purification will be identified
with wisdom which, Socrates then says, is available here and now. We
must consider why Socrates' defense takes this unusual turn.

Socrates claims that only the genuine philosopher, the philosopher
of the sect, achieves this wisdom, and that he does so in this world. In
order to maintain this claim, Socrates must substitute for the body-soul
distinction the distinction between the nonphilosopher and the philosopher. Previously, the incompleteness of the philosopher, which caused him
to long for his object and fear that it was unattainable, was attributed to
the philosopher's being like all other people in his being embodied. Mere
separation of soul from body happens to everyone, with the ambiguous
consequence that everyone becomes wise. But now the hope that Socrates
offers to Simmias depends on a view that the philosopher is radically distinct from all humans in a way that allows him to achieve his goal in this
world. At the beginning of the passage, Socrates calls attention to this alteration by saying, first, that the philosopher is "especially" eager to release the body from the soul, but then he immediately corrects himself by
saying that the philosopher "alone" is eager to bring on this release
(67d7–8). Prior to explicating this radical distinction between the philosopher and all others, however, Socrates engages in a digression. This
digression has the effect of casting doubt on the truth of such a distinction, at least on the grounds offered in the present passage.[79]

In this digression, Socrates presents a view of philosophy that, surprisingly, assimilates the philosophers to other great lovers (68a2–7). He
speaks of those who

> have been willing to enter Hades of their own accord, in quest
> of human loves, of wives and sons who have died, led by this
> hope, that there they would see and be united with those they
> desired. (68a4–7)

Socrates draws the comparison to the philosopher who would do likewise, for there they "may hope to attain what they longed for throughout

life, namely wisdom" (67e9–a2). He will do this "if he's truly a lover of wisdom" (68b2–3). Immediately prior to offering an explanation of the philosopher's hopes that is confined to this world, Socrates thus briefly opens a window through which we can see those longings which convince us that our hopes can only be satisfied in the next world. Socrates ends the digression asking Simmias: "If you see a man resentful that he is going to die," isn't this proof enough for you that that man is "no lover of wisdom" but a "lover of the body"—that is, "a lover of wealth and of honor, either one of these or both"(68b8–c3). Socrates can only say that the man who is vexed by death *is not* a lover of wisdom. He cannot make the more specific claim that the man who is not vexed by death *is* a lover of wisdom. The one who is not vexed by death, the one for whom something is more important than death, might be a lover of a variety of objects or individuals. Desire characterizes humans as such, not merely philosophers.

Having opened this window, Socrates now closes it and returns to his initial line of argument. But there is an ambiguity as to Socrates' referent when he begins again to make the radical distinction between the philosopher and all other humans. Socrates asks: "Isn't it also true that what is named courage belongs especially to people of the disposition we have described?"(68c5–6). Only when he subsequently asks a similar question regarding moderation do we see the claim that Socrates is making. It is that the virtue of the many, as opposed to the genuine virtue of the philosopher, is a sham, nothing but calculative hedonism.[80] Most humans do not pursue virtue for its own sake, but rather as a means of avoiding pain and gaining pleasure. Such people, states Socrates, are "courageous through fear and cowardice" and "moderate through a kind of immoderation" (68c8–69a4). They are courageous only through avoiding a more fearful object, and moderate only to ensure their enjoyment of a greater pleasure.

But does the philosopher escape the same characterization of his activity? For example, the argument maintains that all except the philosopher consider death a great evil; courageous nonphilosophers only abide it through being afraid of greater evils. Thus, they are courageous through fear. This assumes that one takes the lesser evil only out of fear. But can't this be applied also to the philosopher who would avoid that which Socrates later calls "the greatest evil," misology? Why shouldn't it be said that he does so out of fear of misology? To the extent that his activities involve fear at all, it seems that the argument cannot be prevented from impinging on the philosopher. Similar problems exist with Socrates' proof concerning moderation. Socrates' argument that the many are mod-

erate through immoderation, that they only forego one pleasure in order
to enjoy another, can again be applied to the philosopher insofar as he
forgoes, say, the pleasure of drink for the pleasure of thinking.

Resting as it does on such questionable proofs, this version of the
radical distinction between the philosopher and the nonphilosopher
must be similarly questionable. It is rendered more so by Socrates' understanding of what accounts for the distinction: the possession of wisdom
by the philosophers. In the much-vexed concluding passage of Socrates'
defense, the precise status of wisdom seems to undergo an alteration.
Socrates states:

> Yes, Simmias, my good friend; since this may not be the right
> exchange with a view to virtue, the exchanging of pleasures for
> pleasures, pains for pains . . . like coins; it may be rather that
> this alone is the right coin, for which one should exchange all
> these things—wisdom; and the buying and selling of all
> things for that, or rather with that, may be real courage, mod-
> eration, justice, and, in short, true virtue in company with
> wisdom . . . ; but as for their being parted from wisdom . . . vir-
> tue of that sort may be a kind of illusory facade. . . . (69a6–b7)

He concludes that "moderation, justice and courage may in fact be a kind
of purification of all such things, and wisdom itself a kind of purifying
rite" (69b8–c3). As many commentators have recognized, the ambiguity
of the passage lies in the question as to whether wisdom replaces all the
virtues—with the philosopher not having even to deal with those virtues
pertaining to fear and pleasure—or whether wisdom is precisely the necessary means to dealing with those passions.[81] This ambiguity reflects the
problem inherent in Socrates' attempt to replace the body-soul distinction
with the distinction between the nonphilosopher and the philosopher: it
is difficult to maintain that the philosopher is completely free from those
desires and feelings that we have insofar as we are not pure mind alone.

Socrates maintained this position in order to argue that wisdom is
attainable here and now, that what the young men had thought is only
available in the next world is, in fact, available here. But the untenable
arguments used to support this position—the proofs of the philosopher's
true virtue and the ambiguous statement concerning wisdom—lead us to
question again the possibility of attaining perfect wisdom in this world.
The indications of the untenability of the radical distinction between the
philosophers and nonphilosophers point, at least on the grounds offered

here, to the way in which the philosopher, like all other humans, is not pure mind. To this extent, the more accurate picture is that presented in the digression which assimilates the philosopher to other humans in being incomplete and therefore longing for an object that is elusive in this world. Socrates himself indicates the wider perspective when, after referring to his attempts to become an initiate into this purifying rite, he says: "Whether I have striven aright and we have achieved anything, we shall, I think, know for certain, God willing, in a little while, on arrival yonder"(69d4–6).

Though Simmias is the interlocutor for Socrates' defense, it is Cebes who grasps the problem presented therein. He, unlike Simmias, cannot be satisfied with the too-easy hope that Socrates dangles before his interlocutors. The hope of the concluding passage of Socrates' defense is tendered at the cost of denying the human problem, those "evils" of our terrestrial existence that seem to impede the attainment of our good. It thereby dissolves the very conditions which lead to our uncertainty and thus our need for hope.[82] In response, Cebes refers to the *doxa* and specifically to "those evils you were recounting just now" (70a7–8). Cebes wishes specifically to speak about the posthumous career of the soul, seeing that the 'evils' are inherent in this world. Cebes reports the "fear that when it's [the soul] been separated from the body, it may no longer exist anywhere, but that on the very day a man dies, it may be destroyed and perish" (70a1–3). Only "if it did exist somewhere, gathered together alone by itself" would there be "plenty of hope, Socrates, and a fine hope it would be, that what you say is true" (70a6–b1). Cebes sees the need for a demonstration of the soul's immortality.

Simmias can be satisfied with this-worldly hope because his concern is less for certain knowledge than for justice, or—in more accurate terms—for getting what he thinks is his due. He does not dwell on the question of whether his good can be known to be available in this world. Whether he receives it in this world or the next matters less than that it is received. Simmias' concerns remain human concerns in the most mundane sense. He does not rise to the level of the potential philosopher because he does not yet appreciate the way in which his human concerns, the concern for his good, might, in light of the questions concerning the meaning and availability of this good, lead him to the questions concerning the transhuman order. Cebes does appreciate this connection. He cannot rest satisfied with a hope that is contained within this limited horizon. Indeed, as we have seen in his interest in suicide, Cebes is all too fervently aware of the trans-human order, with the result that he neglects the human concerns.

We do not yet know how far Cebes will be willing to follow the argument, wherever it may go. But with Cebes' request, Socrates' defense has brought it about that Cebes has at least begun to consider the grounds for his hopes. Specifically, Cebes' reference to "those evils you were recounting just now" returns the argument, in effect, to the alternatives expressed at the end of the *doxa*. Socrates' defense has brought it about that Cebes sees the orientation on pure wisdom as questionable, in need of support. He is moved to wonder: what exactly is the relationship between the human and the trans-human? There is no more serious *human* question. The rift between philosophic doctrine and the concerns of human existence has been narrowed. Perhaps for this reason, Socrates alludes to his old accuser:

> I really don't think anyone listening now, even if he were a comic poet, would say that I'm talking idly and arguing about things that don't concern me. (70b10–c3)[83]

The Proofs of Immortality

Overview

(70c4–88b8)

Among the commentators on the *Phaedo* there is near unanimity that the first three proofs of the immortality of the soul are defective.[1] This judgment reflects the view of the participants in the dialogue themselves who call attention to this inadequacy. The question that must be addressed is why should Plato choose to have Socrates spend a significant portion of his waning moments making bad arguments?

The first proof rests on a principle of causality that is to be applied to everything that comes to be and passes away. The second proof focuses directly on the soul in its capacity as knower. The defect of each proof can be traced to its oversimplification. More specifically, the first proof raises doubt that any particular being can be fully explained by reference to a *single* principle of causality, and the second proof suggests that the character of the soul is not exhausted by an understanding of the soul as pure mind alone.

The third proof of immortality faces head-on the suggested complexities of the first two proofs as it attempts to show that the soul is immortal because of its incomposite nature, a nature that it is said to share with the intelligible principle of nature. But this proof too is less than adequate. In its inadequacy, however, the third proof serves rather to confirm the complexities of the soul and of the beings.

As we have seen in the preceding chapter, one goal of a proof of immortality is to substantiate the harmony between the human mind and the intelligible structure of the whole—in other words, to show that it is possible for us to attain perfect or pure wisdom. Socrates' defective proofs suggest, therefore, that there exists only an imperfect harmony between humanity and nature. At the conclusion of the third proof, both Simmias and Cebes express their misgivings in the form of objections to the argument as it has unfolded thus far. In response to these objections, Socrates begins to explore the implications of this imperfect harmony. Sharing a defect that Socrates attributes to his predecessors, the proofs might then be characterized as a 'first sailing,' an account of the whole that proceeds as if the principle of the whole were unitary and immediately available.[2] Through indicating the inevitable distortions of this procedure, distortions of both humanity and nature, Socrates indicates the necessity that we embark on the less direct route of the 'second sailing.' Let us now consider these proofs in detail.

Opposites

Socrates' interlocutors consider the first proof of immortality the least adequate of any of the proofs. Cebes, its addressee, exhibits diminishing enthusiasm as the proof progresses. At its conclusion, without a moment's hesitation, he recommends the doctrine of Recollection as a supplemental basis of the soul's immortality. Likewise, later in the dialogue, Simmias almost explicitly repudiates this first proof (77b1–3). The unpersuasiveness of the first proof might be attributed to its unsatisfactory arguments. Consisting of an old saying, a questionable analogy, tendentious examples, and hypothetical propositions, it hardly qualifies as a proof at all. Yet, in the *Phaedo*, faultiness of reasoning is not always an index of unpersuasiveness.

R. S. Bluck's characterization of the proof as being based on "mechanistic principles" suggests a more likely source of this unpersuasiveness: the first proof is decidedly un-Socratic.[3] Absent is the doctrine that these Pythagoreans find so compelling—namely, the doctrine of the eternal intelligibles or the Ideas.[4] Instead, Socrates speaks here in the accents of those of his predecessors who offered accounts of the whole of nature in terms of a perpetual generation and decay. Specifically, Socrates maintains that all coming into being and passing away, the whole of nature, can be explained in terms of a translation of opposites: opposites come to be from, and pass into, opposites. Such an account, relying as it does on mechanistic explanations, must ring discordantly in the ears of those schooled in the doctrine of eternally existing incorporeal intelligibles.

The absence of the Ideas, however, rests on a related and more basic neglect; Socrates' principle flies in the face of what we observe everyday. Dogs give birth to dogs, and humans to humans; generation is not from opposites, but from like to like. Socrates' principle denies the evidence of the visible world, the world as it appears to us. This world is the world of things, the world of individuals distinguishable one from another as different kinds of things. The absence of the Ideas from this first proof rests on this more basic rejection of the visible world insofar as the Ideas, in their heterogeneity, reflect the visible world.[5]

But why does Socrates choose this particular proof, questionable as it is, as his first attempt at a proof of the immortality of the soul? We can begin to answer this question by reflecting upon the conversation that precedes the proof. In response to Cebes' question concerning the enduring existence of the soul, Socrates asks, "Would you like us to tell myths about these very questions," the questions relating to the immortality of the soul (70b6–7)? Cebes responds: "As for me anyway, I'd gladly hear whatever opinion you have about them" (70b8–9). In his wish to hear *whatever* Socrates might say about these issues, Cebes displays his dependence on Socrates. Perhaps part of Socrates' intention in beginning with a decidedly un-Socratic argument is to help Cebes overcome that dependence. Socrates will soon be gone, and thus Cebes will soon be compelled to rely on his own powers. He will have to think through on his own the arguments that oppose his familiar way of thinking. The sooner he becomes self-reliant, the better.

The proof challenges Cebes' familiar way of thinking, as well as our own, in a still more specific way. Although the first proof may be unpersuasive in itself, it introduces far-reaching questions, questions that should trouble one such as Cebes who yearns for pure wisdom. These questions challenge what we might take to be the orthodox Socratic position. Indeed, they challenge any view that would claim to offer a certain and comprehensive account of the whole of nature. The first proof attempts to explain the coming into being and passing away not only of living things, but of all things, by reference to the unitary principle of opposites. But it fails, and in this failure the first proof suggests that such an explanation would require a diversity of causes, causes different in kind. This requirement for what I will call heterogeneous causation raises an abiding question of the dialogue: is there *any* unified account that reconciles this heterogeneity? In other words, is there a single account of why any thing (and everything) comes into being, passes away, and exists—an account that would therefore explain completely our coming into being, passing away, and existence? This question raised by the first proof remains alive throughout the dialogue, even to the end of the final proof.[6] It is one of the nettlesome questions that calls forth Socrates' alteration in philosophy. We have yet to see why Socrates raises this question in such an oblique manner. But insofar as it introduces this question, the present proof is properly the first of the proofs of immortality, and Cebes, though he may not realize it, is properly its addressee. At the conclusion of this proof, Cebes rushes to the safe haven of more familiar Socratic ground. But *we* must resist the temptation to scant this first proof in favor of what we take to be more recognizably Socratic views.

With Cebes' approval, Socrates begins the proof. Moving easily between myth and reason, a distinction of which he is well aware, Socrates asks whether things are such that "the souls of men exist in Hades when they have died" (70c4–5).[7] In support of an affirmative response to his question, Socrates offers an ancient saying which holds that "they do exist in that world, entering it from this one and that they re-enter this world and are born again from those who have died" (70b6–8). Socrates concludes, if this is true,

> if living people are born again from those who have died, surely our souls would have to exist in that world. Because they could hardly be born again if they did not exist; so it would be sufficient evidence for the proof of these claims, if it really became plain that living people are born from the dead and from nowhere else; but if that isn't so, some other argument would be needed. (70c8–d5)[8]

Why is it necessarily the case that that which Socrates variously calls "our souls" or "the dead" exist in Hades? The implicit presumption, later made explicit, is the principle that nothing can come to be from, nor pass away into, nothing.[9] Thus, if we are born, if we come to be, we have to come from something that exists; likewise, when we die, we must pass into something that exists.

Socrates now introduces the principle of causality, that opposites come to be from their opposites. Given that nothing can come from, nor pass into, nothing, all change must be simply an alteration into some other state, an alteration that takes the form of a translation of opposites. Socrates recommends this principle of causality because it will enable his interlocutors to understand more "easily" (70d8). He does not say that it will enable them to understand more truly. This ease of understanding follows, perhaps, from the principle's purportedly universal application. In a breathtakingly rapid ascent to a bird's-eye, or better, a god's-eye view, Socrates invites Cebes to consider the matter

> in connection not only with mankind but with all animals and plants; and in general for all things subject to coming-to-be, let's see whether everything comes to be in this way: opposites come to be only from their opposites. . . . (70d8–e2)

Socrates concludes this expression of his principle of causality with an important qualification to which I will return. He states that the principle applies "in the case of all things that actually have an opposite" (70e2).

As the proof continues, Socrates offers examples rather than arguments in support of his principle. It is important to note that the first set of examples—beautiful–ugly, just–unjust—are a type of opposite known as contraries. Characteristic of such opposites is that the denial of one does not necessarily entail the other: if something is not beautiful, it need not be ugly. This type of opposite, then, does not necessarily lend support to the view that opposites always translate into one another. Therefore, Socrates offers another set of examples that better supports the idea that all change is the translation of opposites into one another. These are a type of opposite known as comparatives. Included within this type are such opposites as worse–better, faster–slower, or (to take Socrates' final example) more just–more unjust. Relying on *this* type of opposites, Socrates' claim that everything comes to be from its opposite is made a matter of logical necessity: if something becomes more unjust, it must have done so from being more just.[10] Again, as with Socrates' qualification of his principle mentioned above, it proves to be important to recognize that Socrates would have been unable to maintain the existence of such a necessity had he stopped to examine the first set of opposites.

Socrates asks: "Are we satisfied then that all things come to be in this way, opposite *things (pragmata)* from opposites?" (71a9–10). At the beginning of the proof, Socrates was somewhat ambiguous about whether he meant his principle to apply to subjects or attributes or both.[11] Clearly, the principle of opposites works best (or perhaps only) with regard to an attributional change in an enduring subject as expressed in Socrates' first example: "When a thing comes to be larger, it must, surely, come to be larger from being smaller before" (70e10–71a1). But with the present question Socrates speaks of *things* without further explanation. He thus glides over still other thorny issues that would be raised if Cebes had asked, for example, what the precise status of a *thing* would be in a world that can be explained in terms of the translation of opposites. Nevertheless, on the basis of such 'evidence,' Cebes agrees that "all things come to be in this way, opposite things from opposites"(71a9–10).

With this refinement of the principle established, Socrates brings the principle to bear on the relevant opposites, life and death. More specifically, he offers the pair of opposites, sleeping–being awake, along with the reciprocal processes of going to sleep and waking up as analogous to the opposites life and death. Through a series of questions, Socrates induces Cebes to complete the analogy. The exchange runs as follows:

Socrates:	You say, don't you, that being dead is opposite to living?
Cebes:	I do.
Socrates:	And that they come to be from each other?
Cebes:	Yes.
Socrates:	Then what is it that comes to be from that which is living?
Cebes:	That which is dead.
Socrates:	And what comes to be from that which is dead?
Cebes:	I must admit that it's that which is living.
Socrates:	Then it's from those that are dead, Cebes, that living things and living people are born?
Cebes:	Apparently.
Socrates:	Are our souls in Hades? Then our souls do exist in Hades?
Cebes:	So it seems. (71d5–71e3)

Clearly, the analogy Socrates urges upon Cebes is a dubious one. It assumes precisely what is in question—namely, the ongoing existence of a subject. In other words, the question at hand is precisely whether or not the change from living to dead is an example of attributional change, a change in which there is a subject that endures throughout this change.[12] Yet Socrates studiously avoids facing the question of the change involved in the coming into being and passing away of a thing as such, what I will call essential change. His efforts in this regard suggest that the principle of opposites is particularly inappropriate to the explanation of essential rather than attributional change, the coming into being and passing away of things rather than of qualities. We must put together the several qualifications and anomalies that Socrates throws into the argument in order to discern what point is suggested by this inappropriateness.

I have mentioned several other ways in which Socrates has expressed reservations regarding the application of this principle to essential change. When introducing his principle of causality, Socrates had glanced at the possibility that not everything has an opposite when he added the qualification, "In the case of all things that actually have an opposite." And after some initial ambiguity about its application to things, he subsequently assumes, without discussion, that it is in fact applicable to things. Yet he never explains what might be meant by the opposite of a *thing*. Most important, in his treatment of the crucial opposites, life and death, Socrates never claims in his own name that they are opposites. Even after Cebes has affirmed that they are indeed opposites, Socrates keeps his distance from this claim, stating it only hypothetically (71c6). By recurring to still another of Socrates' qualifications concerning this principle of causality—namely, the examples given when he first introduced the principle of opposites—we can begin to understand the precise way in which the principle of opposites is inadequate to explain life and death.

Socrates' first set of examples offered in support of his principle were of a type of opposite called contraries. Contraries, in distinction from contradictories, may both be legitimately denied of a subject: the privation of one does not necessarily entail the existence or definition of the other.[13] Something that is not beautiful is not necessarily ugly. It may rather be not-beautiful. Socrates' reticence regarding life and death is thus warranted because they also are contraries rather than contradictories.[14] The denial of one does not necessarily yield the other. That which is not alive is not necessarily dead; it may be neither alive nor dead. This point becomes crucial in the last proof of immortality. There, it is seen that the privation of the supposed opposite of life—namely death—does not entail life. For this reason, Socrates is required to prove not only that the soul is immortal, but that it is imperishable: something may be immortal—not-dead—*whenever* it exists. An example taken from the last proof is: although fire is always hot, it can be extinguished. Fire does not admit cold and, by analogy, soul does not admit death—that is, soul is deathless or immortal. But deathless soul might be destroyed, just as hot fire can be extinguished. The crucial distinction raised by the use of contraries is the distinction between being this or that on the one hand, and being simply on the other.[15] A living thing *is* both as it exists simply and in its being alive.

These senses of being are not opposite to one another but simply different from one another. And, as Socrates maintains in the final proof of immortality, they derive from causes which are not opposite but different. These heterogeneous senses of being—expressed in the difference between essence and existence—are necessary in order to explain a thing as such insofar as each thing both simply *is* and is this particular kind of thing. For this reason, such heterogeneity comes to light especially when we consider essential change, the coming into being and passing away of a thing as such, rather than mere attributional change. In light of the need for heterogeneous senses of being, a unitary explanation of causation such as the principle of opposites, a single principle that claims to explain all coming into being and passing away must fail as an explanation of essential change. It must also distort the visible world insofar as that world is the world of things differentiated by kind. Such distortion is nowhere more evident than in the claim that generation is from opposites rather than from like to like.

The present passage exemplifies clearly the aforementioned failure through the fluctuations in Socrates' terminology. Socrates uses a variety of terms to refer to the subject that undergoes the transition from being alive to being dead and back again. He does choose at times to call this subject our souls. Yet nothing he has said supports this specific designation. Given the universal applicability of the principle, it is difficult to see how that which undergoes change in human generation is distinguishable from that which undergoes change in animals or even in rocks.[16] Along these same lines, we should recognize that, were the soul such as to be dispersed upon death, it would as well satisfy the premise of nothing coming from nothing. For, although the components of the soul have been scattered by the wind, they nevertheless continue to exist—a fact that should assuage hardly anyone's fear of death. The point is that, on the basis of the principle that nothing comes to be from or passes into nothing, one can claim *that* something continues to exist. But one cannot on this basis alone define *what* this something is. Only on the basis of the recognition of heterogeneous senses of being, and thus, of causation, could one hope to provide an adequate account of this change. Cebes' responses exhibit, I think, the diminishing enthusiasm appropriate to an argument which applies equally well to rocks and to humans.[17]

Socrates' proof reflects a temptation that seems to entice Cebes, and it also seemed to have enticed Socrates' predecessors. It can be stated in the following way. If one wishes to attain the perfect wisdom expressed in a unitary view of nature, as Cebes apparently does, then one must explain, or explain away, all that stands in the way of that unity—namely, the manifest existence of significant differences in nature. The principle of opposites is an expression of this desire: those which we think most different from each other—opposites—in fact pass into one another. In working through this unitary principle with a view toward its providing a basis for a proof of the immortality of the soul, Cebes' desire for perfect wisdom comes into conflict with his desire for a proof of immortality, at least one that could apply to *his* soul. Perhaps he will at least begin to wonder whether just any unitary principle of causality can satisfy him. This is the first step in questioning the adequacy of all such unitary principles. In what follows, Socrates indicates the necessity of this questioning by suggesting the difficulties and distortions into which his philosophic predecessors were led because of their failure to see this inadequacy.

Specifically, Socrates points to the potential danger that threatens philosophy if the philosopher fails to recognize the need for heterogeneous causation. If the philosopher, driven by the desire for certainty, posits a unitary principle of causality that lacks a *demonstrable* connection to our everyday experience of ourselves and the world, philosophy would become indistinguishable from myth-making. As is evident in Socrates' intellectual autobiography, it is precisely this error that characterized Socrates' predecessors.

The foregoing points emerge from a new tack that the argument takes. Socrates maintains that this new line of argument, bearing on the reciprocal processes of coming to be, supports the conclusion of the preceding proof. In particular, Socrates wishes to affirm the specific point that the path between life and death must be a two-way street. Socrates asks: "One of the relevant processes here is obvious, isn't it? For dying is obvious enough, surely?" (71e4–6). But Socrates does not ask of the most obvious process opposite to dying—namely, being born. In the service of his one principle of causality, he again ignores that which is truly apparent to us. When Socrates had introduced the reciprocal processes of coming to be earlier in the proof, he had asked: "Even if in some cases we do not use the name, still in actual fact mustn't the same principle everywhere hold good?" (71b7–8). With a similar neglect of our experience as that experience is expressed in speech, Socrates now asks: "What shall we do (*poiēsomen*) then? Shan't we assign the opposite process to balance it? Will nature (*phusis*) be lame in this respect?" (71e8–10).[18] Cebes agrees to posit such a process, devising the name, "coming-to-life-again" (71e14).[19]

In this dialogue, whose centerpiece is Socrates' discussion of his varying views of nature, the first use of the word *nature* is noteworthy. But in this first use of the word, there is something unusual. Nature here does not refer to the causes of our world, accessible or discoverable by reason. Rather, in the midst of this argument, Socrates reverts to his poetizing and personifies nature. He presents nature in the image of an animate being that can be either able-bodied or lame. Moreover, nature is clearly presented as a product of human making or convention insofar as its wholeness depends on Cebes agreeing to make it whole. The subsequent passage of the proof reinforces this notion that nature is considered here as a human creation.

Socrates concludes:

> We're agreed that living people are born from the dead no less than dead people from the living; and we thought that, if this were the case, it would be sufficient evidence that the souls of the dead must exist somewhere, whence they are born again. (72a4–8)

Cebes responds rather half-heartedly: "That must follow from our agreements" (72a9–10). In order to show Cebes "that our agreements were *not unjust*," Socrates asks Cebes whether he realizes that "*if* there were not perpetual reciprocity in coming-to-be . . . all things would ultimately have the same form . . . and they would cease from coming to be?" (72a11–b5, emphasis added). In this question is expressed the aforementioned premise that nothing can come from or pass into nothing. It is clear why Socrates must support this premise. On the basis of the principle of opposites, it would seem that something could, perhaps necessarily would, pass into nothing.

Yet, Socrates expresses this premise as a hypothetical. And this hypothetical is adduced to support the justice rather than the truth of the previous argument.[20] When Cebes confesses that he does not follow Socrates' line of argument, Socrates retorts that it is not difficult to understand, and he presents three examples of what he means. But these examples take the same form as his initial statement: *if* there were not perpetual becoming, all might eventually end up fixed permanently in one state, all might end up asleep or "*if* everything were combined but not separated, then Anaxagoras' notion of 'all things together' would soon be realized" or all might end up dead (72b7–d2, emphasis added).

Neither Socrates' initial statement concerning the perpetuity of the world nor his subsequent examples *prove* anything. But they do point to the existence of a problem for philosophy. If philosophy is understood as the attempt to discover the nature of all things, it must be problematic when the existence of the natural order depends upon what we happen to desire or hope, upon our view of what is good or just. This dependence is precisely a denial of that orderedness insofar as these desires are now more fundamental than the only source of their rational explanation—namely, the natural causes. In this case, philosophy becomes indistinguishable from myth-making, positing a view of nature in order to assure ourselves of the fulfillment of our desires.

That the proof should have this outcome is not accidental, because such an outcome is intrinsically related to the initial premises.[21] In light of the need for heterogeneous causation, to begin from the first cause of all things (as Socrates has done in this first proof) is to assume what the philosopher cannot assume—that there is a unitary first cause accessible to humans. Again, it is not at all clear how, or even if, the heterogeneous senses of being can be reconciled. Thus, those who *begin* their accounts from the standpoint of such unity—beginning from the principle of causality that applies to all things—raise the suspicion that their desires, their ambitions, have led them to create rather than discover such unity. They arrive at nature as they wish it to be rather than as it is. These considerations make intelligible the otherwise meandering course that this first proof takes from its initial premises to its conclusion: there exists a connection between *beginning* with the one cause of all things and the indistinguishability of philosophy from myth-making.

Yet the recognition of this connection brings in its wake an equally troubling outcome for philosophy. How, in light of the recognized need for heterogeneous causation, can philosophy ever attain the perfection of its object in some unified account of all things? Reflection on Socrates' reference to Anaxagoras in the present context sharpens the point. According to Aristotle, Anaxagoras—the only pre-Socratic philosopher named in a dialogue concerning Socrates' relation to his predecessors—spoke like a sober man among lunatics when he saw the need to use not only body but also mind in his account of nature.[22] Only in this way could one speak of the significant differences in nature; only in this way could one avoid lumping "all things together" (72c3–5). If all were undifferentiated, separation and combination would be indistinguishable from decrease and increase. Only if there are significant differences in nature does it make sense to speak of separation and combination, as Anaxagoras apparently did. In particular, this distinction suggests the existence of form as distinguishable from matter, because only on this basis could one tell that there was a thing being separated rather than there simply being more or less of some undifferentiated material. To speak of the heterogeneity manifest in the visible world, to speak of things, seems to require Anaxagoras' innovation—namely, that something other than body be causal.

In the *Phaedo*'s other reference to Anaxagoras, Socrates chides Anaxagoras for not supplying a reconciliation of these heterogeneous causes (99b2–4). Instead, Socrates maintains, Anaxagoras simply relies on one type of causation, material cause. But does Socrates succeed any better than Anaxagoras in reducing that difference which Anaxagoras rightly introduced in order to explain the whole of nature? Of course, we cannot yet answer this question. But in pointing to the need for heterogeneous causation, the first proof raises a question that will be at the core of Socrates' intellectual autobiography: if there is necessarily heterogeneous causation, if things *are* in heterogeneous senses, then is there a unity that reconciles the diverse causes that stand behind these senses of being?

This question clearly must be asked both for a thing as such and for nature as a whole. Moreover, if this diversity persists, then is it not the case that nature understood as manifesting a variety of causes is imperfectly ordered? The first proof raises this question in its treatment of the ultimate principle of intelligibility. The notion that nothing comes to be from nothing is the ultimate principle of intelligibility, for it maintains that each thing (and all things together) has a discernible cause and thus a discernible explanation. In the present proof, this principle appears as a hypothetical, posited in response to what we desire. It remains to be seen whether Socratic philosophy differs from a construction intended to cure a 'lame' nature. In other words, it remains to be seen whether beginning as one must, from recognition of the heterogeneity of beings it is possible to achieve the purported goal of philosophy, a nonhypothetical account of the whole of nature. The non-Socratic character of the first proof makes for an appropriately suggestive introduction to the tremendous difficulties that confronted philosophy after it had taken this momentous step of recognizing the heterogeneity of the beings.

It is the failure to provide a ground for the manifest differences in the world which lies at the heart of the unpersuasiveness of the first proof. Among these differences is that between the human and the nonhuman, a difference which is necessary in order to give an account of what is *specifically* human. The word *soul* is usually attached to that which is specifically human. But reflecting the effacement of these differences, soul in the first proof is simply a name which can be applied to some undifferentiated substrate indistinguishable from anything else in the whole of nature. The final words of the proof run: "And it is better for the good souls and worse for the bad ones" (72e1–2). Editors almost always omit these words as, to quote Gallop, "an edifying enrichment of the text which is, however, logically . . . out of place."[23] Whether or not the omission is correct, the widely shared view that these words are unsupported by what precedes them is a reflection of the dissatisfaction expressed also by Cebes. This dissatisfaction arises from the fact that the soul 'proved' to be immortal is not recognizable to Cebes as a human soul, as a soul that could be his, a soul to which the terms 'good' and 'bad' could apply. Accordingly, immediately after Socrates asserts the conclusion, Cebes brings up the doctrine of recollection as a supplemental basis for immortality. Cebes is drawn to a proof that pertains to that activity dear to him—namely, learning. Apparently, Cebes has learned that not just any causal principle will satisfy his desire for certainty. He wants a principle that will satisfy his desire for personal immortality as well. Accordingly, in his suggestion to Socrates, we find the first use of the word *immortal*.[24] It remains to be seen whether an explanation of immortality based on that which is unique to soul succeeds any better than the explanation that understands soul in the same terms as everything else.

Recollection

Before becoming immersed in the details of the argument, it is useful to say a few words about the structure of the argument. The Recollection argument divides into three sections, of which only the central section is a proof of immortality. The argument begins with a passage preliminary to the proof itself in which there is an allusion to the doctrine of Recollection as presented in the *Meno*. This is followed by a series of examples and conditions meant to explicate what Socrates means by recollection. Only after this passage does Socrates relate the proof of the soul's prenatal existence, a proof that depends upon *all* humans necessarily grasping the intelligibles such as the equal itself, the good itself, and so on. After the proof proper comes the third section of the argument in which Socrates explains why, if all humans grasp the intelligibles, some are more knowledgeable than others. Interpreting the argument as a whole requires that we understand the relationship between these sections of the argument.

Cebes alludes to the *Meno* as he briefly recapitulates the argument that Socrates "habitually" (72e4) states:

> If it's true, what we are now reminded of we must have learned at some former time. But that would be impossible, unless our souls existed somewhere before being born in this human form. (72e4–73a1)

Hearing this, Simmias asks Cebes to remind him of the proofs of this argument, since he doesn't recollect them at the moment. In his response, Cebes speaks of an excellent questioner asking questions whereupon the one questioned responds with the truth—that is, "knowledge and a correct account" (73a9–10). This occurs if one takes diagrams or anything else of that sort to the respondent—a procedure much akin to Socrates' teaching of the slave boy in the *Meno*.[25]

In case Simmias is not persuaded, in case he doubts that learning is recollection, Socrates offers him another way of looking at the argument. This presentation consists of a series of examples of recollection meant to illustrate the conditions and character of recollection. Socrates thus fastens onto what Simmias says, and so, although it is Cebes who first raises the recollection argument, it is Simmias rather than Cebes who becomes Socrates' interlocutor for this particular proof.

It is Simmias more than Cebes who needs to reflect on the activity of learning.[26] At the start of the proof and elsewhere, Simmias shows that he thinks of learning as a passive process of recalling doctrines which he has once been taught. Simmias does not seem to be motivated by a desire to know nor even by a desire for certainty. In response to Socrates, Simmias is quick to deny that he doubts anything: But he needs "to undergo just what the argument is about, to be 'reminded'" (73b7). Indeed, he is almost reminded and nearly convinced by what Socrates has already said.[27] But of course he would like to hear how Socrates, the authority, explains the doctrine. Simmias' view of learning does comport well with the proof proper, yet before and after that proof Socrates presents quite a different view of learning, reflection on which could profit one such as Simmias.

The understanding of learning in the proof proper involves the necessary and universal movement from perceivable to intelligible.[28] There is a significant difference between such an understanding and the understanding implicit in the initial section of the argument. Clearly, if learning occurs necessarily, the skill of a questioner, or even questioning, would be irrelevant, as would discourse itself. Moreover, the all-or-nothing character of perception renders irrelevant such notions as being "almost reminded," or the taking of many paths to one outcome, or the existence of error at all.[29] Indeed, the proof proper maintains that the outcome of the perception is an intuition and not, as here, a correct account (*orthos logos*). The allusion to the *Meno* suggests what is ignored in a doctrine of learning based upon perception: the particular character of the soul involved in the process of learning. The conditions and examples of recollection that Socrates presents in order to jog Simmias' memory, especially insofar as they dwell on recollection from dissimilar objects of knowledge, likewise suggest the importance of the particular character of the soul. Let us consider the first section of the proof in detail.

Socrates states: "If anyone is reminded of a thing, he must have known that thing at some time previously" (73c1–2). He follows this statement with a longer one defining recollection, a statement that makes crucial not the temporal difference between the two instances of knowledge, but the difference in content between the two. Socrates defines recollection in this way:

> If someone on seeing a thing or hearing it, or getting any other sense-perception of it, not only recognizes that thing but also thinks of something else which is the object not of the same knowledge but of another, don't we then rightly say that he's been reminded of the object of which he has got the thought? (73c4–d1)[30]

Simmias confesses that he does not understand. Perhaps this is because Socrates' definition of recollection does not focus on familiar aspects of the doctrine such as the temporal difference between the two thoughts or the role of forgetting. In any case, Socrates provides examples to assist Simmias' understanding. He asks:

> You know what happens to lovers whenever they see a lyre or cloak or anything else their beloveds are accustomed to use; they recognize the lyre and they get in their mind, don't they, the form of the boy whose lyre it is? (73d5–8)[31]

Socrates adds to this example that of someone seeing Simmias and being "often" reminded of Cebes. He maintains that "there are countless other examples" (73d9–10). Simmias enthusiastically agrees that there are indeed countless examples, as well he should (73d11). Socrates' description does not apply only to how we are reminded; recollection that involves forgetting and being reminded is only one species of what Socrates is explaining. Rather, Socrates speaks here of how we are minded at all. He has described the consequential association of thoughts.[32]

Precisely what is significant in this consequential association—the recollection from dissimilar objects of knowledge—is the particular character, the capacity and experience, of the one recollecting.[33] In his first example, for instance, Socrates speaks of someone seeing a lyre or cloak and being reminded of a boy. It was, however, not just anyone seeing and not just any boy who was remembered. The connection of the lyre or cloak to the particular boy lay in the fact that it was the lover of the boy viewing the object which the boy "habitually" used. Again, Socrates spoke of someone seeing Simmias and "often" being reminded of Cebes. This connection, clearly, is not a necessary one; it happens not always, but often. The connection depends upon the contingency that the one viewing Simmias happens to know that he habitually associates with Cebes. We could add to these examples the event at the outset of this argument: an associate of Socrates seeing Socrates and being reminded of that doctrine which he "habitually" sets forth. What is important to see is that the connection between dissimilar objects of knowledge is not then automatic; the connection does not exist in the objects themselves. Therefore, the particular character of the one recollecting becomes important insofar as the connection is made in his or her mind.

What I mean by 'the particular character of the one recollecting' is well-illustrated by Socrates' examples. Socrates speaks of the connection being made by habit—that is, by the particular experience which the recollector happens to have. He further specifies such experience when he speaks of lovers and their beloveds. These examples point to the dependence of knowledge on experience, on having lived in this particular place and time, on having had these particular perceptions, on being moved by a particular set of desires.

Because many commentators read the Recollection argument as a whole in the light of the proof proper, they wonder at Socrates' dwelling upon recollection from dissimilars. Their perplexity is engendered especially by the character of the final example and condition of recollection which Socrates presents prior to the proof itself. Socrates speaks of the case in which one "seeing Simmias depicted [is] reminded of Simmias himself." He asks whether in thinking about recollection from similar things one must not also "think whether or not the thing is lacking at all in its similarity in relation to what one is reminded of?" (73a9–74a7). This example and condition of recollection are usually taken to be the model for the relation of particular and intelligible in the forthcoming proof.[34] Indeed, the movement of the argument lends itself to this impression as it culminates in this example and condition of recollection from similars. Gallop expresses this view concisely:

> The further examples of Recollection given here are so arranged as to lead up to the case of Simmias and his picture which best illustrates the relation between forms and sensible particulars. But it is hard to see why so many examples are given, and in particular why 'being reminded by dissimilars' is illustrated at such length, since cases of this sort will play no part in the coming argument about forms and particulars. Why does Socrates insist that there is Recollection from dissimilar things as well as from similar?[35]

In order to answer Gallop's question, we must appreciate the difference between the first and second sections of the argument.[36] This is especially important because the proof itself (the second section) raises doubt as to whether the relationship between particular and intelligible is the same as that expressed in the example of Simmias' picture and Simmias himself. In other words, it raises doubt about whether the relationship between particular and intelligible is equivalent to the relationship between the perceived image and the previously known original. The proof thus leads us to question whether the whole is organized simply for the sake of intelligibility such that the whole perceivable world is necessarily and for all humans like a diagram of a triangle representing the Pythagorean theorem.[37] In the face of this doubt, Socrates' dwelling on dissimilars makes more sense: he is presenting *the* alternative understanding to that understanding which takes the connection between perceivable and intelligible to be automatic. The alternative is that this connection is made by a particular human mind and is affected by that mind in its particularity—that is, by the experiences, capacity, and desires of that mind. This alternative re-emerges in the third section of the proof. Now, however, we must turn to the second section of the argument, Socrates' proof of the pre-existence of the soul, in order to see precisely what is problematic about the proof such that we are driven back to the alternative presented in the first and third sections of the proof.

The argument for the pre-existence of the soul runs as follows. We know the equal itself and it differs from the equal particulars that we perceive. More specifically, this difference is an inferiority of the equal things to the equal itself. The thought of the equal itself, however, cannot have arisen from the equal things precisely because the latter are inferior to the former. Therefore, we must have obtained the equal itself prior to the perception of the equal things. But we are perceiving as soon as we are born. Thus, if we received the thought of the equal itself prior to our perception of equal things, we must have received it prior to birth in some prenatal noetic perception. Let us consider this argument in detail.

Socrates asks Simmias whether we say there is something equal itself, something beyond the equal things. Simmias affirms most fervently not only that we say there is such an entity, but he also affirms that we know what it is (74a9–b3). Socrates thus begins the proof from the standpoint of the supposed original rather than from the supposed image. He proceeds to speak of two sticks, considered with respect to equality, as leading to the equal itself. Yet we can well wonder whether two sticks do necessarily lead to the equal itself. Do they not as well lead to the dual itself, length itself, wood itself, or perhaps to nothing beyond themselves?

The point is that it is not clear that two sticks, or any other perceivables, are *necessarily* an image of an underlying intelligible such that we are always led to the intelligible. If they were, we should have expected Socrates to begin with what is first encountered, the perceivable, as he did with all of his preceding examples. We should have expected him to begin with what is supposed to be an image and move to the original.

Socrates begins to ask where we get knowledge of the equal itself but interrupts himself to emphasize not the likeness but the difference between the intelligible and the particular (74b6–7). It is established that, although equal things sometimes seem equal to one but not to another, the equal itself never seems unequal. It is difficult to discern the ground of either similarity or dissimilarity in this much-vexed passage. If, as seems to be the case, Socrates claims that the equal itself is equal, then that group of problems which goes by the name of self-predication emerges. Must the equality of the equal itself be accounted for by reference to a still higher intelligible, and this latter by still another intelligible, in infinite regression?[38] Or is the first intelligible perfect equality? But what would perfect equality mean? Would it be equal to everything? Or if it is not equal to everything, is it in some respect unequal and then not different from the particular instantiations of equality? Socrates perplexes the issue still further by asking: "Did the equals themselves ever seem to you unequal or equality inequality?" (74c1–2). Is the plural intended to be equivalent to the intelligible or is Socrates suggesting that the intelligible is *in* each of the particulars?[39] But can something which is supposed to be eternal and unchanging be a multiplicity? Finally, is equality the same as the equal itself? Is there then also the unequal itself? If so, it would seem to be perfectly expressed in the many unequal particulars (74c1–9).[40] None of these questions disturbs Simmias' devotion to the doctrine of self-subsisting intelligibles. However, if the relationship between particular and intelligible is that expressed in the example of Simmias' picture and Simmias himself, between an image and its known original, it is certainly not clear how this might be the case.

Socrates himself confirms the ambiguity of the relationship when immediately following the preceding passage he asks whether the equal particulars lead to the equal itself,

> it being either similar to them or dissimilar? Anyway, it makes no difference so long as on seeing one thing, one does, from this sight, think of another whether it be similar or dissimilar, this must be recollection. (74c11–d2)[41]

In beginning with the intelligible rather than with its supposed image, and in emphasizing the difference between the intelligible and particular, Socrates leaves the relationship between the two in all its ambiguity. To use the phrase later used by Socrates, the relationship appears to be between objects of knowledge that are "dissimilar but related" (76a2–4). Of course, the question then is: What provides for the relationship if it is not provided by similarity?

Socrates asserts that the difference between the intelligible and the particular is one of inferiority on the part of the latter in comparison to the former. Therefore, when we view the equal things we are affected in the following manner: we see a thing and think that it falls short of being whatever intelligible the particular thing strives to be (74d4–d7).[42] Whereas previously, in the case of the image and original, we were said to think 'whether' the one resembles the other, here we are said to think necessarily of their difference.[43]

What then is the connection between the particular and the intelligible? One obvious possibility would be to return to the connection made in some of the examples in the first section of the argument, the connection that is made by the particular character of a human mind. But Socrates avoids this option. In order to join the perceivable and intelligible—that is, to account for the whole—he does reintroduce elements of the individual soul, but he does so in a peculiarly questionable manner. He does not find these elements in the character of individual souls. Rather, he takes what we usually regard as human characteristics and attributes them to the things of the world. Specifically, Socrates takes the desire of the human individual which joined the cloak to the boy in the mind of the lover and places it in the particular things. Socrates eroticizes the perceivable world. Thus, we are asked to believe that the perceivable world is joined to the intelligible because "the thing that I now see wishes to be like another of the things that are," or that all the equal things are "striving to be like the equal," or that "all things are desiring to be like" the intelligible.[44]

When we think through the connection between the particulars and the intelligible offered in the proof proper, we are left uncertain of the connection. Socrates calls attention to this difficulty in the act of covering it up. Through his personifying—or, more specifically, his eroticizing—of the particulars, Socrates leads us to ask why he goes to such lengths to avoid the more obvious solution. What are the implications for understanding if it is the eros of individual humans that is involved with the connection of the perceivable and the intelligible—if, that is, the aforementioned example of the lover viewing the form of the beloved plays an integral role in the process of understanding?[45]

In thinking through this question, it is useful to consider briefly the *Symposium* where this issue is dealt with in detail. In that dialogue, Socrates relates how his teacher in erotic matters, Diotima, describes the progress of human understanding as an ascent from the love of one beautiful body to the love of all beautiful bodies to the love of beautiful souls and eventually approaching the beautiful itself.[46] For the present purpose, it is crucial to see that this description makes evident that success in the ascent depends upon the particular capacity of the student. Only rare students will progress even to the second rung of the ladder; most will be consumed by corporeal desires. And only the very rarest will have the capacity and the desire to complete the ascent. But can we account for these considerations—one's capacity and one's desire—if we conceive of the soul as mind alone—that is, as pure mind? It seems that the soul would have to be conceived as itself partaking of differences if we are to explain how one soul could differ so significantly from another, how one soul could be better or worse than another.[47] Moreover, as Diotima's account makes clear, there are not only corporeal desires, but desires of the soul, as for example the desire for pure wisdom.[48] Again, only if soul is conceived as complex could we explain how it is that the soul could reflect on itself and become aware of what it lacks, much less that soul could fail to be complete. At the very least, such a lack implies an imperfection that mind alone—pure mind, unchanging and eternal—would not exhibit.

In light of such considerations, we can appreciate why Socrates would avoid an explicit discussion of the effect of eros on human understanding. In sum, if human desire plays a role in understanding, then we must have a more complex conception of the soul. On the basis of such a conception, it becomes difficult to maintain the eventual union of pure mind with the likewise pure intelligibles. As Diotima makes clear, the apprehension of wisdom is, to say the least, not for everybody. Indeed, it is not certain that anybody reaches this goal; the apprehension of the ultimate intelligible remains wrapped in mystery.[49] According to her account, the question remains whether beings such as we experience ourselves to be can communicate with wisdom understood as incorporeal and unchanging.

Socrates now states that, since apprehension of the intelligible is prior to perception, and we were perceiving as soon as we were born, then we must have apprehended the intelligible prior to birth. Everything that is necessary in order to prove the soul's prenatal existence is now available. Yet not until after another Stephanus page of argument does Socrates draw this conclusion.[50] In the intervening passage, Socrates presents explicitly that chasm between the soul that automatically and necessarily apprehends the intelligible and the soul that exists in human form. In order to maintain that our souls as such have access to the ever-existing intelligibles, it is necessary to bridge this chasm. This is the purpose of the doctrine of Recollection which Socrates now introduces in its full-fledged form. Only now does he define forgetting and learning. It is important to consider the basis of this doctrine upon which now rests the harmony of the human mind and the intelligibles.

Socrates offers Simmias a choice: either we obtained the intelligibles before birth and are born knowing them all, or, having obtained them before birth, we forget them at birth and later recollect them (75d7–e7). The first alternative, that all are born knowing all, follows more directly from the proof than does the second alternative. However, both alternatives are, strictly speaking, irrelevant from the standpoint of the soul's prenatal existence insofar as both assume that existence.[51] Perhaps for this reason, Simmias cannot decide between the alternatives.

In order to help him decide, Socrates asks Simmias a question directing him to what is staring him in the face: "If a man knows things, can he give an account of what he knows or not?" (76b5–6). Having secured Simmias' assent to the point that this man could give an account, Socrates asks: "And do you think everyone can give an account of those objects we were discussing just now?" (76b8–9). Contrary to his earlier position, which maintained that each soul necessarily intuits the intelligibles (74b3), Simmias now affirms that only Socrates could give such an account or *logos*. With this example of great human diversity before him, Simmias agrees that humans must have forgotten what they once apprehended and are therefore reminded of these intelligibles.

However, we need to recognize, as Simmias does not, the vast difference between the notion of knowledge as a 'correct account' or *logos,* and the notion of knowledge as the intuition of the intelligibles. The former would seem to aim at the sort of discursive account undertaken by Socrates in several dialogues in order to answer his characteristic question, "what is . . . ?" Such an account requires that one articulate the distinctive aspects of the idea in question, those aspects which differentiate it from other ideas, and relate it to still more general ideas. This process of comparing and contrasting, relating and distinguishing, is the process of reasoning. It occurs in and through speech or conversation, whether through an internal conversation or one such as that in which Simmias and Socrates are presently engaged.[52] It occurs through the questioning and answering that Socrates mentions in the present context (75d2–3).

Crucial to such a notion of knowledge are those considerations raised in Diotima's speech and those that Cebes had mentioned when, at the beginning of the argument, he too had spoken of the object of learning as "knowledge and a correct account" (73a9–10). The success of such a conversation depends very much on the innate capacities of the participants. As Cebes says in introducing the Recollection doctrine, the process of question and answer reaches its goal "if the questions are well put" (73a8). Conceiving of knowledge in this way, then, we would also be much more aware of the extent to which our differing capacities affect our understanding of the objects of knowledge. Our experience tells us, as Simmias' experience tells him, that not everyone is equally capable of providing an account of the degree of depth and comprehension that a Socrates is able to provide. Moreover, the successful outcome of such a conversation is not assured; it has the character more of an ascent toward complete understanding than a noetic perception of the intelligible that one has either completely or not at all. Conceiving of knowledge in this way, then, we would also be much more aware of the tentativeness of our knowledge because we are still on our way to wisdom rather than in complete possession of it. Perhaps the recognition of this tentative and hypothetical character of our understanding explains the unusual manner in which Socrates refers to the intelligibles in the present context. He speaks of them as that "on which *we set this seal*, 'what it is', in the questions we ask and in the answers we give" (75d1–3, emphasis added).

But Simmias does not notice the enormous difference between these two notions of knowledge. Rather, he takes Socrates' question as a reason to believe in the doctrine of Recollection. The doctrine of Recollection bridges two views of the soul and, as we see here, the difference that must be bridged by the doctrine of Recollection is indeed vast. It is the difference between what Simmias' experience tells him—that only Socrates truly knows the intelligibles—and what follows from the proof of the soul's prenatal existence—that each soul has intuited the intelligibles. The difference is expressed in Socrates' conclusion: "Then our souls (*psuchai*) did exist earlier, Simmias, before entering human form (*anthrōpou eidei*), apart from bodies, and they possessed wisdom" (76c11–13). This distinction between "our souls" and "human form" occurs throughout the second proof (73a1–2, 76c6–7, 76c11–13, 76e3–4, 76e6–7, 77a1, 77a10–b1 and 77c2–3). It expresses nicely the great difference that must exist between the soul which knows all and the soul which explains our human existence as conscious life, only the rarest of which knows the intelligibles. The harmony of humanity and the intelligibles depends now on the doctrine of Recollection. It does so because the doctrine of Recollection aims to explain how the soul we infer from our experience can be the soul that communes with the unchanging intelligible.

But why should we believe in the validity of the doctrine of Recollection? The ensuing exchange between Socrates and Simmias at least makes clear the premise of this doctrine. In response to Socrates' conclusion, Simmias asks: "Unless maybe, Socrates, we get those pieces of knowledge at the very moment of birth; that time still remains" (76c14–15). Simmias' question poses the possibility that our souls did not pre-exist the body, that we are simply born with varying capacities. In response, Socrates asks tersely: "At what other time do we lose them [the intelligibles]?" (76d1).[53] Simmias drops his objection, but he does so too easily.[54] Socrates' response assumes precisely what is in question—namely, that our souls existed before birth so as to possess the wisdom they later lose. And they must have existed earlier because of the character of the intelligibles which are such as not to be available through perception. The premise behind the doctrine of Recollection is precisely that such intelligibles exist.

Without the doctrine of Recollection, the proof of immortality based on the soul's capacity to know lacks a connection to our self-experience; the soul has little in common with that which occupies the 'human form.' Yet the doctrine of Recollection is not demonstrated. It rests on the premise that the intelligibles are necessarily prior to any experience, precisely the premise that it was called upon to help substantiate. If this latter contention became questionable, if the existence of such intelligibles were put into doubt, then clearly the harmony of the soul and the eternal intelligible would become likewise questionable. It is just this contention that Socrates encourages the young men to question. He asks:

> Then is our position as follows, Simmias? *If* the objects we are always harping on exist, a beautiful, a good, and all such being, and *if* we refer or liken all our sense-perceptions to them, finding again what was formerly ours, and *if* we compare these things with that, then just as surely as those objects exist, so also must our soul exist before we are born. *On the other hand, if they don't exist, this argument will have gone for nothing.* Is this the position? Is it equally necessary that those objects exist, and that our souls existed before birth, and if the former don't exist, then neither did the latter? (76d7–e4, emphasis added)

So convinced is Simmias of the existence of the intelligibles and of the corollary pre-existence of the soul that he does not even comment on the troubling possibility Socrates has raised in presenting what he calls "our position"—namely, that the intelligibles *so understood* do not exist. Simmias does not yet seem to desire to engage in learning in the sense of striving for a correct account. But perhaps we should not be surprised that Simmias does not seem to hear this possibility. After all, neither did he seem bothered by the notion that only Socrates knows those intelligibles which so easily gain Simmias' assent. Instead, Simmias states that "it is abundantly clear" to him that

> there's the same necessity in either case, and the argument takes opportune refuge in the view that our soul exists before birth, just as surely as the being of which you're now speaking. Because I myself find nothing so plain to me as that all such objects, noble and good and all the others you were speaking of just now, are in the fullest possible way; so in my view it's been adequately proved. (76e8–77a5)[55]

Simmias is correct in drawing together the soul's immortality and the existence of the unchanging intelligibles. For in order to prove immortality, there has been an attempt to establish a harmony of the human soul and these intelligibles. But Socrates ends the argument by casting doubt on the existence of these intelligibles. We can appreciate why he does so: that we are such as to have access to these intelligibles depends on a doctrine—the doctrine of Recollection—whose premise is precisely that such intelligibles exist. We can also appreciate why Socrates is not more forthcoming about this disharmony if we recall that the doctrine of immortality of the soul was intrinsically related to the attainment of pure wisdom.

But Simmias does not question our access to the ever-existing intelligibles. As suggested by his addition of the Noble itself and the Good itself to the Equal itself, this doctrine of the ever-existing intelligibles, or the Ideas, is most important for Simmias to the extent that it enables him to maintain his unquestioned assumption that there is trans-human support for the human good which, of course, includes his good.[56] Simmias is content to define that which transcends humanity in whatever way will serve what he 'knows' to be his good.

Simmias' interest is circumscribed by his self-concern. Unlike Cebes, he does not challenge Socrates to present an account of the whole of nature. But Simmias is the proper addressee of this proof insofar as reflection on the issue it implicitly raises could lead one such as Simmias to see the need to transcend his characteristic concern. The tension between the several sections of the proof, as well as the recurring distinction between our souls and the human form, point to an issue papered over by the doctrine of Recollection. The issue concerns the way in which the soul must be conceived in order to explain our self-experience. The doctrine of Recollection acknowledges the problem in its attempt to provide a link between the soul conceived simply as knower and the soul as it accounts for the variety of human capacities and characteristics. Most prominently, Socrates compels Simmias to acknowledge the existence of vast inequality among humans in reminding him of the chasm between Socrates and all other humans. In light of this inequality, the question of human good must be more complicated than Simmias is willing to admit. Is his good the same as Socrates' good or is it akin to the good of most humans? What common good could join such diverse beings (63d1)? What understanding of the soul could account for these vast differences? And in what way could the intelligibles support Simmias' good if only Socrates can give an account of them? In short, the proof shows how Simmias' characteristic concern for his own good ought to lead him to reflection on the wider questions of the nature of human beings and the place that we occupy in the whole of nature. Simmias does not pursue these wider questions. But it is important for us to see that this is Socrates' lesson for Simmias. For in his forthcoming reply to Simmias' objection, Socrates makes even more clear the dialectical necessity that leads from the examination of the soul to the examination of the whole. As is evident from this second proof, this necessity derives from the complexity that the soul must have in order to explain our self-experience.

While Simmias is satisfied with aspects of the foregoing argument, he wants further assurance that what he knows to be his good will be his. Accordingly, while accepting that the soul pre-exists its embodiment, Simmias asks for further assurance against "the popular fear that when a man dies, his soul may be dispersed at that time, and that that may be the end of its existence" (77b2–5). Cebes agrees that "if the proof is going to be complete," post-mortem existence must be demonstrated (77c1–5).

Socrates advises the interlocutors simply to combine the preceding proofs, in order to obtain what they seek (77c6–9). But his recommendation is obscure in its details: he proceeds to speak only of the first proof which by itself pertains to the soul's existence both before birth and after death. Socrates' recommendation, however, does serve to focus on the difficulty at hand: precisely how could one combine the first and second proofs? Specifically, in what way could the complexity of nature and the complexity of the soul harmonize?[57] The third proof addresses this problem in speaking about both the soul and nature. It attempts to show that, in fact, both the soul and intelligible nature share the same simple, incomposite nature.

Prior to undertaking still another proof, Socrates recognizes the fear in his interlocutors. It is a fear which must be growing in light of the less-than-satisfying arguments offered so far. Socrates says to Cebes: "I think you and Simmias would like to thrash out this argument still further; you seem afraid, like children" (77d5–7). In response, Cebes sheepishly asks Socrates: "Try to reassure us, Socrates, as if we were afraid; or rather, not as if we were afraid ourselves—but maybe there's a child inside us who has fears of that sort" (77e3–7). Cebes seems to want to put some distance between himself and this fear. Socrates, in turn, says: "You must sing spells to him every day until you've charmed it [the fear] out of him" (77e8–9). Cebes asks plaintively; "And where shall we find a charmer for such fears, Socrates, now that you're leaving us?" (78a1–2). Thus, although Cebes seems to want to distance himself from this fear, his dependence on Socrates and his desire for some new charmer, indicate that he's still drawn to the hope that there exists some wiser being who will explain away the fact of death.[58]

Socrates recommends first that they search both Greece and the foreign lands for such a charmer, "sparing neither money nor trouble, because there's no object on which you could more opportunely spend your money" (78a5–7). As we learn in the *Crito*, Simmias and Cebes are already willing to spend their money for Socrates' sake. But Socrates concludes by saying: "You may not easily find anyone more capable of doing this than yourselves" (78a8–9). Perhaps it is *only* by ourselves, one at a time, that we can truly reconcile ourselves to death insofar as such reconciliation means finally to acknowledge that *I* will no longer exist. Socrates, it seems, has at least made progress in this direction. For, contrary to Cebes' expectation, Socrates would be pleased to continue to think and talk about the topic that cannot help but remind him of his own mortality.

Likeness

Socrates begins the third proof by laying out the program he will follow in considering the issue at hand. He asks:

Mustn't we ask ourselves something like this: What kind of thing is liable to undergo this fate—namely dispersal—and for what kind of thing should we fear lest it undergo it? And what kind of thing is not liable to it? And next, mustn't we further ask to which of these two kinds soul belongs and then feel either confidence or fear for our own soul accordingly? (78b4–9)

The proof aims to consider the nature of the soul in order to determine whether it is the kind of thing that does not pass away. In order to exemplify such entities, Socrates refers to the unchanging intelligibles. The proof bears on that possibility raised at the end of the preceding proof concerning the existence or nonexistence of the unchanging intelligibles. Simmias was unprovoked by this possibility, but Cebes, with his characteristic willingness to follow the argument, asks Socrates to "go back to the point where we left off" (78a10–b1). Cebes again becomes Socrates' interlocutor for this proof which, like the first, investigates the availability of a certain and comprehensive account of the whole of nature.

In the announcement of his program, Socrates already voices a premonition of failure; an airtight argument would make irrelevant fear and hope, which are, after all, responses to uncertainty. But the argument is not airtight. It reaches the conclusion that the "soul must be completely indissoluble, *or something close to it*" (80b9–10, emphasis added). The nature of soul does not seem to guarantee its immortality. Following this conclusion, there occurs a passage, akin to the third section of Socrates' defense, that elucidates the grounds upon which the philosopher might reasonably hope to earn very great benefits in the next world. The premise of this passage is in tension with the conclusion of the discursive portion of the third proof insofar as it seems to assume a harmony between the human and the trans-human. In the detailed examination of the proof that follows, we shall have to see whether Cebes' willingness to follow the argument brings him to recognize this tension.

Approaching the question of what kind of thing is not liable to dispersal, Socrates considers first the qualities of incompositeness and compositeness. The relation of these qualities to the question of dispersal is clear: that which does not consist of parts cannot suffer dispersal of parts or decomposition. But as several commentators recognize, Socrates' treatment of these qualities in fact raises doubts about the status of the incomposite.[59] Socrates begins speaking of the composite rather than the incomposite, and he evinces far more assuredness about the existence of the former than the latter. For example, he goes out of his way to indicate that there is a composite *by nature,* referring to the composite as "what has been put together and is by nature put together" (78c1–2). Yet, although Socrates clearly thinks that nature provides for the composite, the same cannot be said for the incomposite. Speaking of the latter, Socrates states: "*If* there happens to be something incomposite, it alone is liable, *if anything is,* not to experience [dispersal]" (78c3–4, emphasis added).

Socrates' hesitancy concerning the incomposite appears also in the next step of the argument as he links the incomposite with the unvarying.

Instead of offering an argument for this link, he asks an ambiguous question that contains the point that the unvarying is "likely" to be incomposite. The form of the question implies greater certainty on Socrates' part concerning the range of the unvarying than of the incomposite (78c6–8).[60] But, Socrates exhibits no such hesitation regarding the connection between the composite and the varying. He asserts the existence of this connection categorically. Socrates never offers an example of the incomposite nor, more remarkably, does he ever apply this category, decisive as it is, to the soul.

Socrates moves to the next set of opposite qualities, the varying and the unvarying, and he suggests that they "go back to those entities to which we turned in our earlier argument", the intelligibles, in order to exemplify that which is unvarying (78c10–d1). Socrates asks:

> Is the Being itself whose being we give an account of in asking and answering questions, unvarying and constant or does it vary? Does the equal itself, the beautiful itself, what each thing is itself, that which is, ever admit of any change whatsoever? Or does what each of them is, being uniform alone by itself, remain unvarying and constant, and never admit of any kind of alteration in any way or respect whatever? (78d1–5)[61]

Cebes affirms that this is the case. Turning to that which varies, Socrates asks:

> But what about the many beautiful things, such as men or horses or cloaks or anything else at all of that kind? Or equals, or all things that bear the same name as those objects? Are they constant or are they just the opposite of those others, and *so to speak* never constant at all, either in relation to themselves or to one another? (78d10–e4, emphasis added)

Socrates articulates here the full-blown 'two-world' theory that contemporary thinkers consider to be his final word.[62] According to this understanding, the cosmos is rent by such irreconcilable distinctions as that between the unvarying and the varying or, to be more specific, between the beautiful itself and the beautiful things, the good itself and the good things. However, while Cebes affirms this understanding without reservation, the same cannot be said of Socrates. A careful consideration of the foregoing statement reveals the basis for Socrates' qualification—"so to speak" (78e4).

Socrates' statement that the things we confront in our everyday experience "bear the same name" as the intelligibles suggests that the things cannot be simply consigned to the category of the varying (78e2). How could that which is constantly changing in relation to itself nevertheless "bear the same name as those objects"—the intelligibles? A thing must be sufficiently stable to permit us to recognize it as the same thing and thus to name it as a certain kind of thing.

A similar question arises in relation to what Socrates says about humans in this context. Socrates includes humans as examples of beings which are, "so to speak," constantly varying. But, if we are in constant flux, how can we have the contact with the intelligibles that involves "asking and answering questions" in our account of them. These questions do not occur to Cebes, or if they do he does not raise them.[63] But Socrates makes Cebes face them through his introduction of still another pair of opposite qualities, the seen and the invisible.

Socrates asks:

> Now these things you could actually touch and see and sense with the other senses, couldn't you, whereas those that are constant you could lay hold of only by reasoning of the intellect; aren't such things, rather, invisible and not seen? (79a1–4)

This speech tacitly endorses my preceding critique concerning Socrates' categorization of humans; given that we are in touch with both the particular things and the intelligibles, we cannot be understood to fall simply into one or the other absolute categories. As becomes evident in what follows, the same conclusion must be reached with respect to the particular beings or things.

Socrates asks Cebes: "Would you like us to posit two kinds (*duo eidē*) of beings, the one kind seen, the other invisible?"(79a6–7). Cebes agrees to this point as well as to Socrates' identification of the invisible and the unvarying. But in the subsequent discussion, the hard and fast distinction between two kinds of beings is made dubious. The form of Socrates' argument itself belies this absolute separation. Kenneth Dorter rightly notes that the mode of argumentation in the third proof involves "reasoning by analogy from the known to the unknown."[64] To be more specific, it involves inference from that which is seen to that which is invisible. Understanding is presented as a process of noting similarity and difference. This process of inference becomes clear as Socrates asks, at last, into which category does the soul fit? More specifically, he asks this question with respect to both body and soul after having asserted that "we ourselves are part body and part soul" (79b1–2). Body, it is decided, is "more similar and more akin" to the seen (79b4–6). But what about the soul? The relevant exchange runs as follows.

Socrates:	Well, but we ourselves are part body and part soul, aren't we?
Cebes:	We are.
Socrates:	Then to which kind do we say that the body will be more similar and more akin?
Cebes:	That's clear to anyone: obviously to the seen.
Socrates:	And what about the soul? Is it seen or invisible?
Cebes:	It's not seen by men, at any rate, Socrates.
Socrates:	But we meant, surely, things seen and not seen with reference to human nature; or do you think we meant any other?
Cebes:	We meant human nature. (79b1–11)

Cebes' answer ("It's not seen by men, at any rate, Socrates") entertains the possibility that we could perhaps adopt a perspective other than the human. Socrates' pointed retort ("But we meant, surely, things seen and not seen with reference to human nature or do you think we meant any other?") seems intended to emphasize for the self-forgetting Cebes that we see and think in accordance with "human nature."[65] There is no stepping outside of our own skin. We must begin with the world as *we* experience it. In the exchange that follows, it is made more clear that we come to know through a process of inference.

Socrates:	What do we say about soul then? Is it seen or unseen?
Cebes:	It's not seen.
Socrates:	Then it's invisible?
Cebes:	Yes.
Socrates:	Then soul is more similar than body to the invisible, whereas body is more similar to that which is seen. (79b12–16)

Socrates establishes that soul is "not seen" and, next, that it is "invisible."[66] Again, the latter is presented as an inference from the former. Socrates has indicated that by the invisible he means a kind of being that is constant and perhaps incomposite, exemplified above all by the intelligibles (79a1–10). But to the extent that the invisible is an inference from our experience, its absolute separation from the perceivable is made dubious. It must be possible to move from the particular things to the intelligibles somehow understood; to the extent that we know by inference, the things and the intelligibles must be connected in some way.[67] The things must be more complex than Socrates' absolute distinction implies. Socrates' cautious conclusion concerning the soul reflects the foregoing point. This conclusion, the only one drawn by Socrates himself in this passage, runs as follows: "Then soul is more similar than body to the invisible, whereas body is more similar to that which is seen" (79b16–17). Body is not simply equal to that which is seen; after all, there are processes of the body that are not seen by men. But neither is soul simply equal to the invisible. Indeed, as regards the soul, Socrates does not even permit himself to draw the same conclusion that he had drawn with respect to body. He does not say that soul is more similar to the invisible. Rather, he states that soul is simply more like the invisible *than is body*. If, as is the case with the other objects of our understanding, the soul must be understood as an inference from our experience, the claim that it is identical with that which is "invisible" becomes more difficult to sustain.

Socrates next considers the soul and body in relation to the opposites, unvarying–varying. He asks Cebes whether it had not been maintained that whenever the soul uses sense-perception,

> it is dragged by the body towards objects that are never constant; and it wanders about itself, and is confused and dizzy, as if drunk, in virtue of contact with things of a similar kind. (79c6–8)

The opposite occurs whenever soul communes with things of an unvarying nature—namely, the unchanging intelligibles (79d1–8). Most impressive in this portrayal, however, is the degree to which soul is affected by those things that Socrates attributes to body. In fact, far from unvarying, the nature of the soul seems determined by the company it keeps. Depending on its objects, the soul has the potential to be either "confused and dizzy as if drunk" or "always constant and unvarying" (79c7–8, 79d5).

Cebes is led to the conclusion that soul is "totally and altogether more similar to what is unvarying" (79e2–5).[68] This odd locution—"totally and altogether more similar"—serves to highlight the character of the conclusion being drawn here. The soul is *similar* to that which is unvarying; it is *similar* to those intelligibles which are *the* examples of that which is unvarying. It is *not identical* to them.

We expected Socrates, at some point, to apply the crucial polarity, incomposite–composite, to the soul. But given the need to consider our self-experience in understanding the soul, we can well understand why Socrates avoids facing directly the question of the soul's incompositeness. How can soul be incomposite and simple if it must be held responsible for those activities we do as humans? How can it be responsible for life as well as thought, for moral activity as well as contemplative activity? In this light, we can understand why it is that when Socrates considers the case when "soul and body are present in the same thing," he applies to the soul and body the opposite categories of divine–mortal rather than the categories incomposite–composite (79e8–9). The former pair is better suited to explaining what soul must be given the activities of which it must be capable.

As he begins this application, Socrates is even evasive concerning which of this pair applies to soul. Without stating explicitly whether he means soul or body, Socrates first says that "nature ordains that one should rule and the other serve"(80a1–2). Because each has had its turn in the driver's seat—we've just heard about the soul being dragged about by the body—we must conclude that nature's command is not unbreachable; nature is more equivocal than we might wish it to be. Only after having made the foregoing statement concerning nature does Socrates introduce the divine and mortal, associating the former with rule and the latter with servitude. He then likens soul to the divine and body to the mortal, thereby avoiding ever directly stating that soul rules and body is ruled (80a1–7). As for the question of the soul's incompositeness, it is answered, I think, by Socrates' silence on this subject in the present context.

Socrates concludes the argument by listing the qualities that the soul resembles and those that the body resembles. It is perhaps worth noting, as does Burnet, that the pairs of opposites are not perfectly symmetrical.[69] Socrates inverts the pairs of monoeidetic and polyeidetic, and intelligible and foolish. Certainly, body as such cannot be characterized as foolish. But if this quality were attributed to soul it would become necessary to rethink whether soul is properly considered monoeidetic or polyeidetic.

Again, soul is "most similar" to what is "intelligible" and "unvarying." Humanity is not in perfect harmony with intelligible nature; there is no certainty concerning the relationship between the human soul and the whole of nature. Socrates can only say that "soul must be completely indissoluble, *or something close to it*" (80b9–10 emphasis added). In support of this contention, Socrates offers one more inference derived from what we can observe. He notes that when the body is embalmed as it is in Egypt, it "remains almost entire for an immensely long time" and some of its parts are "practically immortal" (80c9, d2). Socrates asks, if body is capable of this,

> can it be, then, that the soul, the invisible part, which goes to another place of that kind, noble, pure, and invisible, to "Hades" in the true sense of the word, into the presence of the good and wise God—where, God willing, my own soul too must shortly enter—can it be that this, which we've found to be a thing of such a kind and nature, should on separation from the body at once be blown apart and perish, as most men say? (80d5–e1)

That our knowledge must depend on this kind of reasoning, on inference from experience, testifies against the perfect harmony of the soul and the Ideas. Socrates' pun on the word *invisible* (*aidē*) and Hades (*Haidou*) prepares the next stage of the proof as he moves from discursive argument to mythic presentation. The failure of the proof makes this movement necessary. It remains unproved that either the soul or the beings possess the incomposite nature that would render them indissoluble.

At this point, Socrates presents another version of the religion for philosophers that we saw in his defense. Again, he turns to an account of rewards of the philosophic life. Like that earlier presentation, this religion rests precisely on the premise that was left undemonstrated in the immediately preceding argument—namely, that there is a harmony of the human soul and intelligible nature. Socrates' defense had culminated in an alternative: either prove that the soul is immortal and thus has access to perfect wisdom or inquire into the possibility of philosophy that does not presume the accessibility of perfect wisdom. In offering the present religion for philosophers, Socrates again sets before the young men a choice: either *believe* in a premise that supports your hopes for reward in the next world or face the uncertainties left by the inadequate proofs. The choice is now all the more vivid, coming as it does hard on the heels of the failed third proof. That is, reasoned argument has failed three times to supply demonstrable proof of immortality. To this extent, reason points to the dubiousness of such a proof. In what follows, Socrates sharpens the choice between reason and belief even more by making the requirements of the religion for philosophers more stringent than ever and the ground of hope, therefore, ever more dubious.[70]

Socrates speaks of that place to which the soul will go, journeying to "another place of that kind, noble, pure, and invisible, to 'Hades' in the true sense of the word," a place that is akin to its own nature (80d5–7). Having said this, however, he interrupts himself (80e5).[71] He does so to dwell not on the next world but on the practice necessary in this world, the practice necessary to become what he calls one of the initiates (81a8–9). Involved in this practice is a depreciation of our terrestrial existence exceeding even that of the earlier *doxa*.

Socrates offers the familiar advice that the initiate is to avoid as far as possible any contact with the body. But he is even more vivid than he was in his defense concerning the many "ills of the human condition" (81a7–8). Moreover, the philosopher is advised to abstain not only from all desires but from pleasures and pains as well. The recommended practice regarding the senses is equally demanding. The philosopher's disdain of the senses should reach as far as "not to regard as real" the "sensible and the seen" (83b3–4). Only in this way can one avoid what Socrates here calls, "the greatest and most extreme of all evils":

> that the soul of every man when intensely pleased or pained at something is forced at the same time to suppose that whatever affects it in this way is most clear and most real, when it is not so; and such objects especially are things seen. (83c2–8)

Following this program, one would presumably merit treatment as an initiate after death. Again, however, this program involves a mode of existence that finds little reflection in Socrates' own life. Moreover, the requirements ignore the limits of the human perspective upon which he had just insisted. In fact, the requirements seem all but impossible. In presenting such an extreme program, Socrates aims, I think, to bring about a confrontation with the premise of that program, a premise so compelling that for most people almost any regimen would be preferable to abandoning it.

The premise is most clearly revealed by Socrates' inclusion of a doctrine of reincarnation in the speech. This doctrine begins from Socrates' claim that those who have had commerce with the body during their lives are encumbered by corporeality (81c4–6). They cannot move to Hades, the region of the invisible and incorporeal. Rather, they are dragged back to earth, and we see them wandering around tombs and graves as ghosts (81c8–d4). Their ghostly careers end when "they are once more imprisoned in a body; and they're likely to be imprisoned in whatever types of character they may have cultivated in their lifetime" (81e2–3). A particular way of life leads to reincarnation in a particular kind of animal; for example, gluttons, lechers, and drunks enter the forms of donkeys.

As Socrates continues to match ways of life with appropriate animals, it becomes clear that the reincarnative process redounds to the benefit of the philosopher, who differs from all others in avoiding reincarnation altogether. Even "those who have practiced demotic and political virtue . . . developed from habit and training but devoid of philosophy and intelligence" are consigned "to go back into a race of tame and political creatures similar to their kind, bees perhaps, or wasps or ants" (82a11–b7). Only after serving time in this form can these be born again as "decent men" (82b8). But the philosophers' destiny lies beyond the earthly realm. It lies in the company of gods. The philosophers earn this reward because they have departed in "absolute purity" (82b10–c1). The distinction between the philosophers and all other humans is even more starkly drawn than it had been in Socrates' defense. But attention to the premise of the doctrine of reincarnation shows that precisely where Socrates distinguishes most radically between the purified philosophers and the nonphilosophers, there is evident a deeper ground on which they agree.

The doctrine of reincarnation is a system of reward and punishment on a cosmic scale. It maintains that a moral intent governs the very coming into being and passing away of all animate beings. The premise of this view is, then, that the whole is organized with a view to human goodness. Necessary to maintain this view is a doctrine of personal immortality. On the basis of our earthly experience alone, it would be hard to maintain what might be called the providential view of the whole: here the unjust prosper, and the most just of humans is put to death. Another realm must exist, therefore, in order to remedy the terrestrial lack of support for human good, "another place" to which we go after our stay in this world (80d5). In this way, the desire for personal immortality is a corollary of the providential view of the whole.

But should philosophers accept the premise behind such a view of the whole? If they do, then it is difficult to see the way in which the philosophic life differs essentially from other ways of life.[72] Socrates suggests this difficulty when he states that "lovers of riches" abstain from bodily desires out of "fear of poverty or loss of estate," whereas "lovers of rule and honor" do so "through dread of dishonor or ill-repute" (82c2–8). The true philosophers do so, however, in order to join the company of gods. "It's *for the sake of* (*heneka*) these things" that the philosopher repudiates those things of the body that seduce other humans (83e5, emphasis added). But this means that the philosophers, like all other humans, think of their activity as instrumental. They think of it not as rewarding in itself but as a means by which certain goods may be earned. In other words, according to this understanding, they share the providential view of the whole, the view that through reward and punishment that which is transhuman supports certain ways of life. Certainly, the philosophers so understood differ from the nonphilosophers with respect to the specific way of life that is rewarded. But this difference rests on the deeper agreement concerning the more fundamental issue—namely, the character of the whole in which humans exist. This agreement was implied at the start of the myth where, by means of his pun, Socrates referred interchangeably to the intelligible and to Hades. This providential view of the whole underlies philosophy understood as "a release and purifying rite," as a practice by which one can earn the benefits of the next world (82d6).

At the end of the proof, Socrates completes his program by addressing whether they should "feel either confidence or fear" for their souls (78b7–9). He states: "With that kind of nurture, surely, Simmias and Cebes, there's no danger of its fearing that on separation from the body it may be rent apart . . ." (84b4–6). Socrates has not shown that the soul is the kind of thing that is not in danger of dispersal. He does claim, however, to have shown the kind of nurture that should quell the fear of this dispersal. Yet, to repeat, Socrates has made this practice seem well-nigh impossible.[73] In doing so, Socrates might induce the young men to question the premise—that the whole of nature is organized with a view to human good—which leads one to think of the world in this way, a premise which, after all, remains undemonstrated. He might lead them to focus on the conclusion to which the discursive portion of the proof led—the imperfect harmony of humanity and the whole of nature—rather than on the rewards of the practice of philosophy. He might cause them to heed the distinction between that which we can know insofar as we are human and that which, based on our hopes, transcends human limits. In short, he has sharpened to the extreme the difference between the path of reason and the path of belief.

But if this should prove not to be the immediate outcome, we should not be surprised. For although the portrayal of the practice of philosophy might make nearly superhuman demands on the young men, the demands of the alternative are hardly less severe. To undertake that alternative, to doubt what I have called the providential view of the whole, entails that the young men entertain the possibility that what they think they want most deeply, and what is apparently not provided in this world, may not be provided in "another place." And it might well be asked: for what should one relinquish this hope? Should one do this in order to experience Socrates' plight? Those "ills of the human condition" that make us yearn for this other place are real enough. Less clear in the present circumstances are the countervailing goods of this world. This applies with special force to the potential philosopher because what has not yet been made clear is how the practice of philosophy can be defended if it is not joined to the attainment of pure wisdom.

The third proof attempts to establish the harmony of the soul and the ultimate intelligibles by showing that they share the same composite nature. In its failure to make this case, it in fact lends support to the indications of the preceding failed proofs that the particular beings on the one hand, and the soul on the other must be considered to be in some way complex. This necessity makes elusive a certain and comprehensive account of the whole of nature, for it is not clear that we can give a unified account of either a particular being or of the soul, much less an account of the unity of the soul and the whole of nature.

Simmias and Cebes are clearly troubled by this outcome. Accordingly, they express their reservations with the argument thus far. Socrates had indicated at the start of his defense that the ground of the *true* distinction between the philosopher and the nonphilosopher, contrary to the doctrine of reincarnation, lies precisely in the willingness to confront directly the issue of mortality. In what follows, we have an opportunity to consider whether either Simmias or Cebes is willing to undertake this confrontation.

Objections

Simmias and Cebes speak together in low voices (84c3–4). They still have questions about immortality. Socrates himself says that the argument "certainly still leaves room for many misgivings and objections, if, that is, one's going to examine it adequately" (84c6–7). Whether Socrates would have broken the long silence to explore further these objections we cannot know. At least he does not offer this observation for a long time, not until he sees Simmias and Cebes talking together (84c2). Socrates does seem willing to pursue the argument further, but if they are to continue the discussion then the topic will remain the immortality of the soul and related issues. Socrates says: "If it's something else you're considering, never mind" (84c7–8). He apparently thinks that inquiry into the issue of immortality is what those in the cell, himself included, most urgently require.

Simmias responds to Socrates by saying:

For some time each of us has had difficulties, and has been prompting and telling the other to question you, from eager-

ness to hear, but hesitating to make trouble, in case you should
find it unwelcome in your present misfortune. (84d5–7)

Simmias and Cebes require that Socrates urge them to voice their objections. Though they are eager to hear, they do not want to make trouble
for Socrates. Socrates laughs at the extent to which Simmias and Cebes are
impervious to his arguments concerning his disposition toward death. In
order to encourage Simmias and Cebes to speak, Socrates offers a reinterpretation of a myth which, though presented in a jocular manner, expresses a serious warning regarding the obstacle to clear thinking. This
warning clarifies even more why the philosopher and the potential philosopher must focus on the issue at hand.

Socrates maintains that they are mistaken in thinking that he regards
his present lot as a misfortune. To impute this understanding to him mis-
takes his view as surely as do those who mis-characterize the swans' song.
According to Socrates: "Humans, because of their own fear of death, ma-
lign the swans, and say that they sing their farewell song in distress, la-
menting their death" (85a2–5). Socrates reinterprets the swans' singing
in a benign way: the swans sing out of joy at the blessings of Hades which
await them (85b1–3). In this way, Socrates provides a gentle warning for
the young men against viewing the world through the lens of their fears.
The potential philosopher must strive to avoid the distortion that results
from this perspective. This is essential if one wishes to pursue the way of
reason versus the way of belief.

Encouraged to speak, Simmias prefaces his objection with general
reflections that manifest a certain brand of skepticism. He maintains that
"with respect to these matters, certain knowledge is either impossible or
very hard to come by in this life" (85c2–4). And, he continues, one's investigation into these questions must have one of two possible results:

> Either learn or find out how things are; or, if that's impossi-
> ble, then adopt the best and least refutable of human doc-
> trines, embarking on it as a kind of raft, and risking the
> dangers of the voyage through life. (85c7–d2)

Simmias seems unaware of the vast difference between these two possibilities. Neither does he indicate a preference for the former over the latter. He seems able to be content with either one. Such complacency must
cast doubt on Simmias' potential as a philosopher, for the difference between the alternatives is precisely the difference between philosophy,

which is based on reason, and other ways of life which are grounded in belief. But this difference seems less important to Simmias than does his prime concern, a concern which emerges as he continues his prefatory remarks.

Forgetting the number of alternatives he had just laid down, Simmias unwittingly adds a third possibility to the previous two, the possibility that "one could travel more safely and with less risk on a securer conveyance afforded by some divine doctrine"(85d2–4). This, it seems, is what Simmias truly desires—to live safely and with less risk, to have assurance that the dangers of this life won't touch him. Again, his concern with justice is rooted in self-concern. Simmias cares about that which transcends his self-concern only to the extent that he wants substantiation for his belief that he is a special individual who as such will also be granted benefits in the next world. For this reason, he prefers above all "some divine doctrine."

Simmias possesses an easygoing skepticism; it is not born of the fact that he truly cares to know. It is true that Simmias is famous as a great generator of speeches.[74] But Simmias' desire for speeches is based on his appreciation of their variety and novelty; after Cebes has fallen silent, Simmias still wants to hear the novel things that Socrates has to say about the earth (108d1–3). Simmias seems to regard speeches more generally as a means to satisfy his desires. Whether these speeches are true or not is less important than that they support his desires. His desires, his life, have not yet become a question for him.

Simmias shares the fears of the many and thus looks to philosophy for a nonphilosophic purpose—for reassurance in the face of those fears. He therefore does not distinguish between philosophy and some "divine doctrine." As for Socrates, he sidesteps Simmias' invitation to join him in agreement on these views, directing Simmias back to the issue at hand. But Simmias' prime concern is reflected in the objection he now raises and in the manner that he raises it.

Simmias uses the mode of argument of the third proof. He begins by comparing the character of the soul to that of a *harmonia* of the strings of a lyre.[75] In so doing, he seems to be repeating bits and pieces of the argument he has heard, likening the lyre to the "composite and earthy" and the *harmonia* to what is "unseen and incorporeal" in the manner of the preceding proof (85e5–86a3). He develops the argument in accordance with his understanding of what Socrates has said—"by the same argument as yours" (86a5). But it leads him to the conclusion that the *harmonia* must last beyond the lyre. At this point, however, Simmias interrupts himself and speaks more clearly and in his own name:

And in point of fact, Socrates, my own belief is that you are aware yourself that something of this sort is what we actually take the soul to be. (86b5–6)

He finally gets to the view with which he's truly concerned. As is evident in what follows, his personal worries break through his attempt to work through the argument.

Simmias presents the view of the soul that is called epiphenomenalism. This view maintains that the soul is really a particular arrangement of matter and thus exists only as long as the matter is arranged in the proper way. So, although the matter constituting it may last a long time, the soul so constituted lasts only as long as this matter is properly arranged—a fragile existence indeed. Although Simmias says that this is what 'we' take the soul to be, he asks for an argument against this view. His fears come into conflict with his own doctrine. He desires an answer to an argument denying personal immortality. Simmias is still concerned with an argument to use against those who would undermine his assurance. He certainly has not proceeded to a questioning of immortality itself.

As he had done earlier, Socrates responds to Simmias using legal terminology, perhaps thus recognizing that Simmias' desire lies in finding arguments to support the side to which he has already committed himself. But Socrates says that, before answering Simmias, "I think we should first hear from Cebes here what further charge he has to bring against the argument" (86d8–e1). In this way they will be able to judge whether the two arguments are "at all in tune" with one another (86e3).[76]

Cebes states that he too requires an image (87b3). Cebes rejects Simmias' notion that soul predeceases body; rather, it may endure through several incarnations. Relying on the image of a weaver and his cloaks, Cebes holds that although the weaver qua human is longer-lived than any of his cloaks, qua this particular human he may not outlast the cloak he weaves on his last day (87b4–d3). Thus, in the case of the soul, it may be such as to animate several bodies but one cannot be sure that this particular soul is not animating its last body prior to perishing itself (87d3–88a7). Cebes' objection brings up the distinction suggested in the first proof between the different senses of being, between *what* soul is and *that* it is. This distinction requires that Socrates in the final proof attempt to prove not only that the soul is immortal but that it is imperishable, that it not only is such as to be alive, whenever it is, but also that it always is.

Cebes, then, unlike Simmias, is moved by the preceding discussion not to ask for a new proof of immortality but to offer reasons for thinking that "anyone who's confident in face of death must be possessed of a fool-

ish confidence" (88b3–4). At this point, Cebes seems to heed the requirement expressed in the discursive portion of the preceding proof that we
investigate in accordance with the character of the human perspective; he
does not heed Socrates' advice, offered in the religion for philosophers,
not to regard as real what can be perceived. Cebes says that such confidence would be foolish because "no one can know this death or detachment from the body which brings perishing to the soul—since none of us
can possibly perceive it" (88b2–3). Cebes' objection, then, faces the possibility of intrinsic limits on human understanding especially with regard
to our knowledge of what happens after death. In raising this possibility,
Cebes' objection compels those in the cell as well as those hearing the
story later on to face the crucial alternative: whether to derive our understanding from that which can truly be known or from how we wish things
to be.

Socrates' 'Second Sailing'

Overview

(88c1–102a9)

Following the objections of Simmias and Cebes, the dialogue returns to the conversation of Echecrates and Phaedo. Plato makes us aware that there is an audience hearing the story of Socrates' death. The story is told, as Echecrates later remarks to Phaedo, "to us who were not there but are now hearing it" (102a8). Plato makes especially clear that we are part of the audience, perhaps to alert us that we have to judge the adequacy of the arguments with greater perspicacity than do Phaedo and Echecrates. As for these two, the doubts engendered in them by the objections are transformed into reassured certainty by Socrates' response to the objections. This transformation becomes evident when, following Socrates' intellectual autobiography, Echecrates again breaks into the narration saying, "It seems wondrous to me how clearly he put things, even for someone of small intelligence" (102a3–5).

Echecrates' interruptions serve to delineate the central section of the dialogue (88c8–102a2).[1] The section has many striking features, two of which need to be emphasized at the outset. First, in this section Socrates articulates the peculiarly Socratic mode of philosophizing. Second, this section contains no proof of the immortality of the soul. I will argue that the connection between these features lies in the nature of Socratic philosophizing; because it is not oriented on the attainment of pure wisdom, Socratic philosophy does not require the doctrine of the immortality of the soul.

Socrates formulates this understanding of philosophy through his reply to the objection of Simmias and through the first portion of his reply to Cebes' objection. These objections do reflect the respective concerns of Simmias and Cebes, and Socrates replies to them in kind. An important omission in his reply to Cebes makes evident, however, that the character of the reply is dictated by Socrates himself. Specifically, I will argue that in his reply to Simmias, Socrates treats Simmias' image of the soul and, in so doing, indicates what soul must be in order to account for human activity. In the reply to Cebes, however, Socrates is silent concerning Cebes' image of the soul and concentrates instead on the cause of all coming into being and passing away—that is, he speaks of nature as a whole. As Kenneth Dorter notes, Socrates suggests in several ways that his replies are to be understood as two aspects of one argument.[2] In my interpretation, these two aspects relate Socrates' understanding of the soul on the one hand, and his understanding of the beings on the other.[3] Together they describe what I will refer to as the human situation, the place of humanity in the world. It is the knowledge of this human situation that is reflected in Socrates' 'second sailing.'

Before embarking upon his replies to Simmias and Cebes, however, Socrates must rally those in the cell to undertake any rational inquiry whatsoever. The troubling doubts raised by the objections of Simmias and Cebes have made reason itself questionable to those gathered in the cell.

Misology

Phaedo reports that all were "disagreeably affected" by the objections (88c1–2). The objections lead those in the cell to doubt not only the arguments they had heard but also forthcoming arguments and indeed to wonder whether these things are intrinsically dubious (88c4–7). Echecrates, for his part, asks: "What argument (*logōi*) shall we ever trust now?" (88d1). It seems puzzling that the objections should render reason itself dubious. If Socrates had failed to provide an irreproachable argument proving, say, that humans must be able to fly, would Phaedo and Echecrates then come to the conclusion that reason itself must therefore be defective? Probably not. They would instead accept that we cannot fly and live their lives without the hope of flight. Their unwillingness to accept a similar conclusion in the present context indicates how deeply they yearn to believe that the soul is immortal; they are more ready to question reason than to abandon the hope for immortality. Reason is impugned not because it is inherently defective but because it cannot deliver what

Phaedo and Echecrates desire; it cannot provide the assurance, the trust, that Echecrates desires. Echecrates, therefore, says:

> I very much need some other argument that will convince me once again, as if from the start, that the soul of one who has died doesn't die with him. (88d7)

If this need for reassurance is deeper than the need to know, then when the conclusions of reason conflict with the more deeply felt need, they will be set aside. In fact, reason itself may become an object of scorn. In this way misology, the hatred of reason, arises.

Socrates now confronts misology "because there's no greater evil that could befall anyone" (89d2–3). Socrates had earlier claimed the greatest evil to be

> that the soul of every man, when intensely pleased or pained at something, is forced at the same time to suppose that whatever most affects it in this way is most clear and most real. (83c2–8)

The two are, I think, related in the following way. The intense pain engendered by thoughts of one's own annihilation makes the need to believe in a doctrine of personal immortality most clear and real. This need, engendered by such pain, overcomes the attachment to reason. In response to this first evil, Socrates had recommended that the philosopher resist both pleasure and pain altogether. Now he counsels that the philosopher resist the hatred of reason. To resist the hatred of reason does seem less daunting than to resist the testimony of both pleasure and pain.[4] However, it is important to see that what follows is an exhortation against misology rather than a demonstration of its falsehood. Surely, though, the proper antidote to misology is not an exhortation but a demonstration. Socrates' hesitance in providing a demonstration raises the suspicion that the case for reason might not be made so easily as we would hope. Reflection on the mythic allusion with which Plato begins the misology passage lends support to this suspicion.

Following up on Echecrates' desire to begin "as if from the start," Phaedo takes up the story of Socrates' death day. This portion of that momentous day must be especially vivid for Phaedo because he now takes center stage. What follows is Phaedo's report of his own conversation with Socrates on his death day.[5] As he did in the opening scene, Phaedo emphasizes Socrates' deeds more than his words. Specifically, Phaedo re-

ports that Socrates stroked his hair and rallied him to confront "the argument of Simmias and Cebes" (88c3–4). But Phaedo responds that
"even Heracles is said to have been no match for two" (89c5–6). The incident to which Phaedo alludes is the battle of Heracles with the many-
headed Hydra, in the midst of which Heracles was also attacked by a sea
crab. Heracles had to call upon his nephew, Iolaus, for assistance. Socrates
advises Phaedo: "Summon me as your Iolaus; while there's still light"
(89c7–8).

The only other mention of this incident in the Platonic corpus occurs in the *Euthydemus*. There Socrates uses it to refer to those against
whom Socrates is about to warn Phaedo—namely, the sophists. Those
controversialists exploit the ambiguities of rational discourse for the sake
of victory in speech.[6] The very possibility of the sophists' art expresses,
therefore, something important—and something disturbing—concerning
the nature of reason itself. Clearly, if sophists exist, reason must be such as
to allow the practice of this art; it must give rise to contradictions, to the
antinomies that Socrates also mentions in the present context (90c1).
That reason should be so exploitable by the sophists, that it should so
readily lend itself to confusions, ambiguities, and deceptions, manifests
what Plato calls in the *Seventh Letter* "the weaknesses of reason."[7] Reason
docs not necessarily lead to the truth of the beings; it exists largely in the
element of falsehood.[8] This problematic character of reason helps to explain why Socrates delivers an exhortation against misology rather than a
demonstration of the solidity of reason. If such a demonstration is possible, it surely requires a long and complicated presentation.

But why does Socrates not present this demonstration straightaway?
The answer to this question becomes clearer in Socrates' analogy—or
rather his disanalogy—between misology and misanthropy that is the fo-
cal point of his exhortation. Asserting that misology and misanthropy
"both arise from the same source," Socrates describes the origins of, and
the cure for, misanthropy:

> Misanthropy develops when without art one puts complete
> trust in somebody thinking the man absolutely true and sound
> and reliable and then a little later *discovers* him to be bad and
> unreliable ... and when it happens to someone often ... he
> ends up ... hating everyone. (89d3–e2, emphasis added)

The truth about humans, a truth that would prevent misanthropy, arises
from a certain art concerning humans:

Because if he handled them with art (τεXνης) he'd surely have recognized the truth, that extremely good and bad people are both very few in number and the majority lie in between. (89e7–90a2)

Socrates considers the origin of misology, but he does so in a peculiar way. After having secured Phaedo's assent to the notion that "if a contest in badness were promoted . . . those in the first class would be very few," Socrates immediately adds: "Yes, probably, though in that respect arguments aren't like men, but I was following the lead you gave just now" (90b1–2, 90b4–5). Phaedo, of course, did not lead anyone anywhere. Rather, Socrates whisks the chair away after having asked Phaedo to sit down. This bit of crudely sophistic reasoning should make us wary of the rest of Socrates' analogy.

Socrates speaks of the source of misology, and though there is a surface similarity with the source of misanthropy, the differences run deeper. With respect to misanthropy, the humans once trusted were "discovered" to be false, but with regard to misology, the argument "*seems* to him false, sometimes when it is and sometimes when it is not"(90b8–9, emphasis added). In the case of misanthropy, Socrates had related the art that prevents misanthropy, but in the case of misology he does not provide such an art, at least in the present context.[9] That art, and more importantly the truth on which it is based, only emerge in Socrates' complete response to the objections of Simmias and Cebes.

Instead of presenting that truth, Socrates interrupts himself; he supplies no apodosis to the protasis of the crucial sentence (90b9).[10] He interrupts himself to speak of the sophists, "those who have spent all their time on contradictory arguments"(90b9–c1). According to Socrates, these men believe that

there's nothing sound or secure whatever, either in things or arguments; but that all the things that are are carried up and down just like things fluctuating in the Euripus and never remain at rest for any time. (90c2–6)

But are there arguments that endure in a way that things do not? In response to this question, Socrates offers only a hypothetical statement. He states:

It *would be* a pitiful fate, *if* there were some true and secure argument, and one that could be discerned, yet owing to association with arguments of the sort that seem now true and now false, a man blamed neither himself nor his lack of skill but finally relieved his distress by shifting the blame from himself to arguments, and then finished out the rest of his life hating and abusing arguments, and was deprived both of the truth and of knowledge of the beings. (90d6–7, 90c8–d1, emphasis added)[11]

Yet, to forestall this possibility, Socrates does not now provide the one true and comprehensive argument guaranteed to dispose of misology. Were Socrates in possession of the perfectly rational account of the whole, he could simply dismiss the sophists by offering that rational account as proof against the sophists' deceptions. Given the urgency of his circumstances—"while there is still light"—we would have expected Socrates to relate this account first in his defense of reason (89c7–8). He would thereby insure that the potential philosophers possess this certain antidote (89c7–8). But again Socrates offers an exhortation against misology rather than a theoretical refutation. The existence of the "true and secure argument" remains only a possibility. Moreover, inherent in reason are those antinomies exploited by the sophists that could exasperate the lovers of reason and lead them to the conclusion that reason is futile, manipulatable to any end, worthy only of scorn. Socrates does encourage those in his cell to blame themselves rather than reason when faced with these dilemmas. But his self portrait at the end of the misology passage makes us wonder all the more at the adequacy of reason.[12]

Socrates admits that in his present circumstances, he himself is especially in danger of abandoning the commitment to reason. Because his own imminent death is one concern that he "may not be facing as a philosopher should, but rather as one bent on victory, like those quite devoid of education" (91a1–3), he differs from the latter individuals only to the extent that he wants to persuade himself more than anyone else (91a6–b1). One plausible conclusion from this statement is that Socrates is now in inner conflict, attempting to resist lower desires for the sake of what is higher and more noble. His next statement belies this view, however:

Because I reason (*logizomai*), my dear friend—watch how anxious I am to score—that if what I say proves true, it's surely well to have been persuaded; whereas if there's nothing for a dead man, still, at least during this very time before my death, I'll distress those present less with lamentation, and this ignorance of mine will not persist—that would be evil—but will in a little while be ended. (91b1–7)

Socrates admits that he is not acting in strict accordance with the requirements of philosophy, but he does not consider this a defect in his character, a weakness of will. Instead, he presents it as a conclusion of reason and indeed makes a show of his selfishness. It is reason that leads him to consider *his* good, here and now. It is reason that leads him to relax his devotion to philosophy. Reason does not lead him to the view that philosophizing is good everywhere and always; reason tells him that this devotion may not be good in his present circumstances.[13] Perhaps one ought to write poetry instead.[14]

But doesn't reason lead us to knowledge of The Good, the self-subsistent, absolute good in the light of which we can assess our lives? Or does it only lead us to what is good for each of us, here and now? If the latter is the case, misology must be a constant threat. We cannot help but want what is good for ourselves, the things that we as humans cherish— our own existence, the existence of our loved ones, honor, and a noble life. The authoritative teachings of the community are designed to offer transhuman assurance that these goods will, in fact, be provided. If one is unwilling to accept these authoritative teachings and turns instead to reason for such assurance, it must be disappointing when all that reason can tell us is that there either is or isn't a life after death, when the only sure good is the reasonable assessment of what is good for oneself here and now (91b2–7).

There would perhaps be consolation in the knowledge that one's life is based on what can be *known* to be good rather than merely imagined, as Socrates knows that the persistence of ignorance "would be an evil thing" (91b6). But, how can we even be sure of this conclusion? The question remains: how can Socrates defend the life of reason on these grounds— that is, on the grounds that we can attain only of knowledge of good rather than knowledge of The Good? This is the question left by the proofs of immortality and the objections to them. In presenting an exhortation against misology rather than a demonstration of its untruth, Socrates introduces the question to which he now must respond.

Socrates' Reply to Simmias: Soul as *Harmonia*

Socrates responds to Simmias' objection with three separate but related arguments. The first argument is, in actuality, a display of the opposition between the image of *harmonia* and the doctrine of Recollection. This display moves Simmias to abandon his objection. Despite Simmias' concession, however, Socrates argues the soul as *harmonia* thesis for two more Stephanus pages.[15] In the continuation of the argument, Socrates considers the character of the soul itself rather than its immortality.

Although Socrates' account of the soul occurs in the continuation of the argument, the preceding conversation between Socrates and Simmias has an important bearing on an issue related to the character of the soul, the issue of the status of the knowledge of the soul. Plato makes Simmias' remarks—despite Simmias' contrary intention—suggest that in order to understand the soul we must finally rely on a likelihood, on what is here called an image but will later be called a hypothesis. These remarks are made in the course of Socrates' drawing the contrast between the *harmonia* image and the doctrine of Recollection.

Socrates asks Simmias and Cebes about the Recollection argument, and both indicate their attachment to it. According to Socrates, however, they will have to reject the Recollection argument if they continue to maintain the soul as *harmonia* thesis. The Recollection doctrine requires that the soul exist prior to the elements of which it is composed, and this a *harmonia* cannot do. Simmias then rejects the *harmonia* image and explains his reasons for the rejection:

> I acquired the latter [the soul as *harmonia* thesis] without any proof, but from a certain likelihood (*eikotos*), and plausibility about it, whence its appeal to the many; but I am aware that arguments basing their proofs upon likelihoods are impostors, and if one doesn't guard against them, they completely deceive one, in geometry as well as in all other subjects. But the argument about recollection and learning has come from a hypothesis worthy of acceptance. Because it was, of course, asserted that our soul existed even before it entered the body just as surely as its object exists—the Being, bearing the name, 'that which is.' (92c11–d5, 92d6–9)

Simmias remarks on the plausibility of the image, as did Echecrates before the misology passage.[16] Perhaps its plausibility derives from its being the inference or hypothesis that most obviously represents our experience. We experience ourselves engaging in the disparate activities of speaking and moving. We also experience conflict within ourselves. The soul understood as a harmony of disparate elements seems plausible as an explanation of the experience that we have of ourselves as partaking of such differences while remaining a whole.

But Simmias rejects the notion that soul is but an inference or an image formulated to explain that which is confusing in our experience. Even though Simmias rejects the *harmonia* image as a mere "likelihood," some details of his rejection raise the question whether such likelihoods should be so easily rejected. His rejection presumes that something more certain than likelihoods or hypotheses are available with respect to the soul. However, as I have already stated, Plato makes Simmias' own remarks unwittingly cast doubt on this presumption.

For example, Simmias rejects these likelihoods in geometry, but Simmias was a member of that school famous for undermining absolute certainty in geometry. Furthermore, in stating the ground of his own certainty, Simmias inadvertently states the principle of the third proof of immortality instead of the second.[17] That is, Simmias' remark implies that he accepts the pre-existence of the soul on the basis of the nature purportedly shared by the soul and the intelligibles rather than on the basis of the doctrine of recollection. The intervening proof, however, suggested that the soul was only akin to "that which is" and not, as Simmias states here, equivalent to Being. In other words, the third proof made dubious the notion that the soul is equivalent in its nature to the Ideas.

In these ways, then, Plato has Simmias unwittingly suggest that we should not overestimate our ability to replace likelihoods with absolute certainty in our accounts of the soul. Accordingly, in the present context Socrates calls the *harmonia* image a hypothesis (94b1). In his reply to Cebes, Socrates indicates that our understanding is in general dependent upon hypotheses. This limitation on our understanding is intrinsically related to the character that soul must have in order to explain our diverse activities. This character emerges in Socrates' continued treatment of the soul as *harmonia* thesis.

Several elements of Socrates' discussion point to the need to examine more closely the *harmonia* thesis. As I have stated, the conflict of the thesis with the doctrine of Recollection does not in Socrates' view alone suffice to dismiss it because he continues to address the *harmonia* thesis well after this has been established. Nor does the defect of the soul as *harmonia* thesis lie simply in its materialistic account of the soul because the thesis does not necessarily entail such an account. In the *Republic,* for example, there is a prominent example of soul understood as a *harmonia* composed of other than corporeal elements.[18] And Socrates suggests a similar understanding in the present context when, for example, in restating the objections, he attributes to Simmias the view that soul is "*a* form (*eidei*) of *harmonia*" (91d1–2, emphasis added). Socrates thus raises the possibility that there are other forms of *harmoniai*. Still another example occurs when Socrates presents to Simmias the choice between soul as *harmonia* and the doctrine of Recollection. He states:

But you will have to think otherwise, O Theban stranger, if
you stick to the supposition that *harmonia* is a composite
thing, and soul is a kind of *harmonia* composed of the bodily
elements held in tension. (92a6–9)

This statement separates the point that *harmonia* is a composite from the
point that soul is a form of *harmonia* composed of bodily elements. Such
a separation opens up the possibility that there may be *harmoniai* which
are composite but which are not necessarily composed of bodily elements—for example, those harmonies of arguments to which Socrates alludes when he asks Simmias how "this theory of yours is going to
harmonize with that one [the Recollection theory]?" (92c2-8)[19] In the
Phaedo, Socrates does explicitly push the understanding of *harmonia* in the
direction of a corporeal composition. This makes the image more easily
dismissible. However, an examination of Socrates' continued treatment of
the thesis shows that Socrates dismisses it not because of its conflict with
the doctrine of Recollection nor because of its materialistic explanation
but ultimately because it is overly sanguine concerning the unity of the
soul. Let us now consider Socrates' argument in detail.

Socrates presents a complex argument concerning the complexity
of the human soul. As many commentators recognize, between the premise and conclusion of one argument, Socrates sandwiches another argument.[20] The 'outer' argument concerns whether *harmonia* is a proper
image of soul if soul is to be understood as leading the body. In the course
of denying the appropriateness of this image, Socrates implicitly questions
the adequacy of the simple distinction between soul and body as a means
of explaining the struggle to live a moral, soul-guided life. As befits a
struggle, Socrates also makes clear that we vary in our success at living
such a life. The 'inner' argument concerns how soul must be in order
to account for this variance in human souls. Accordingly, it deals with
the issue of whether a *harmonia* can be more or less of what it is. I will
first consider the whole of the "outer" argument before moving to the
"inner" argument.

Socrates secures Simmias' assent to the points that a *harmonia* cannot be "in any state other than that of the elements of which it's composed" nor can it "act or be acted upon in any way differently from the
way they may act or be acted upon" (92e4–93a5). This being the case, a
harmonia "should not properly undergo contrary movement or utter
sound or be opposed in any other way to its own parts" (93a8–9). A *harmonia* must follow, in both deed and speech, rather than lead its components. At this point, the new argument intervenes. The first argument is

not resumed until Socrates asks Simmias: "Again now, would you say that of all things in a man it is anything but soul, especially if it is a wise one, that rules him?"(94b4–5). Socrates builds on the contention that if soul is *harmonia*, it could not possibly lead or rule that of which it is composed.

Socrates' presentation of the relation between the body and the soul that strives to rule it casts doubt on the tenability of the simple soul-body distinction. Socrates asks:

> Does it comply with the bodily feelings or does it oppose them? I mean, for example, when heat and thirst are in the body, by pulling the opposite way, away from drinking, and away from eating when it feels hunger; and surely in countless other ways we see the soul opposing bodily feelings, don't we? (94b7–c1)

For soul to oppose body necessarily suggests that there is communication between soul and body, as there must be between any ruler and ruled. Moreover, while Socrates speaks of heat and thirst and hunger as bodily feelings, surely only ensouled body rather than body alone is capable of these feelings. The line between soul and body becomes more blurred as Socrates asks:

> Well now, don't we find it, in fact, operating in just the opposite way, dominating all those alleged sources of of its existence, and opposing them in almost everything throughout all of life, mastering them in all kinds of ways, sometimes disciplining more harshly and painfully with gymnastics and medicine, sometimes more mildly, now threatening and now admonishing, conversing with our appetites and passions and fears, as if with a separate thing? (94c9–d6)

The appetites, passions, and fears are even less clearly attributable to body alone. The possibility that the soul can not only admonish and threaten but also converse with these implies a soul more akin to that of the *Republic* (allusions to which are numerous in this passage) than the simple and separable soul that is so prominent in the *Phaedo*.[21] For this reason, Socrates offers the qualified conclusion that soul speaks with these "*as if* with a separate thing" (94d5–6, emphasis added). And at this point, in order to buttress his case, Socrates quotes the *Odyssey* to support the notion that soul rules body (94d8–e1). The same quote is used in the *Re-public* to support the view that reason rules the other parts of soul.[22]

Socrates has described the experiences of inner conflict and the struggle for self-control. To the extent that this is a struggle, lasting "throughout all of life," neither of the contestants secures a final victory. Rather, there are only varying degrees of success. Socrates indicates this conclusion by his language in the context. For example, soul is said to rule "*especially* if it's a wise one"(94b5, emphasis added). In this same vein, addressing Simmias as "best of men" (*o ariste*), Socrates notes that if they approved of the *harmonia* thesis, "we should agree neither with the divine poet, Homer, nor with ourselves"(94e8–95a2). In the words of the *Republic,* the possibility of disagreeing with oneself implies that, "concerning the soul, in the same human being there is something better and something worse."[23] The "inner" argument addresses the wondrous fact that there can even be better and worse souls, all of which are nevertheless souls.

Socrates asks Simmias: "Again now, isn't it natural for every *harmonia* to be a harmonia just as it's been tuned?"(93a11–12). Perhaps because Socrates introduces a new argument with this question, Simmias does not understand. Socrates follows his first question with another:

> Isn't it the case that if it's been tuned more and to a greater extent, assuming that to be possible, it will be more a *harmonia* and a greater one, whereas if less and to a smaller extent, it will be a lesser and smaller one? (93a13–b2)

Socrates then asks Simmias this same question concerning soul:

> Well, is this the case with soul—that even in the least degree, one soul is either to a greater extent and more than another, or to a smaller extent and less, just itself—namely, a soul? (93b4–6)

Simmias responds emphatically in the negative. It is not clear, however, that this is the proper answer, especially given the definition of good and bad souls that Socrates expresses in his subsequent question:

> Well, but is one soul said to have intelligence (*noun*) and virtue (*aretēn*) and to be good (*agathē*), while another is said to have folly (*anoian*) and vice (*mokhthērian*) and to be bad (*kakē*)? (93b–c1)

Socrates' question, reporting what is said, suggests that soul partakes of a variety of capacities and does so in varying degrees. It would seem that only if soul were complex could it meet these requirements. For how could that which is simple be capable of a variety of capacities? And how could that which is simple be capable of being more or less of what it is— namely, soul? In light of these questions, it would seem that the image of *harmonia,* a unity of diverse elements, represents nicely the soul's complex unity. Socrates, however, rejects this image. Let us consider why he does so.

Socrates had left open whether *harmonia* could be more or less, to a greater or smaller extent—"assuming that to be possible." Now he denies this possibility, but he does so in a manner that deserves close scrutiny. Socrates states: "It has been agreed that no one soul is more or less a soul than another"(93d1–2). But he goes on: "This is the admission that no one *harmonia* is either more or to a greater extent or less and to a smaller extent a *harmonia* than another"(93d2–6). In this way, Socrates defines the image, *harmonia,* by reference to the alleged original, soul.[24] At 92b7–8 Socrates prefigured this unusual procedure when he told Simmias: "Your *harmonia* is not in fact the same sort of thing as that to which you liken it." Commentators have noted the peculiarity in Socrates' procedure at 93d2–4. C. C. W. Taylor, for example, calls this "one of the most problematical passages in the argument." Taylor continues:

> Socrates says that premise B3 [No soul is more or less of a soul than any other] is the same as the proposition (B7) that no *harmonia* is more or less (of) a *harmonia* than any other, and Simmias agrees. Of course B3 is not as it stands equivalent to B7 and the question is what additional assumptions Plato must have used to produce what he regarded as a valid equivalence.[25]

Taylor concludes that Plato,

> assuming the soul to be a *harmonia,* took this to imply that whatever is true of soul is also true of *harmonia* . . . In effect this is to confuse implication with equivalence which seems a possible error for Plato to commit at this stage in his philosophical development.[26]

I agree with Taylor concerning the existence of an odd argument in the text at this point. It seems to me, however, that this oddity can be understood in terms of Socrates' intention rather than as an error. The notion that *harmonia* is simple, or rather is insufficiently complex to be more and less of what it is, becomes a sort of stalking horse for the *soul* as simple or as insufficiently complex to be more and less of what it is.

Socrates secures Simmias' assent to the propositions that

> what is neither more nor less a *harmonia* has been neither more nor less tuned" and that "that which has been neither more nor less tuned participate(s) in *harmonia* . . . to an equal degree. (93d6–11)

He now applies this conclusion to soul:

> given that no one soul is either more or less itself, namely a soul, than another, it has not been more or less tuned" nor could it participate more either in non-*harmonia* or *harmonia*. (93d12–e6)

Now assuming badness to be non-*harmonia* and goodness to be *harmonia*, a soul, being *harmonia*—which is by Socrates' definition simple—could not participate in non-*harmonia*. Soul, therefore, could not be bad. Socrates draws the following conclusion:

> By this argument, then, we find that all souls of all living things will be equally good, assuming that it's the nature of souls to be equally themselves, namely souls. (94a8–10)

He asks Simmias: "Do you approve of this assertion, or think this would happen to the argument, if the hypothesis that soul is *harmonia* were correct?" (94a12–b2).

Socrates finds the "scientific" *harmonia* image inadequate due to its inability to account for our common experience. In other words, Socrates finds *harmonia* an inadequate image of soul precisely because being simple, being unable to be more or less, or to a greater or smaller extent, *harmonia* cannot account for the empirical fact of there being good and bad humans. But, of course, *harmonia* was limited in this way following from Socrates' own definition of the soul as simple. The limitation does not necessarily apply to *harmonia;* surely, we are familiar with the possibility that a *harmonia* might be more or less well-tuned. Socrates' backward reasoning—defining the image by reference to the purported original which the image is supposed to explain—allows him to critique and dismiss the *harmonia* image as inadequate because it is too simple while at the same time pointing to the difficulty that then arises: whatever image is presented concerning soul, it must be able to be what it is, and more and less, to a greater and smaller extent.

Several times in the inner argument, Socrates uses these phrases— "more or less", and "to a greater or smaller extent"—in reference to the soul. They suggest that it must be possible for there to be souls that differ in the degree to which they represent the true nature of soul. In other words, soul must be capable of both being and not being what it is, namely, soul. Souls must have the potential to be what they are—namely, souls—but also to be other than they are, so far as they do not achieve the perfection of soul.

How is this possible? How can it be that a particular soul is fit to be called a soul yet falls short of being what a soul truly is? Such questions arise when we reflect on the empirical fact of human inequality, the inequality between Socrates, who can give an account of the intelligibles, and nearly all others who cannot. In his reply to Simmias, Socrates explores further the issue that is thematic in the one proof addressed to Simmias. The inner argument raises the question of the relation between that which the soul truly is and the many souls of diverse potentials. It raises the question of the one and the many.

This question necessarily arises also for anyone who reflects on the proper standard for human activity. Specifically, if we wish to move beyond mere description of human activity to a determination of which among the many possibilities open to us we ought to pursue, it is necessary to invoke some standard of judgment, some *measure* of the soul. In short, we must have some idea of what it means to be human. What then is the relationship between the standard of judgment on the one hand, and the variety of activities and the individuals who pursue them on the other? Is there a single model for the perfection of the soul that brings order to this variety? Is there a highest good that reconciles the diverse and even conflicting subordinate goods? These questions are of obvious importance to the political community in its attempt to articulate some common good in which the individual goods can find satisfaction.[27] Perhaps for this reason, Socrates begins his reply to Simmias by referring to the city of his origin, addressing Simmias as the Theban stranger (92a6). And the many allusions to the *Republic* in this context are appropriate because the sovereign question of the *Republic,* the question of justice, is precisely an examination of the possibility that the many individual goods can be reconciled in a single overarching good.

In attempting to achieve this reconciliation should we refer to that which all humans share? Should we, in other words, measure humans according to the sliding scale of "more and less" which assumes a basic commensurability among humans? How then do we explain the great rift that exists between Socrates and all other humans? This and other serious inequalities would seem to call for measurement by reference to "a greater and lesser extent" which, as Dorter notes, suggests measurement of individuals with reference to some paradigm.[28] This kind of measurement raises the question of the manner in which may individual souls are related to the one paradigmatic soul. We wonder how there can be such a great difference between the many souls and this one.

This question becomes especially vexing when we recognize that there is great controversy concerning what constitutes the paradigmatic soul. Plato has repeatedly called our attention to the vast difference between the various qualities that are called virtuous; it has been suggested that this difference is as vast as that between animals and gods (82b). The question that Socrates asks in the present context raises this controversy once again.

> Well, but is one soul said to have intelligence (*noun*) and virtue (*aretēr*) and to be good (*agathē*), while another is said to have folly (*anoian*) and vice (*mokhthērian*) and to be bad (*kakē*)? (93b4–c1)

Should virtue be understood in terms of intelligence or of goodness? Whether these qualities are perfectly reconcilable may well be doubted.[29] That these terms are at least potentially different becomes evident by considering, for example, that from the standpoint of political or moral virtue it is doubtful that misology would be considered "the greatest evil" (89d2–3, see also 82a10–c1). There is no clearer representation of the implications of this difference, however, than the trial and execution of Socrates, whose pursuit of knowledge fit him for execution by his fellow citizens, and *necessarily so* in his view.[30] Accordingly, the conflict between Socrates and his fellow-citizens, this political problem, can be understood as reflecting a conflict within the human soul, a conflict that leaves in question the character of the perfection of the soul. In this light, Socrates' rejection of the *harmonia* image reflects not only that it is too simple but that it obscures the degree to which the coherency of the soul remains a question.

The foregoing considerations suggest the inadequacy of Simmias' position. These considerations also provide a clue to the subsequent movement of the argument. To the extent that the coherence or unity (that is, the harmony) of the soul remains a question, the examination of the soul points beyond the soul. In undertaking this further investigation the philosopher hopes to find more comprehensive or more basic causes and explanations that might reconcile or reduce and thus explain the conflicts within the soul. Perhaps the wider view of nature will show that in fact soul can be reduced to some more basic element. Or a study of nature may reveal that there is a cosmic ruling intelligence that indicates an order for the conflicting qualities of the soul. The key point is that, given the soul's complex character, the attempt to know the soul leads to the attempt to know nature more generally. This being the case, the study of human affairs, political philosophy, is inseparable from a consideration of the whole in which we reside.

But the question remains: why should Socrates present this picture of the soul so obliquely? We can begin to answer this question by recognizing that Socrates does not direct Simmias to the Idea of soul for the true understanding of soul. Socrates' silence in this regard is all the more striking given that he reminds Simmias of his allegiance to the doctrine of Recollection at the start of his reply to Simmias' objection. Socrates' silence casts doubt on the possibility that the explanatory principles featured in the doctrine of Recollection, the Ideas, pertain to an explanation of the soul. Indeed, on the basis of the *Phaedo* we would have to conclude that there is not an Idea of the soul.[31]

Socrates' curious reversal of image and original bears on this point. The "misstep" in the argument occurs when Socrates defines the image by reference to a definition of soul. The "misstep," I contend, is intentional because it causes us to reflect on the fact that we are relying on images precisely because the original is elusive. Such reliance would be unnecessary were we able to appeal to the Idea of soul. But contrary to Simmias' contention, we cannot judge the soul by reference to Being itself (76e8–77a2). Rather, the image is judged by how well it explains the various things that are said about the soul. Socrates does not suggest that the soul is intelligible other than by reference to an image or a hypothesis.

As we try to understand the soul in terms of something other than soul, we can be led to subhuman explanations as easily as to super-human ones. Perhaps it is easier to move to the former—to a materialistic, "scientific" view—than the latter, especially for those who want to rely on what they can know for themselves. As Echecrates says in commenting on the notion of soul as *harmonia*, "This theory that our soul is a kind of *harmonia* has a strange hold on me, now as it has always done . . . " (88d3–4). Socrates himself was attracted to such explanations early in his career. This attraction is all the more powerful if the doctrine of the Ideas, is not available as an explanation. In presenting his investigation of the soul so obliquely, Socrates disabuses Simmias of an understanding of the soul that would make dubious the notion of moral responsibility (94b4–e6). By this manner of presentation he also suggests those complexities of the soul that might induce Simmias to see the need for more comprehensive reflection without confirming him in his easy-going skepticism.

We do not know whether Simmias has yet taken his life seriously as a question.[32] Socrates cannot compel Simmias to do this; just as we participate in the construction of our own prisons, so must we participate in our own liberation (82e5–83a1). Socrates can only present to Simmias the wondrous character of the soul that could lead to such an outcome. Socrates turns to Cebes' objection and says: "we seem to have placated the Theban lady, Harmonia, moderately well" (95a4–5). Socrates divinizes Simmias' "scientific" account of the soul, treating it as a goddess belonging to his city. Perhaps, Simmias' search would have to begin from a serious consideration of the merits of the scientific view as opposed to the view of his community. In any case, Socrates' mythic reference suggests the wondrous character of that which the "scientific" account aimed to explain. He suggests also that something about the soul escaped such an explanation.

Socrates now follows the course indicated by the argument. The examination of the soul has led to the necessity to go beyond the soul, to consider the whole in which the soul resides. Accordingly, Socrates relates the investigations into nature as a whole upon which he embarked in order to understand life and thought (96b2–8). As we follow this new investigation we must remember that there is necessarily a link between that which the soul must be and the way in which the soul is intelligible. The character of that which is called soul is such as to be accessible only by inference from experience, inferences that are expressed in the variety of images or hypotheses used in the *Phaedo* to describe the soul. Socrates' response to Simmias has done nothing to alter the conclusion that the soul is not transparent to itself. In considering the examination of nature that follows, then, we cannot forget that our access to nature is through the problematic soul.[33]

Socrates' Reply to Cebes: The Second Sailing

Socrates' Varying Views of Nature

Cebes wondered how it could be known that an individual soul, although surviving many incarnations, does not ultimately disintegrate.

Socrates makes clear that Cebes' objection requires a proof of the soul's immortality and, he adds, of its imperishability (95b8–96a4). After having looked into himself for a long time, Socrates announces that such a proof in turn requires an account of the whole of coming to be and passing away—that is, an account of the whole of nature (96a1–4).

Although this requirement is admittedly not easily satisfied, the unusual tentativeness of Socrates' subsequent response is striking, especially if one believes that Socrates has a ready answer in his doctrine of Ideas. But he does not immediately offer Cebes this account of nature. Instead, Socrates tells Cebes a story—"my personal experiences." He says: "If any of the things I say seem helpful to you, you can use them for conviction on the points you raise" (95b5–96a5). In the ensuing intellectual autobiography, Socrates recounts the way in which his view of nature altered from one based on material and efficient causation to a hope for a teleological understanding, until he finally settled on a new *approach* to nature. Socrates refers to his new approach as a 'second sailing,' a course dictated by a failed first sailing.[34] The defects of his previous views shape the character of his new approach. With this in mind, let us consider first what one commentator has aptly called the "pre-Socratic Socrates."[35]

Socrates begins by noting that he had a "wondrous desire for that wisdom (*sophias*) gained by the inquiry into nature."[36] This wisdom is not exhausted by knowledge of coming to be and passing away, but also includes knowledge of why something exists (96a7–10). As is evident in what follows, Socrates did not abandon his desire for wisdom gained by inquiry into nature. The character of this goal, however, and thus also the means to it, had to change because of the elusiveness of the whole of nature.

Socrates wondered especially about those human activities that he usually attributes to the soul—living and thinking. But Socrates does not mention soul or speech here. Instead, Socrates reports that he addressed these questions in terms of material and efficient causation, with life developing out of heat and cold and blood, and blood or air or fire giving rise to thought. He speaks of the brain (*enkephalos*) as the seat of the senses, and of knowledge coming to be when memory and judgment have stopped moving, when they have become stable (96b2–8). However, Socrates eventually judged these conclusions as inadequate. They left him with certain perplexities which continue to trouble him; Socrates' tentativeness is not, as some commentators think, ironic.[37] These perplexities led him to conclude that he had "unlearned even those things I formerly supposed I knew" with the result that he was "utterly blinded" (96a10–96c5). The word *blinded* occurs again in Socrates' description of his turn from his predecessors. Socrates states that he turned to speeches to avoid being "blinded" (99e2–3). An examination of Socrates' perplexities can help to reveal the precise inadequacy that Socrates was trying to avoid in his 'second sailing'—the threat of being blinded.

As the first example of his perplexity, Socrates cites his understanding of the growth of a human being. The cause of this growth, a cause he supposed was "clear to all":

> was because of eating and drinking, whenever, from food, flesh came to accrue to flesh and bone to bone, and similarly on the same principle (*logon*) the appropriate matter came to accrue to each of the other parts, it was then that the little bulk (*onkon*) later came to be big, and in this way the small human being comes to be large. (96c3–d5)

Cebes affirms that this is a reasonable explanation, but Socrates clearly thinks something is amiss. He speaks of eating and drinking as leading to the growth of various parts of the body, but it is not evident how the thing eaten is properly altered and distributed so as to become flesh and bone. Specifically, what determines that the thing eaten will be distributed so as to maintain and enlarge this certain form, the human form? Socrates suggests this question when he describes the process of growth in two different ways. He says first that "the little bulk comes to be large," and second that "in this way the small human being comes to be large." Why does the accrual of matter not simply lead to a larger bulk, a larger heap, rather than to a larger human being? And why is there a limit as to how large a human being can grow and still be a human being?

Socrates indicates the answer to these questions when he mentions the principle (*logon*) that determines that the matter accrues in the proper way. This principle might be called the formal cause or the class-character, an invisible cause or explanation which is manifest in the visible form. It functions as a cause in its determination of *what* something can be. Specifically, it places limits on the possibilities inherent in a particular thing. To take the example mentioned above, a human cannot continue to accrue matter indefinitely and still remain a human. Relying on material and efficient causation alone prevented Socrates from recognizing this cause. But without this form of explanation, it is difficult to explain accurately the difference between a human and a heap, a man and a mound. Socrates' reliance on what is "clear to all" did, paradoxically, lead to blindness. Explanations that remain on the level of perception cannot by themselves explain that which is manifest. They cannot explain the articulation of the world into different kinds, an articulation manifest in visible form.[38] An examination of Socrates' further perplexities confirms that what he missed in his investigations was the need for more than one type of causality.[39]

Socrates states: "I used to suppose it was an adequate view whenever a large man standing beside a small one appeared to be larger just by a head; similarly with two horses" (96d8–e1). Socrates' account of being larger considers the head as a unit of measurement. But as his apparently unnecessary mention of horses suggests, the head is not fully understood only as a body occupying a certain space. This latter understanding neglects the qualitative difference between the head of a horse and the head of a human, a difference just alluded to in Socrates' explanation of knowledge inhering in the brain (*enkephalos*). But the head so considered *is* in a different sense than the sense in which it can be considered as a unit of measurement.

This difference in senses of being is most evident with respect to number and it is for this reason, I think, that Socrates calls his first mathematical example "clearer":

> It seemed to me that ten was greater than eight because of the accruing of two to the latter, and that two cubits were larger than one cubit, because of their exceeding the latter by half. (96e1–4)

In the case of ten being greater than eight, two is considered as a unity— that is, as a certain number having definite properties as that number. Two is thus considered in its twoness. Contrarily, with respect to two cubits, two is considered as composed of so many units. For this very reason, Socrates speaks of "cubits," giving the units a material character as representative of *things* instead of the idea of twoness. The crucial point, however, is that number, above all, exhibits the dual senses of being: on the one hand something is considered in terms of what it shares with all else, as a multitude of units, while on the other hand it may be considered in terms of what distinguishes it as a number having properties specific to that number.

The primordial example of this distinction is seen in the nature of two. The number two is, in one sense, two units, but in another sense it is one, the one idea of twoness. This example occurs throughout the Platonic corpus as the exemplar of the heterogeneous sense of being—that is, as the exemplar of the problem of the one and the many. As seen in Socrates' reply to Simmias, this problem is raised by the possibility that one idea can be found in or expressed by a multitude of individuals.[40] Socrates rediscovers the problem of the one and the many in nature as a whole.

Socrates suggests the severity of his perplexity when, swearing by Zeus, he states that he is perplexed as to whether

> when you add one to one, it's either the one to which the addition is made that's come to be two; or the one that's been added and the one to which it's been added that have come to be two, because of the addition of one to the other. (96d8–97a1)

In a statement of his curiosity, striking for its directness, Socrates continues:

> Because I wonder (*thaumazō*) if when they were apart from each other, each was one and they were not two then; whereas when they came close to each other this then became a cause for their coming to be two—the union in which they were juxtaposed. (97a2–5)

In this statement, Socrates exhibits the perplexity that arose when he cast the attempt to understand the cause of the notion two—what I have called twoness—in terms of a kind of cause appropriate to two, understood as two units or things. His use of the verb *come to be* (*egeneto*) his use of the word *cause* (aitia), his use of words connoting locality, all are suggestive of the confusion: we cannot refer to the components of twoness to understand *what* it is. This explanation misses the character of twoness as a unity, a unity that has properties belonging to it only as this unity and not to either of its components. It is a mistake to point to two units as that which came to be twoness because the idea of twoness is always the same. It always has the same definition. Two, as twoness, is not then the result of the juxtaposition or proximity of two units but of their being thought as twoness.

These different senses of two—as twoness and as two units—depend upon similarly heterogeneous causes. Socrates' summary of his perplexity expresses the problem that this difference raises. He states that following his original method of inquiry, "I cannot even persuade myself that I know *one* account of why it is that anything comes to be, or perishes, or exists" (97b4–6, emphasis added). The explanation of an entity must, again, account both for its existence as this particular individual and as this *kind* of individual. In his reliance on what is "clear to all," Socrates missed these different senses of being, senses so different that causes different in kind are required for explanation. To repeat, being blinded then seems to mean missing what is, strictly speaking, invisible. It means to miss the need for formal causation or the class-character or idea of something as a cause. On the basis of this understanding of causation, Socrates would be hard-pressed to explain the existence of a human kind distinct from other kinds. Socrates' remarkable desire, his ambition, for wisdom concerning nature blinded him to the complexity of nature.[41]

Clearly, this complexity raises a further question: can an explanation of the nature of an individual being, or *a fortiori* of nature as a whole, be complete if this explanation involves a variety of causes, a variety of accounts?[42] It is crucial to see that there exists an incoherence in our understanding if we cannot articulate the principle by which the several causes unite to form a single entity. In this case, moreover, there remains a gap between our understanding and intelligible nature. It was precisely Socrates' improvement upon his original view of nature, his recognition of the inadequacy of a reductionist account of nature, that left him with this new problem.

To solve this problem, Socrates turns to teleology. A teleological view would resolve that incoherence in our understanding by joining mechanical and efficient causation and formal causation into a single cause— a cause which, as Socrates says, both "orders and effects" (97c2). But further, it might provide that information for which Socrates had turned to nature in the first place. Socrates' initial questions were questions about himself, about the causes of human life and thought. His first attempt to turn to nature as a whole in order to understand himself culminated in incoherence; it is not at all clear how nature so understood makes more intelligible our puzzling human existence. But it is clear how a teleological account would respond to this desire. As Socrates indicates, teleology appeals to him precisely because it promises a unity of human and cosmic *nous,* the latter ordering all with a view to good (97d5–7). A successful teleological account of nature would resolve perfectly the question of humanity's place in the cosmos and thus provide the unity or fulfillment that we lack.

Yet there already exist indications that Socrates' hopes may go unfulfilled. After Socrates had presented the first mathematical perplexity, Cebes asked concerning his perplexities: "Well, *now* what do you think of them?" (86e5, emphasis added)[43]. Socrates replied that he "is far from supposing I know the reason for any of these things" (96e6–7). And after relating the problem of two, Socrates states that he "rashly adopts a different method, a jumble of my own and in no way incline toward the other" (97b6–7). We expect to hear of Socrates' new method at *this* point. But this impression serves to reinforce the fact that Socrates has described his present state—his continuing perplexity—without yet speaking of his former experience with teleology. Apparently that experience did not lead him to adopt the teleological view. Let us consider the reasons for this disappointing conclusion to such a promising possibility.

Socrates reports that one day he heard a man reading from a book by Anaxagoras. In the book, Anaxagoras expressed the view that *nous* both "orders and causes all things" as it is best for each thing to be, a cause which "seemed good" to Socrates (97b8–c6). Socrates makes the serious pun that he was "pleased to find in Anaxagoras an instructor to suit my own *nous*" (97d5–7). What suited Socrates was the perfect harmony of human and comprehensive *nous*. Socrates goes on to express the hope that Anaxagoras

> in assigning the cause for each individual thing and for things
> in general, would go on to expound what was best for the in-
> dividual thing and what was the common good. (98b1–3)

To know any individual being, one need only know what is best for that being. In pursuit of these hopes—which he would not "have sold for a large sum"—Socrates reports that he "hurriedly acquired these books" (98b3–5).

Lamentably, however, "these marvelous hopes of mine were dashed" (98b7). On examination, Socrates found Anaxagoras using no *nous* at all but rather relying on such "absurdities" as air, ether, and water (98b8–c2). Socrates proceeds to show the inadequacy of relying only on material causation when explaining, for example, his own activity; surely, one has not explained Socrates' decision to remain in jail if one only understands the physiology which made the realization of this moral decision possible. But this is exactly what Anaxagoras did, relying ultimately only on material cause and not, as advertised, on mind alone.

Summarizing Anaxagoras' thought, Socrates notes his failure to reconcile the two kinds of causation: "Imagine being unable to distinguish two different things: the cause proper and that without which the cause could never be a cause" (99b2–4). This statement, however, is a critique not of teleology itself but of a failed attempt at a teleological understanding.[44] Why doesn't Socrates himself now offer a teleological account, an account that would reconcile the two kinds of causation? Socrates' failure to do so suggests that in his treatment of Anaxagoras' thought lies a reason to think that a teleological account is unavailable.

But precisely what has Socrates said to indicate the unavailability of such an account?

Perhaps Socrates recognizes that the teleological account must, like his previous view, be supplemented by a view of the forms or ideas as causes. In order to know what is best for something, one must surely know the kind of thing one is speaking about. Yet Socrates does not make this argument in the context. Curiously, Socrates' only discussion in this most cosmological passage is the example of his own moral-political decision to remain in prison. As I will show in what follows, an examination of this example indicates that the problem is not simply that the teleological view needs to be supplemented by a consideration of natures or kinds. It is rather that human nature itself, that complex nature evident in Socrates' reply to Simmias, makes elusive the possibility of the reconciliation of all goods in a cosmic teleology.

We can begin to see the link between Socrates' example and teleology by recognizing that this political example has an etymological connection with the cosmological passage. The key word used throughout the present passage, *aitia*—usually translated as 'cause'—originally meant to be responsible for, in the sense relating to guilt and innocence or honor and shame.[45] In other words, the word originally referred to human causality. Only later was its meaning broadened to encompass causality in general, as it does in the present context. By using his trial as an example of causality, Plato has Socrates return the word to its narrower, political meaning. The significance of Socrates' example lies in the connection between human causality and cosmological causality or teleology.

Guilt or responsibility depends on humans having the possibility of choice. Only if choice exists do those distinctions characteristic of our political existence—guilt and innocence, praise and blame—make sense. If we were absolutely determined in the manner of either body in motion or rational necessity—as say the law of non-contradiction—guilt would be a nonsensical notion. Indeed, the very idea would not arise. We escape complete determination—whether in the form of rational necessity or in the form of the necessary movement of matter—only to the extent that we cannot be completely reduced either to reason itself or to mere body. In other words, freedom of action exists precisely because humanity comprises somehow this duality of reasoning intelligence and corporeality. And in this freedom of action lies the possibility of moral choice to which Socrates has called attention.

But then what exactly is the human unity that comprises this duality? As I stated earlier, the urgent need for an answer to this question, and thus recognition of the difficulty of such an answer, arises first in political life. To know what justice is, to know the proper distribution of human goods, depends on knowledge, first, of the content and rank of the various goods. This knowledge in turn depends on knowing what it is to be human; only in this way can we know what is better and worse for the kind of beings that we are. But the *Phaedo* has given us reason to believe that the human being understood as embodied consciousness, as involving both living and thinking, cannot be reduced to either of its aspects without distortion: life involves motion and thus necessarily body but mind cannot be fully understood if reduced to body. The several proofs of immortality founder precisely on this point. The *Phaedo*—subtitled "On the Soul"—is devoted in large measure to an investigation of the complex irreducible whole which comprises these diverse capacities.[46] But it is a whole whose unity Plato affirms but does not fully explain by attaching to it the one name—soul.

The irreducible aspects of the soul give rise to conflicting goods— the goods related to mind and the goods related to body and the preservation of life. The classical understanding sees politics as undertaking to fulfill both kinds of goods.[47] But it is not at all clear that it can satisfy those more urgent, more widely shared goods of the body without restricting those individuals who would pursue the goods of the mind. It is not at all clear that "what [is] best for the individual and what [is] the common good" harmonize in some unproblematic view of justice (98b1– 3).[48] As Socrates suggests when he says, "I would not have sold these hopes for a large sum," Socrates' goods may be incommensurable with the goods of most humans (98b3–4). Again, we have no better expression of this conflict and its irreconcilability than the example Socrates offers, that of his own trial.[49] Behind the political problem, the problem of justice, lies the complex human soul. It is here too that the source of the elusiveness of cosmic teleology lies.

In order to resolve the problem of justice created by the complexity of human being—that is, in order to overcome the conflict of human goods—political communities look to some trans-human order. Socrates was likewise led from his early questions concerning humanity to his investigations into nature as a whole. In this vein, Socrates states that he hoped a teleological account would reconcile the tension between the good for each and the good for all. But Socrates' account of his own conflict with the Athenians makes this possibility dubious. Socrates reports:

> The Athenians judged it better to condemn me, and therefore I in my turn have judged it better to sit here and thought it more just to stay behind and submit to such penalty as they may ordain. Because, by the dog, as I believe, these sinews and

bones would long since have been off in Megara and Boetia impelled by their judgment of what was best, had I not thought it more just and more noble not to escape and run away but to submit to whatever penalty the city might impose. (98d1–99a4)

Socrates opposes what the Athenians consider just to his view of what is good for him. In this case, the judgment of Athens and the judgment of Socrates happen to coincide, although these judgments are based on divergent rationales. But more important is Socrates' recognition of the conflict concerning what is good. Were the various human goods perfectly reconciled, we would not expect to see political arrangements subject to the great array of possibilities to which they are in fact subject. We would not expect to see everywhere the variety of conventional reconciliations of the diverse individual goods into a common good rather than the predominance of the one true and natural reconciliation.[50] That is, we would not expect that the reconciliation of what is good for each and for all would always be only a humanly contrived approximation of perfection, an approximation that allows or demands that the best, wisest, and most just man be put to death (118a16–17).[51]

Again, in the hope of achieving a solution to the political problem— that is, in the hope of achieving the reconciliation of the diverse individual goods—humans look to gods or nature. But the very existence of political life and its characteristic distinctions—that humans are free to order their existence in a variety of ways—must belie the notion that *nature* orders all as it is best for each and for all. There remains a difference between understanding what is truly good and its actualization. The good does not both order and effect. Socrates' hopes remain only hopes.

Reflection on Socrates' political example explains, I think, why Socrates criticizes Anaxagoras' attempt at a teleological understanding but does not himself offer such an understanding. The example compels reflection on the relationship between human and cosmological causality, a reflection that leads to the conclusion that a teleological account is elusive. In sum, to the extent that it includes mind, soul makes understanding possible. But to the extent that soul is also the source of life and motion—that is, to the extent that the soul is the complex whole indicated in Socrates' reply to Simmias—it makes complete understanding elusive.[52] It remains unclear how this complex whole can be articulated with nature as a whole.[53] Socrates' treatment of teleology indicates the existence of a distance between humanity and the whole of nature, the greatest sign of which is the very existence of political life.[54]

The examination of Socrates' example shows that the teleological view is formulated to respond to the questions we have about ourselves: what are we, and what is our good? The teleology section indicates that these questions, not being resolvable on the strictly human plane, become linked to the question of the good or purpose of the whole of nature. This question goes beyond the need for explanation in terms of the natures or class-characters because this type of explanation leaves open the question of the purpose of the whole, that by virtue of which the whole is a whole: from the standpoint of this purpose, such order as we perceive in the forms or the classes may be only temporary.[55] The question of purpose or good has not been resolved on the cosmic plane.

Socrates now articulates his new approach to nature. The goal of this approach remains the apprehension of the nature of the whole to the extent that it is possible to do so. Socrates continues to act on the desire he expresses at the start. Socrates tells Cebes:

> Now I should have been most pleased to have become anyone's pupil, to learn the truth about a cause of that sort; but since I was deprived of this, proving unable either to find it for myself or to learn it from anyone else, would you like me, Cebes, to give you a display of how I've conducted my second sailing in quest of the cause? (99c6–d2)[56]

Socrates recommends a new approach by which to conduct the inquiry into nature. Unlike Simmias, whose language Socrates here mimics, Socrates embarks on his voyage not with a view toward safety and reassurance but with a view toward continuing his search. Socrates' 'second sailing' does not involve a circumscription of view, focusing only on human concerns. But the character of Socrates' search has been shaped by his earlier errors. He undertakes his renewed search with a greater appreciation of the elusiveness of the goal and the reasons for that elusiveness. Specifically, Socrates must face the question of how one ought to conduct such a search in light of the complexity of the soul on the one hand, and the complexity of the beings on the other. Socrates' momentous alteration in philosophy is the response to this question.

The 'Second Sailing'

Socrates describes his famous 'second sailing' in a passage that begins with a discussion of the proper beginning point of any investigation. In order to make his point clearer to Cebes, Socrates immediately adds a discussion of his method that is usually referred to as the hypothetical method. In accordance with this method, he then formulates a hypothesis—that the intelligibles themselves exist and that they alone are causal—which he then applies to his previous perplexities.

The passage raises many difficult questions. First, what exactly is the new beginning point of Socrates' investigation? Second, what is the relationship between the new starting point and the hypothetical method? Third, what is the relationship between this method and the first hypothesis—the existence and causality of the intelligibles themselves? Fourth, how does Socrates' new mode of philosophizing ground rational inquiry even in the face of those uncertainties that the dialogue has brought to light? And fifth, why is Socrates' alteration in philosophy traditionally understood as the origin of political philosophy? To begin to answer these questions, we need now to consider the passage in detail.

Socrates states that he had to

> take care not to incur what happens to the people who observe and examine the sun during an eclipse; some of them, you know, ruin their eyes unless they examine its image in water or something of that sort. I had a similar thought: I was afraid I might be completely blinded in my soul by looking at things with my eyes and trying to lay hold of them with each of my senses. So I thought I should take refuge in speeches and study in them the truth of the beings. Perhaps my comparison is in a certain way inept; as I do not at all admit that one who examines in speeches the beings is any more studying them in likenesses than one who examines them in deeds. (99d5–100a3)

Socrates states that he took refuge in speeches (*logous*) in order to study in them the truth of the beings (*ontōn*). He opposes this course of investigation to one that would rely on direct perception of the things (*pragmata*). In the course of the description of his new approach, Socrates responds to an expected objection to this approach: doesn't one miss the object itself—the sun—if one looks only at its reflection in water? In other words, aren't the speeches or ideas images of the more 'real' perceivable things? Am I not more sure of the stick I trip over than the invisible speech that expresses the idea of a stick? Socrates denies that this is the case. He maintains that the perceivable things can as well be regarded as images of the speeches. Behind this claim lies the argument—learned through his previous investigations into nature—that true understanding of a thing requires knowledge of the class or nature of a thing; that class or nature limits or defines what the thing I see before me now can do and be. To sense the perceivable thing is not yet to *understand* the thing as a particular kind of being. It is not possible to tell *what* a thing is, what kind of thing it is, simply by looking at the thing. We could see, for example, innumerable trees, and each would remain a discrete individual unless and until the idea of tree occurs to us. We, therefore, do not know *what* the individual things are until this idea arises in the mind.[57] It is this idea or class-character or nature that is expressed in speech, in the common noun.[58] Accordingly, Socrates denies that "one who examines in speeches the beings is any more studying them in likenesses than one who examines them in deeds" (100a1–3).[59]

Through its use of the image of the sun, the passage suggests, moreover, that this lesson concerning perceivable things applies as well to the possibility of grasping the whole of nature through an immediate mental perception. Socrates' use of the image of the sun recalls its use in those famous images of the *Republic*, the images of the divided line and the cave.[60] There it represented The Good or the Idea of the Good, that by which the whole is a whole, that by which the whole is intelligible as a whole. Socrates' doubt concerning direct access to the sun in the present passage carries with it the implication that the whole of nature too resists immediate perception. This point will be substantiated in Socrates' forthcoming discussion of hypothesis, a discussion that also has its parallel in the *Republic*. At present, the point is that the initial object of Socrates' investigation is not an object of immediate perception, whether sensory or mental.

However, while this passage makes clear that knowledge is not simply perception, it does not maintain that ideas occur to us without any basis in perception. Several elements of the passage substantiate this point. First, it is significant that Socrates does not refer here—as he had done earlier—to the doctrine of Recollection or its companion doctrine, the Immortality of the Soul, in order to explain how these intelligibles, *prior to any sensory perception*, come to be in the mind (74a9–75c6). Second, Socrates denies that studying beings in speeches is *any more* studying them in images than is studying them in deeds. This qualification suggests that the speeches are still to some extent imagistic—that is, they do not completely replace the individual beings as far as causal explanation is concerned. Finally, elsewhere in the dialogue, Socrates severs the connection between seeing and knowing, avoiding his usual term for the intelligible, *eidos* or *idea*, words derived from the simple past of the verb *to see*.[61] But in the present passage, insisting that our speeches convey that which is intelligible, Socrates preserves this connection to the extent that speech reflects the manifest articulation of the world into kinds, an articulation first evident in visible form. In the present passage, our knowledge seems to depend on experience. As with Phaedo's knowledge of the event he describes, our knowledge depends on memory and perception as well as intellection. To the extent that this is so, the implication is that the intelligible is in some sense *in* the particular beings rather than separate from them insofar as our experience is of particular beings.[62]

The foregoing understanding of the focus of Socrates' 'second sailing' runs contrary to the more prevalent interpretation of this famous passage. The latter holds that Socrates' 'second sailing' constitutes a turn to the separate Ideas.[63] In support of this interpretation is the fact that Socrates does soon after the discussion of the 'second sailing' speak of the doctrine of separate Ideas (100b4–5). He does introduce these intelligibles—the beautiful itself, the good itself, the large itself, and so on—apparently in order to exemplify his new approach. He also claims that the intelligibles so understood provide a resolution of his earlier perplexities. But other elements of the dialogue give reason to doubt that this is the most accurate interpretation of the 'second sailing.' In order to substantiate this point, I will first consider Socrates' initial presentation of the intelligibles in this context. Next I will examine his application of these intelligibles to his perplexities. Finally, I will discuss his explanation of the hypothetical method.

Socrates does not refer to the separate Ideas in his initial discussion of his new approach. It is only *following* the description of his new approach that Socrates elaborates the hypothetical method, and it is only at that point that he introduces the separate Ideas, apparently to exemplify this method (100b1–7). Socrates' presentation of the intelligibles—which Socrates calls, those "much babbled-about entities"—begins as he easily secures Cebes' agreement that the intelligibles exist (100b4–5; see also 76d8–9). Socrates says:

> It appears to me that if anything else is beautiful besides the beautiful itself, it is beautiful for no reason at all other than that it participates in that beautiful; and the same goes for all of them. (100c4–6)

This proposition, a proposition that depreciates the whole phenomenal world—"*if* anything else is beautiful besides the beautiful itself"—is agreed to without discussion. Having formulated this understanding of causality, Socrates goes on to deny the need for heterogeneous causation.

He states that he no longer understands those "other wise causes"— "blooming color" or "shape"— which "confuse" him (100c9–d2). In the face of this confusion, Socrates does not advise further study but rather that these causes be dismissed (100d1).

Socrates contrasts his understanding of causality with that of the sophists, calling his understanding "plain, artless, and possibly simple-minded (*euēthōs*)" (100d3–4). The word *simpleminded* was used earlier by Cebes to designate an argument that did not heed the difference between an individual and a class (87c7). Socrates' use of the word in the present context is appropriate because he is aiming, most explicitly, at the obfuscation of the causal heterogeneity that is necessary in the light of this distinction. Socrates' earlier criticism of Anaxagoras—that he does not distinguish a cause and that without which the cause cannot be a cause— applies to his present definition of causality. Socrates limits the notion of causality to a single meaning: something is beautiful "*for no reason at all other than* that it participates in that beautiful" (100c4–6, emphasis added). In order to maintain this definition, Socrates speaks of the intelligibles in the flagrantly inappropriate language of efficient causation. He states at one point that "nothing else makes (*poiē*) a thing beautiful except that beautiful itself" (100d4–5). Surely, it is difficult to maintain that the separate Ideas—the unchanging, eternal, incorporeal intelligibles—make a thing beautiful in an efficiently causal manner.

Aristotle recognizes the difficulty in *On Coming into Being and Passing Away.* He criticizes the understanding of the Ideas set forth in this passage of the *Phaedo* by asking:

> If the Ideas are causes, why do they not always generate things continuously rather than sometimes doing so and sometimes not, since both the Ideas and the things which partake in them are always there?[64]

Gallop maintains that Aristotle's critique is "irrelevant" because "the Forms are not represented as explaining [what causes the acquisition of attributes]."[65] But in the course of insisting that the Ideas alone are causal, Socrates does express the notion of the Ideas acting in an efficiently causal manner. Aristotle's criticism is therefore relevant, especially when the criticism is placed in its context. Aristotle renders this criticism as he denies that *either* the Ideas alone or matter alone can explain all causation.[66] This is precisely the inadequacy of Socrates' present discussion. Socrates raises the same difficulty through his discussion of the Ideas as he raised in the first proof of immortality: just as the principle of opposites, to the extent that it assumed homogeneous causation, could not provide a comprehensive explanation, neither can the separate Ideas; the latter are also misleadingly reductive.[67]

Lending additional support to this conclusion is Socrates' confession in the context that he does not know the mechanism by which this sort of causation operates. Speaking of the notion of participation, the leading explanation of this mechanism, Socrates states:

> Whether it works by "its presence or communion or whatever and however it may be called, I don't go so far as to affirm (*diïskhurizomai*) that . . . (100d5–7)

Socrates had used the word *affirm* (*diïskhurisaimēn*) just prior to his initial defense. There he stated that he would not affirm with certainty the account of the next world that he was about to deliver (63c2). He uses the word once more, in reference to the final myth. Socrates says that it is not reasonable to affirm that things are exactly as he has portrayed them (114d1). In each instance, then, Socrates uses the word to express doubt about his possession of comprehensive knowledge. The uncertainty that Socrates expresses regarding the doctrine of participation is further emphasized by his use of the phrase, "whatever and however it may be called"(100d6).[68] This phrase is used by supplicants unsure of the appropriate designation of the god to whom they pray.[69] In his final hours, then, Socrates states explicitly, and rather casually, that he does not know what joins the separate Ideas to the world that they are supposed to explain. Socrates' confessed ignorance on this matter must raise doubt that Socrates recommends his 'second sailing' as simply a vehicle for the introduction of the separate Ideas. This doubt grows as Socrates now applies the doctrine of Ideas to his earlier perplexities.

Socrates begins by asking whether "it's by largeness that large things are large, and larger things larger, and by smallness that smaller things are smaller?" (101a2–3). Socrates suggests that it is by reference to the idea of largeness that we are to explain not only a thing's being large but also its being larger. It is difficult to see how something's being *large* can be an absolute, but it is impossible to conceive how something's being *larger* could be an absolute. Such a notion would seem to depend on a comparison of two particulars. Further difficulties arise as the passage continues.

Having offered this introduction, Socrates considers the first of his perplexities—how to think of something being larger or smaller by a head. He conjures up a situation in which Cebes would be confronted by one of the lovers of contradiction. Socrates tells Cebes that, when faced with the question of the cause of being larger or smaller, "you'd protest that you for your part will say only that everything larger than something else is larger by nothing but largeness," and similarly with respect to being small (101a1–5). According to Socrates, Cebes would reply in this manner because

> you'd be afraid, I imagine, of meeting the following contra-
> diction: if you say that someone is larger and smaller by a head,
> then, first, the larger will be larger and the smaller smaller by
> the same thing; and, secondly, the head, by which the larger
> man is larger is itself a small thing; and it's surely monstrous
> that anyone should be large by something small; or wouldn't
> you be afraid of that? (101a5–b2)

But why should we necessarily consider monstrous either of these two claims?[70] Neither is inherently contradictory. Socrates' explanation does obscure the distinction between this or that particular thing being large or small on the one hand, and the quality of largeness or smallness on the other. The conclusion that this explanation is monstrous arises, I think, only if one wishes to avoid the complexity of causality behind these different senses of being. It is this complexity, the equivocal character of being, that enables the lovers of contradiction to engage in those sophistications that cause the fear of which Socrates speaks.

As is evident in Socrates' treatment of the problem of two, to which he now turns, the measures taken to avoid this fear come at a great cost. When explaining the cause of two, Socrates tells Cebes:

> You'd shout loudly that you know no other way in which each
> thing comes to be, except by participating in the peculiar be-
> ing of any given thing in which it does participate. (101a1,
> 101c2)

This you would do because you are "scared of your own shadow"(101a5). Specifically, Socrates would have Cebes respond that, as regards two things, there is "no other reason for their coming to be two, save *participation* in twoness" (101c4–5, emphasis added). This explanation could avoid an empty formality if it were possible to understand the relationship between two and twoness. But in order to join the Idea with the particular, Socrates relies on the notion of participation, and he has just confessed that he is in the dark about this notion. Socrates presents the doctrine of Ideas as a source of assurance or of safety against the fear of contradiction.[71] The doctrine can prevent an unwarranted skepticism, preserving the notion that there *are* intelligibles. However, neglecting as it does the real difficulties of explaining causation, on the deepest level it purchases irrefutability at the cost of being uninformative.[72] The doctrine of Ideas qualifies as one of those "least refutable of human doctrines" desired by Simmias. But although it is a consoling doctrine, promising certainty in every respect, it does not constitute the core of Socratic rationalism.

An examination of the hypothetical method offers further evidence that Socrates' 'second sailing' does not finally rest on the separate Ideas. Socrates discusses the character of this method twice in the course of this passage. In the first discussion he states:

> This was how I proceeded: hypothesizing on each occasion the speech I judge strongest, I put down as true whatever things seem to me to accord with it, both about a reason and about everything else; and whatever do not, I put down as not true. (100a3–7)

The widely recognized ambiguity of the passage resides in the question of whether *accord* means 'be consistent with,' or 'is deducible from.'[73] But, as Gallop notes, more important than this ambiguity is that neither interpretation offers a solid ground for thinking a proposition true or untrue.[74] Surely the fact that a proposition is consistent with or deducible from a premise does not necessarily entail that that proposition is true. Although the proposition that cows have wings is a proposition perfectly consistent with the premise that cows can fly, this consistency does not demonstrate the truth of the former proposition. This example manifests the defect inherent in a strictly deductive procedure, which is precisely the way in which this first statement characterizes the hypothetical method.

Some commentators attempt to remedy this defect by maintaining that the speech Socrates "judges strongest," the speech from which he deduces all else, is that which he now announces: the X's themselves exist and a thing is X because of its participation in the X itself.[75] However, we have seen reason to doubt that this hypothesis, stated in this way, is intrinsically tied to Socrates' new approach.[76] Socrates' second statement on his procedure offers further confirmation of this conclusion. Bringing to a close his treatment of the perplexities, Socrates states:

> You'd dismiss those divisions and additions and other such subtleties (*kompseias*), leaving them as answers to be given by

people wiser than yourself; but you, scared of your own
shadow, as the saying is, and of your inexperience, would hang
on (*ekhomenos*) to that safety of the hypothesis and answer accordingly. But if anyone hung on (*ekhoito*) to the hypothesis itself, you would dismiss him and you wouldn't answer till you
should have examined its consequences, to see if, in your view,
they are in accord or discord with each other; and when you
had to give an account of the hypothesis itself, you would give
it in the same way, once again hypothesizing another hypothesis, whichever should seem best of those above, till you came
to something adequate. (101c7–e1)[77]

In this passage, Richard Robinson discerns what he calls an "outrageous
case of . . . ambiguity", in Socrates' use of the same word—(*ekhesthai*)—in
exactly opposite senses.[78] Other details of the passage partake of similarly
outrageous ambiguity and even outright error. For example, Socrates uses
the phrase, "the same way," to refer to what are in fact opposite ways or
movements of the mind. The first way corresponds to the deductive procedure evident, for example, in the movement of the mathematicians from
a hypothesis down to its consequences. But the second way runs in the
opposite direction since it involves the reference of the hypothesis to some
higher, more comprehensive justification.

The present point can be made clearer by a comparison of Socrates'
treatment of these two motions of the mind in the *Phaedo* with his treatment of the same issue in the *Republic*. In the famous 'divided line' passage
of the *Republic*, Socrates speaks of the articulation of the portion of that
line which pertains to that which is intelligible. He tells Glaucon:

In one part of it a soul, using as images the things that were
previously imitated, is compelled to investigate on the basis of
hypotheses and makes its way not to a beginning but to an
end; while in the other part it makes its way to a beginning
that is free from hypotheses.[79]

In this way, Socrates describes the contrary motions of the mind—the
motion that *descends* from an agreed-upon hypothesis to explain the visible
world and the motion that *ascends* from hypotheses toward the beginning,
the first principle, which is most knowable and free of hypotheses. Glaucon does not quite understand Socrates' meaning. To aid his understanding, Socrates offers explanatory examples which pertain to our present
passage. Socrates states:

> I suppose you know that the men who work in geometry, cal-
> culation, and the like treat as known the odd and the even, the
> figures, three forms of angles, and other things akin to these in
> each kind of inquiry. These things they make hypotheses and
> don't think it worthwhile to give any further account of them
> to themselves or others, as though they were clear to all. Be-
> ginning from them, they go ahead with their exposition of
> what remains and end consistently at the object toward which
> their investigation was directed.[80]

Socrates has here described mathematics and, more generally, all the arts
that depend on deductive reasoning. These activities begin from agreed-
upon premises and use these premises as beginnings or first principles to
understand and to work upon what lies 'below'—namely, the conclusions
derived from these first principles.

There is also a motion of the mind running in the opposite direction. Socrates continues:

> Well, then, go on to understand that by the other segment of
> the intelligible I mean that which argument itself grasps with
> the power of dialectic, making the hypotheses not beginnings
> but really hypotheses—that is, stepping stones and spring-
> boards—in order to reach what is free from hypothesis at the
> beginning of the whole.[81]

It is important to see that it is to this *ascent* of the mind that Socrates refers
in his second discussion of his procedure in the *Phaedo*. I quote this passage once more:

> And when you had to give an account of the hypothesis itself,
> you would give it in the same way, once again hypothesizing
> another hypothesis, whichever should seem best of those
> above, till you came to something adequate. (101d3–e1)

It is difficult to make sense of this particular discussion of the hypothetical
method and at the same time to maintain that the strongest speech is that
the separate Ideas exist. To what more comprehensive hypothesis should
one refer in order to substantiate their existence?

Reacting to this difficulty, Gallop states that, at this point,
"Socrates' remarks seem by now to have cut loose from their moorings."[82]
But Gallop's reaction is justified only if the "moorings" of the hypothet-

ical method are understood to be the separate Ideas. If, however, the hypotheses to which Socrates refers are the speeches we express in our everyday existence, then the need for ascent is not so incongruous.[83]

It is in the light of this consideration that we should understand the widely recognized difference between the present passage and the one in the *Republic*. Several commentators have noted that there is one crucial difference between the account of hypothesis in the *Phaedo* and the account in the *Republic*: the presence in the *Republic* and the *absence* in the *Phaedo* of the Idea of the Good.[84] At the end of his life, Socrates leaves in doubt his commitment to the metaphysical doctrine considered to be his deepest understanding—that there exist separable Ideas, hierarchically arranged and culminating in the Idea of the Good, that guarantor of perfect intelligibility. In urging the need for ascent, in omitting mention of the highest principle of intelligibility and being, Socrates makes dubious that he has in his possession a comprehensive account of the whole of nature. For this reason, Socrates characterizes his 'second sailing' as a search (99d1).

I can now summarize the answers to those questions that I have posed concerning the initial object of Socrates' new approach, the relation of this approach to the hypothetical method, and the relation of the separate Ideas to the hypothetical method. Socrates begins his investigation with speeches, with what humans say about the world. He does so out of a recognition of the incomplete intelligibility of sense perception and the unavailability of immediate mental perception. Socrates does not dismiss common opinion, because this beginning point reflects the way in which we really do begin to know the world. The hypothetical method follows from this starting point insofar as it reflects the need both to explain the world on the basis of these speeches—to descend from these speeches—and to ascend from these initial speeches to more comprehensive, more explanatory speeches. In short, the hypothetical method as it is presented in the *Phaedo* is intrinsically related to the beginning point of Socrates' inquiries only if that beginning point is *not* understood as the separate Ideas.

As I stated at the outset, one purpose of my study of the *Phaedo* is to challenge the Nietzschean claim that Socrates is dogmatically rational. So far we have seen that Socrates himself subjects to radical criticism precisely those doctrines on which this portrayal rests. Teleology has been seen to be elusive, and the doctrine of separate Ideas is dubious. But recognition of the nondogmatic character of Socrates' rationalism makes all the more pressing the need to respond to the question that I posed at the beginning of this section—namely, the question of the rational basis of rational inquiry. If the doctrine of Ideas is not available as an explanation of the whole of nature, then our explanations must continue to rely on a variety of causes.[85] Though the nature or class-character of a thing, expressed in speech, might reflect most accurately our experience of the world, this type of explanation leaves important questions unanswered.[86] For example, can the nature or class-character explain the existence, the coming into being and passing away, of any individual? If we know *what* something is, can we predict with certainty the tenure of its existence? It is doubtful that we can. A more complete explanation would have to refer also to material and efficient causation. However, even on the basis of these two forms of explanation taken together, we cannot claim to predict the existence or demise of any individual because as an individual it is—at least in part—a corporeal being subject to the accidental movement of body or chance. Of course this inability bears directly on the issue that is of pressing concern in the *Phaedo,* the issue of the ultimate disposition of our selves as individuals. Realizing this, we are brought face to face with the uncertainty characteristic of our transient, contingent existence; we lack vital information concerning the ultimate disposition of our lives and thus concerning how we should live now.[87] This consideration brings us back to the leading question of the dialogue: why should we think that the Socratic way of life rests on something more substantial than a dream? In other words, why does Socrates think that his turn to speeches provides a substantiation of the philosophic life even in the face of such uncertainties? And, more specifically, why does he believe that it can serve as an alternative to a teleological understanding?

It is also important to see that we have not yet addressed the last of my initial questions. We do not yet know precisely why Socrates' 'second sailing' should give special prominence to the examination of moral and political issues. We would expect that in his intellectual autobiography Socrates would give some explanation for his distinctive interest in these issues. But the connection between the 'second sailing' and political philosophy remains unclear. In what follows, then, I will consider again Socrates' intellectual autobiography in order to begin to answer the questions raised in this and the preceding paragraph.

To begin to respond to these questions, it is necessary to recall that Socrates' new approach arises in reaction to his philosophic predecessors. In other words, Socratic philosophy arises as the result of a failed attempt to follow the way of his predecessors who claimed to have grasped the ultimate principles of the whole. Socrates saw that the failure of his predecessors made philosophy questionable in making the goal of philosophy, wisdom, seem elusive. If the goal is elusive, how could philosophy be anything other than futile? And if philosophy is futile, why pursue such a life, especially in light of the manifest dangers involved in scrutinizing cherished beliefs? In light of these questions, Socrates realized that the task facing him was to provide a vindication of the philosophic life. Socrates conveys the ground of this vindication through his intellectual autobiography.

The apparent disproportion between what Socrates says is required to respond to Cebes' objection—"an account of the whole of coming to be and passing away"—and what Socrates in fact presents—"my personal experiences"—dissolves when we see that Socrates learned something of the utmost importance from these experiences, something that does respond to the heart of Cebes' objection. We can thus appreciate why it is that Socrates does not despair even though in the course of his intellectual career he "had to unlearn many things I thought I knew" (96c5–6). Such disappointments—recognizing the inadequacy of one view of nature after another—could well lead someone to conclude that the human condition is abysmal, that there is no access to knowledge of nature able to guide human existence. Socrates, however, does not draw this conclusion because it was precisely through his disappointments that he gained a certain kind of knowledge, the famous Socratic knowledge of ignorance, the knowledge of what he does not know.[88]

Knowledge of ignorance is far from simple ignorance. Being in possession of it, Socrates knows something of crucial importance. He knows, first of all, that knowledge is possible, because he now knows that his former views were inadequate. Moreover, he must have a sense of what would be required in order to remedy this inadequacy. Most fundamentally, in order to grasp these inadequacies as inadequacies, and in order to apprehend how to remedy them, Socrates must have an idea of what does and what does not qualify as knowledge.[89] That Socrates possesses such knowledge is exemplified by the progress of his intellectual autobiography. But what, more precisely, constitutes this knowledge? The knowledge that provides the ground of Socrates' 'second sailing' does not lie in the speeches to which he says he turned, nor even in the *techne* of the hypothetical method.[90] Rather, the ground of Socratic rationalism lies in the knowledge that substantiates Socrates' conclusion that speeches are the proper beginning point for our investigations.

Socrates' knowledge of ignorance is human wisdom.[91] By human wisdom I do not mean some psychological account of the human soul, at least as the term 'psychological' is used in a contemporary context. As we have seen, especially with reference to the concerns of Simmias, the examination of the soul raises questions that point beyond the soul. A strictly psychological account would not meet the question that the examination of the soul inevitably raises, the question of humanity's place in the whole of nature. In this same vein, neither should Socrates' human wisdom be regarded as knowledge of ourselves as subjects separated from the world as object. It is true that the *Phaedo* does indicate that the soul is not an Idea and that there is not perfect harmony between soul and intelligible nature. But in response to this imperfect harmony, Socrates does not teach that there is an unbridgeable chasm between humanity and nature. Such a teaching would neglect the access we do have to the world, imperfect though this access might be. To maintain that there is an absolute separation of humanity and nature may permit us to avoid examining the vexed question of the relationship between the two, but it does not comport with our everyday experience. Finally, neither should this human wisdom be understood in terms of an epistemological determination of the make-up of the human mind such as that found in the work of Kant. An aspect of the self-understanding that Socrates gains is that there is no stepping outside the mind such that we might speak of it from a vantage point free of the human perspective. As was made clear in the third proof, addressed to Cebes, we can only know in accordance with human nature.

Socrates' human wisdom should be understood, most basically, as an understanding of that which must be true of ourselves and the world, given our experience of ourselves as thinking, living beings. It expresses an understanding of human intellect and of the way in which the world is intelligible to that intellect. More particularly, Socrates' human wisdom reflects what we must be and what the world must be insofar as we experience the perplexity in our understanding of ourselves and of the world that Socrates articulates in his replies to Simmias and Cebes. It is this wisdom which provides, not the conditions of certain knowledge in the manner of Kant, but the conditions of philosophic inquiry.[92] Socrates' new approach heeds the undeniable uncertainties of human existence because it rests precisely on an articulation of the experience of perplexity or of wonder, the original spur to philosophy. If we take Socrates' intellectual autobiography as an example of philosophic activity, we would conclude that the result of such activity is not pure wisdom but rather a more accurate account of the persistent problems and perplexities that characterize our understanding of ourselves and the world.[93] This account, a clear view of the human situation, is the essence of Socrates' human wisdom.

It is necessary to understand the foregoing claim in greater detail. To this end I will, first, outline the configuration of perplexity that describes the human situation in order to show how this configuration manifests the two complexities that emerged from the failed proofs of immortality: the complexity of the human soul and the complexity of beings.

Second, I will consider the way in which an understanding of the experience of perplexity can ground philosophic inquiry. Finally, I will address the last of my initial questions: Why should philosophy so understood focus on the study of moral and political affairs?

As I have interpreted them, the proofs of immortality presented so far lead to the conclusion that what we refer to as soul must be conceived as complex. This conclusion follows from the diverse activities for which the soul is held to be accountable. In the *Phaedo,* the soul is held to be the seat of the intellect on the one hand, and the source of life on the other. The explanations of these diverse functions place equally diverse requirements on the soul. Soul as intellect must be held to be "similar to what is unvarying" insofar as through the soul we understand the ideas or kinds of things that persist even though particular examples of these kinds come into being and pass away.[94] Insofar as soul is responsible for life, however, it would seem to involve corporeality because life involves motion and motion, body.[95] This suggests that soul must be susceptible to change. In addition to the diverse requirements of intellect and life, the picture of the soul is made even more complex by those passages that refer to the soul as responsible for desires, passions, pleasures and sense-perception. These phenomena would seem to be best understood as capacities of ensouled body or conscious life. This conclusion would apply as well to the requirements that follow from the existence of numerous and varying souls, souls varying to such a degree that seem to express a difference in kind.

Responding to this portrayal of soul in the *Phaedo,* Gallop writes that "the dialogue contains no explicit account or consistent image of the term [soul] and it therefore remains unclear exactly what it is whose immortality Socrates is seeking to prove."[96] Gallop then proceeds to offer a brief but lucid account of the various activities attributed to the soul in the *Phaedo.* I think that it is just this type of account that best relates what it is that we know of the soul. In other words, if asked what the soul is, we would have to answer that it is that which is capable (has the potential to engage in) the activities just mentioned. I should add that despite the kind of language used—'that which'—I do not think that the *Phaedo* substantiates the existence of an entity called the soul that exists separately from an entity called the body. It suggests, rather, that for the sake of analysis it is useful to speak of the soul and the body, in the way that it is also useful to speak of parts of the soul. It is useful to understand the human whole in this manner but care must be taken lest we mistakenly reify what are only terms of analysis.

Gallop maintains that the lack of clarity concerning the soul affects the dialogue's presentation of the soul-body relationship so that there is no "single, logically coherent doctrine" that would reconcile the *Phaedo*'s conflicting images of this relationship.[97] While I would agree with this conclusion, I would add that this lack of clarity points to what I take to be an important lesson of the *Phaedo*—that the soul is necessarily complex in its diverse capacities and it is thus elusive as to its precise nature. In never denying that soul is best represented by an image or a hypothesis and in never suggesting that there is an Idea of the soul, Socrates recognizes the peculiar difficulties of saying *what* the soul is, the difficulty of providing a *logos* of the soul. The reliance on images and myths to describe the soul preserves the wondrous character of the soul suggested at the beginning of the dialogue by Phaedo as well as in Socrates' first speech.[98] This reliance on image and myth to describe the soul does not mean that we cannot speak discursively about the soul. It rather means that there are reasons to be wary of a *logos*, offered by some philosophic sects, that claim to provide comprehensive accounts of all things including the soul. Mythic or imagistic speech may be more appropriate to explaining the soul since such speech preserves the diverse and even conflicting potentials of the soul. Such speech prevents distortion in our self-understanding by making us dwell on the undeniable dilemmas that characterize our political and intellectual existence.

The proofs of immortality have suggested that not only the soul but also the beings are complex. This complexity is manifest in the heterogeneous causation, and thus heterogeneous being, of the things that was thematic in the first proof. This heterogeneity is expressed in Socrates' perplexities culminating in the 'perplexity of two.' The beings *are* both as this particular individual and as this kind of being. They *are* in the way in which we confront them in perception, as particulars, but also in the way that they are understood as examples of this or that kind of being. Moreover, as Socrates' reference to the issue of one thing's being larger than another, the beings *are* both in themselves and in relation to one another. In fact, the complexity of beings is what makes reasoning possible insofar as reasoning is commensuration—understanding one being in terms of another—in the mode of the third proof of immortality. We cannot speak of a being "naked as it were and isolated from all the things which are," but only by noting the similarities and differences among the various aspects of the beings under consideration.[99] What makes this possible is that a being is not only itself—this individual—but also possesses characteristics that make it akin to other beings.

Socrates locates the intelligible in the relationship between these two complexities, the complexity of the soul and the complexity of the beings.[100] The precise point of relation, the point that acknowledges both these complexities, lies in speeches, in what we say about things. Speeches reflect our mediate access to the particular beings insofar as they are the result of the intellectual abstraction of that which is common in our perceptions. But even though they express this understanding, these speeches are still distinguishable from a particular being itself. The status of speeches is perfectly captured in Socrates' statement that "I don't at all admit that the one who studies in speeches the beings is any more studying them in images than one who examines them in deed" (100a1–3). The speeches are as real as the things insofar as they convey knowledge of the beings, knowledge that is not available in perception. But they are still to some extent imagistic insofar as they are other than the particular thing in itself. Socrates' locution in the present passage specifies the locus of intelligibility. Recalling a distinction he had made in the misology section, Socrates distinguishes between truth on the one hand, and knowledge of the beings on the other.[101] He states that he had "wearied of studying the beings (*ta onta*)" so that his future study would be of "the *truth (aleitheian)* of the beings" (99d4, 99d5, e6, emphasis added). Speeches do not provide access to the beings themselves. Rather, they provide access to the truth of the beings, to the way in which beings are intelligible to creatures such as we are.

Clearly, this situation can give rise to grave error and overwhelming perplexity. Thinking's dependence on perception is one possible source of error. Perception is always perspectival; nor can we perceive an entire object at once. Moreover, the notion that the intelligible lies in truth rather than in knowledge of the beings themselves suggests that the mind does not wholly become its object. The object always remains in some degree separate from the thought of it. This distance from the object exists also when the object is ourselves. As we saw in Socrates' reply to Simmias, we must rely on images or hypotheses as representative of the soul; the soul itself is not transparent to itself. Finally, our knowledge extends only as long as our embodied existence does.

Again, the beings themselves engender perplexity and also error and uncertainty insofar as they *are* in heterogeneous ways. We know the various aspects of the beings. Furthermore, we know them in relation to one another; the idea of tree arises only after having seen sufficient numbers of trees so as to grasp their similarity to one another and their difference from other beings. Because our knowledge is relational, the understanding we have of a particular thing can change as its relations to other things change, as Simmias may be larger than Socrates but smaller than Phaedo (102b4–5).[102] Reflecting this fact is Socrates' use of the term *speeches (logous)* to describe the intelligible (at least at first) rather than *ideas*. The term *idea* suggests a separability of the objects of knowledge that is perhaps unwarranted. From the fact that the beings present themselves in a variety of ways, there follows a latitude in understanding such that it can even be said that "we set the seal, 'what it is'" on them (75d1–2).

Uncertain and perplexing as the human situation is, however, it is precisely on the basis of an understanding of this human situation that Socrates can provide the ground for rationalism in a way that his predecessors had failed to accomplish. In support of this contention, let us consider one of Socrates' key discussions of his predecessors.

At the end of the teleology section Socrates assimilates his cosmological predecessors to the many (99b4–8). The ground of this assimilation is that the former, like the latter, are doing nothing but erecting a new god, an "Atlas" (99c3–5).[103] The implication is that the Pre-Socratics, aiming to explain nature, arrived not at nature but at another opinion about nature, having no more rational ground than any other "god." But why did these first philosophers, who consciously sought nature, succeed only in erecting an "Atlas," that is, another god?

Socrates' procedure in his treatment of cosmic teleology points to the answer to this question. Socrates judges the truth of cosmic teleology by reference to his moral-political situation. The error of the Pre-Socratics lies in their failure to follow this procedure. They *should have asked:* What must humanity's place in the whole be such that a variety of views of the one nature is possible? How is it possible that there exists that diversity of philosophic views represented, for example, by the philosophic schools in attendance at Socrates' death-bed? They should have begun, in other words, from reflection on the facts of our experience of the world. In beginning as he does, Socrates points to the following consideration as a criterion of knowledge: an explanation that fails to explain or that makes inexplicable our experience of ourselves in the world cannot be true. On this basis, then, we would have to reject an explanation that failed to explain the existence of error or, again, the existence of the variety of views of nature exemplified in Socrates' own intellectual career.[104] Without such an explanation, that which claims to be the one view of nature is indistinguishable from any other of the variety of conventional views.[105] As was evident in Socrates' reference to curing nature's lameness, to the beings wishing to be like the intelligibles, as well as in the Pre-Socratics' appeal to "Atlas," without such an explanation it becomes difficult to maintain the distinction between philosophy and myth-making.

Socrates did ask the question that his predecessors failed to ask. Thus, his rationalism can defend against the charge of myth-making. Socrates can defend against the charge that his rationalism is but another projection of his hopes in the face of uncertainty, a projection that is ultimately arbitrary because it fails to account for the source of these hopes. In other words, Socrates can defend rationalism, even in the face of uncertainty, since his brand of rationalism begins precisely from an explanation of why uncertainty, error, and perplexity exist. In this way, Socrates shows that philosophy is possible as an intellectual endeavor distinguishable from myth-making.

This is particularly evident in Socrates' treatment of the issue of death. Socrates does not claim to know with certainty what awaits us after death. Cebes had reported the view that "no one can know this death or detachment from the body which brings perishing to the soul—since none of us can possibly perceive it" (88a10–b3). Socrates does not respond to Cebes by claiming that he can perceive this, that he can know the soul's posthumous career. He responds rather through the implicit teaching of the failed proofs of immortality by showing what exactly we can claim to know with confidence. Specifically, he responds by articulating an understanding of what we are such that death presents the particular problems that it does for our lives. This understanding exemplifies human wisdom.

Socratic rationalism, then, begins from that which must be true, given the experience of perplexity itself. And it is this explanation which provides the ground for Socratic rationalism. Again, Socrates has admittedly not ascertained the purpose of the whole, thus infecting all of his conclusions with doubt: from the standpoint of the purpose of the whole, such order as we apparently apprehend might be only temporary.[106] And given the tentative character of this knowledge and the resultant variety of possible understandings, we might think that we are then left with competing and irreducible answers to our most serious questions. But such is not the case if these answers—the very fact of their variety as well as the particular content of each—are intelligible precisely in terms of that knowledge we do have, the knowledge of the experience of perplexity or the knowledge of ignorance. If, as with Socrates' treatment both of the immortality of the soul and of Anaxagoras' teleology, the various views of the cosmos could be explained as emerging from or responding to persistent discernible human problems, then it is the case that the human situation, however problematic, would prove to be more fundamental, more explanatory, than these competing views. If this is the case, then even given the uncertainties that death imposes on our understanding, the choice to proceed toward that object through reason may be a reasoned choice insofar as the human situation is open to rational investigation.

Because Socratic rationalism, the 'second sailing,' rests on the human wisdom that is knowledge of ignorance, it can serve as an alternative to a teleological understanding. The knowledge underlying Socrates' 'second sailing' does not constitute a comprehensive account of the whole of nature such that it makes clear "why each thing comes to be or perishes or exists" (97c7). But this knowledge does suffice to judge whether our inquiries are leading to greater understanding of the beings or things, that is, whether we are making *progress* in our understanding. The 'second sailing' then, is not finally intelligible as a turn to the separate Ideas. Nor can it be fully understood as simply a turn to the ideas as class-characters or even to speeches. This turn itself must finally be understood as a turn to the consideration of the situation of the speaker. For it is this situation defined in the *Phaedo* by the dual complexity of the soul and of the beings that determines that the proper starting point of philosophic reflection lies in speeches.

Socrates makes evident the importance of the awareness of the proper starting of reflection in the concise but far-reaching advice that he offers the potential philosopher near the end of the central section of the dialogue:

> you wouldn't jumble things up as the contradiction-mongers do, by discussing the starting point and its consequences at the same time, if, that is, you wanted to discover any of the things that are. For them, perhaps, this isn't a matter of the least thought or concern; their wisdom enables them to mix everything up together, yet still be pleased with themselves; but you, if you really are a philosopher, would, I imagine, do as I say. (101e1–102a1)[107]

Socrates thus all but defines the philosophers by reference to their clarity concerning the proper starting point of philosophic inquiry. In light of Socrates' reminder to Cebes that we only know in accordance with human nature, the heart of such clarity, the heart of Socrates' human wisdom, must be an appreciation of what we are such that we must ascend toward wisdom. The view of humanity expressed in the 'second sailing' maintains that we are not such as to profit from gazing directly at the sun or, less metaphorically, immediate perception of the whole of nature is not within our ken. Having intellect we can gain understanding but, since soul is more than mind alone, this understanding is affected by our corporeality. It is important to see that if comprehensive wisdom remains elusive, if therefore our understanding is tentative and hypothetical, then a clear understanding of the starting point of philosophic reflection remains crucial. For what we know best concerning our ascent to wisdom is that and why we must ascend, that and why a *'second* sailing' is necessary. This knowledge, knowledge of the complexity of the human soul, provides our surest understanding of what nature must be. Following Socrates, we must even dismiss those views of nature that fail to account adequately for it.

The central importance of this knowledge establishes the most fundamental connection between Socratic rationalism and political philosophy. Again, Socrates shows us this connection when, in the midst of his most cosmological reflections, he jarringly recalls his conflict with Athens. He does so because he wishes to make a telling point concerning the failure of cosmological teleology to account for the complexity of human causality. His example shows that this complexity is exhibited in and through the dilemmas characteristic of political life, dilemmas which are expressed in what is said (93b8–c1, 99e5, compare with 71b7–8). In a dialogue that focuses so fervently on themes transcendent of ordinary experience it is possible to neglect the significance of Socrates' legal problems. But by placing this other-worldly discussion in a cave within "The Cave", Plato provides a constant reminder of the significance that the conflict between Socrates and Athens should hold for the philosopher. Socrates' clash with Athens possesses an enduring fascination precisely because it reveals a human conflict, a conflict among goods belonging to divergent aspects of human existence. An understanding of this conflict bears on the very heart of philosophic activity. For its significance, I think, derives less from the dangers that the community might pose for the philosopher than from what this conflict teaches concerning human nature itself. Political philosophy lies at the heart of philosophic investigation because politics reflects human nature and the complexity of human nature provides our surest insight into what nature must be. The philosophic investigation of human affairs, with all its attendant dangers, becomes unavoidable in the light of the elusiveness of knowledge of the whole of nature.

Precisely because nature's unity remains a question, however, political philosophy must remain at the heart of philosophic investigation not only as a window to nature but in order to prevent distortions in our understanding of nature. Given the tentativeness of our understanding, our need to ascend toward wisdom, the inquiry into nature is beset by uncertainty. Here, too, our understanding cannot dispense with images or hypotheses. Moreover, given our distance from an understanding of the whole of nature, these images are inevitably drawn from, and influenced by, what is closest to us, our self-understanding. Of the utmost importance, however, is the character of this influence. Specifically, given the kind of question that animates the inquiry into that which transcends humanity, and given the tentativeness of our understanding, the danger is ever-present that inquiry into the matters of concern will be guided by, and answer to, more urgent desires than the desire to know.[108] The danger is especially acute that, moved by the former desires, we may well arrive at images or hypotheses of nature that neglect and thus distort precisely those human complexities that necessitated the inquiry into nature.

The influence that our heartfelt concerns can have on our understanding is evident throughout the *Phaedo*. An example of such influence occurs early in the dialogue when Phaedo says of the ship whose return delayed Socrates' execution: "It is the ship, as the Athenians say, in which Theseus once sailed to Crete" (58a10–11). But as Burnet writes, "of course, none of the original timbers were left."[109] Burnet goes on to say that "Plutarch tells us the philosophers took it as their stock example in discussing the question of identity. Was it the same ship or not?"[110] Even the apparently simple question of what ship the Athenians see before them is influenced by their hopes in the face of death.

The potential philosopher is not immune to the desires that are answered in and through the political community. The drama of the *Phaedo*, especially the drama of Simmias and Cebes, is the portrayal of the desires that deflect us from reason toward belief, that make us hate reason rather than relinquish our cherished hopes. The dialogue details the desires that make us unwilling to accept that the only wisdom available to us is human wisdom rather than pure wisdom. It is all too tempting to succumb to these desires—the desires, for example, for certainty, for justice, for assurance of the significance of one's life. It is all too tempting to reject human wisdom and to claim to know what we don't know—namely, that there is ultimate satisfaction for these desires. If the good at which inquiry aims is not the good of understanding, the possibility exists that conclusions about the whole of nature may result not from unprejudiced investigation but from the desire to substantiate the otherwise questionable character of one particular view of what is good. Only an acute awareness of the desires that motivate the inquiry into that which transcends humanity can serve to forestall this possibility. Such an awareness depends upon a careful study of our moral and political concerns.

There remains a third, more urgent, reason that this understanding of Socratic rationalism demands a philosophic examination of moral and political affairs. It must be recognized that, in thus locating the ground of rationalism, Socrates makes urgent the need to respond to the question of the goodness of the philosophic way of life, both in itself and in its relationships to other ways of life. The *Phaedo* does not supply the complete answer to this question, but it does enlighten us concerning this question, including why it became of critical importance to Socrates. Certainly in the face of the inadequacy of Socrates' predecessors, their evident failure to provide the complete account of the whole that they had promised, the activity of philosophy could appear futile, a deadend. Yet the Socratic approach, based as it is in the experience of perplexity, might well give rise to the same conclusion. To the extent that Socrates' remedy for his predecessors' inadequacies does not lie in his attainment of pure wisdom, the question of the goodness of the philosophic life remains open. Accordingly, a significant portion of the Platonic portrayal of Socrates involves the scrutiny of this question.

The answer to the general question of the goodness of the philosophic life depends on the answers to two further questions: where does the desire to know rank in relation to other human desires and does the philosophic life best satisfy that desire? The *Phaedo* bears on the first issue in its concentration on death. This concentration brings to light the incompleteness, the lack that we experience as humans. Being embodied consciousness, we desire and we are aware that we desire. And given the lack of a demonstrable proof of the immortality of the soul, we do not know that this lack that we experience as embodied humans will be satisfied in some other realm. The *Phaedo* thus points to the question treated in the *Symposium*, the question of the proper rank of desires for embodied, and thus erotic, humans. In response to this question we want to know which among the many desires takes precedence, which desire ought we to try to satisfy. Because we seriously *desire* that which is good, we want to *know* that which is truly good. The character of specifically human desire, that our desire is inseparable from understanding, points to the desire to know as underlying all other desires.

Yet, though the desire to know may be our fundamental desire, is rational inquiry the best means of satisfying that desire? This question is made all the sharper when the philosophic way of life is confronted by alternative ways of life which, based on faith and supported by civic authority, do not require rational defense. In pursuit of an answer to this question, the Platonic corpus portrays Socrates engaging in conversation concerning what is just, what is pious, and what is good.[111] And it portrays that investigation of the various views of the gods and the afterlife that brought about his execution. As the fate of Socrates attests, the sensitive character of these questions requires that the philosopher study politics for the practical purpose of providing for his own preservation.

In facing these questions Plato's Socrates belies Nietzsche's claim that all previous philosophers ignored the question of the value of philosophy for life.[112] Indeed, Socrates' awareness of the elusiveness of the object of philosophy compels him to defend philosophy precisely *as a way of life* rather than as a set of propositions. I have argued that the reflection on the very experience of perplexity is crucial to any possible defense of philosophy. But it is important to see that as an *experience* there is something irredeemably personal about this defense; that is, it is available only to one who has certain experiences, who lives a certain way of life. Perhaps to emphasize the experiential aspect of philosophy, Plato leaves in doubt whether Cebes or anyone else in attendance will in fact use any of the points expressed in Socrates' "personal experience." Moreover, as I have interpreted the rhetorical character of the dialogue, the *Phaedo* as a whole attempts to engender this experience in the reader through portraying the examination of opinions, the dialectical process, that leads to the experience of perplexity. The dialectical process is evident in Socrates' attempt to find an explanation for what is said concerning the existence of good and bad souls, it is evident in the need to look beyond the soul to nature in order to find such an explanation, and it is evident in the move beyond the various views of nature to the discovery of a new approach to nature.[113] Though commentators speak of Socrates' hypothetical method, this self-portrait of his intellectual progress expresses no fool-proof *techne* leading inexorably to wisdom. Rather, we see a man ascending toward greater understanding through trial and error, unwilling to accept any explanation that fails to account for his self-experience. The crucial point is that the height to which one will ascend, and the appreciation of the insight gained, can only be gained by the one who has traversed this path.

Socrates' path is strewn with discarded doctrines. But these are the evidence of his progress toward the insight into the proper approach to nature. Socrates' turn to speeches, this mediated approach to nature, can be fully understood only on the basis of an appreciation of the inadequacy of an immediate approach to nature. This I take to be the point of locating Socrates' intellectual autobiography at the heart of the *Phaedo*. In so doing, Plato means to convey the idea that in order to grasp this insight for oneself, one must be willing and able to work through the false-starts and dead ends by which one acquires this experience. Furthermore, one must possess the disposition that leads one to focus on the *knowledge* expressed in this experience rather than its culmination in perplexity. Accordingly, there is less benefit to be derived from hearing any particular doctrine than from seeing a man driven by wondrous desires for wisdom, with marvelous hopes for complete knowledge of the whole, pleased by the promise of such knowledge, who nevertheless faced his dashed hopes and did not slide into despair or accept consoling explanations (96a7, 98b7, 97c2–4). The prerequisite for such philosophic courage is perfect clarity concerning those desires which would lead one to prefer certainty to truth.

Plato's appreciation of the experiential character of philosophy, however, raises this question: Can self-understanding mean more than understanding of myself as this particular individual? In Socrates' self-portrait we see someone serious about his life, attempting to explain himself to himself. But perhaps the philosopher deceives himself about the value of this endeavor because he deceives himself about the possibility of self-understanding. Is there possible, in other words, an ascent from the variety of individual perspectives?

To the extent that the various views expressed in the dialogues are placed in the mouths of particular characters having particular desires, dispositions, and circumstances, this question is present in every dialogue. In addition to the reasons mentioned above, however, still other aspects of the *Phaedo* substantiate the conclusion that this question is especially acute in this dialogue. First of all, we are dependent on one particular individual for the entire story of Socrates' death day. More substantively, the treatment of a pre-dominant theme of the *Phaedo,* the immortality of the soul, involves an examination of the way in which our embodied human existence affects our understanding. The tension between comprehensive understanding and the character of human existence, wisdom and life, has been present from the beginning of the dialogue but this tension has been heightened by those limits on our understanding that have emerged from the proofs of immortality. Specifically, we have been led to see that even the character of our souls is elusive, that our understanding of the soul depends on inference from experience, on images or hypotheses, rather than on direct perception.

In light of the foregoing considerations, we can perhaps understand why Nietzsche speaks of his own "unconquerable mistrust of the *possibility* of self-knowledge."[114] Nevertheless, Nietzsche, who rightly considered himself an adept "psychologist," shows himself to be acutely aware of the way in which human needs color our views. He is especially aware of the influence of these needs on the views of philosophers.[115] Based on the foregoing account of Socratic rationalism, the Socratic challenge to Nietzsche would, I think, pose the following questions. Why could not Nietzsche's own reflections on the problematic status of humanity in the world constitute that human wisdom, on the basis of which we can become aware of the needs that distort our views and thus be free of them? More specifically, if it is possible to articulate our perplexity, to discern the sources of the latitude in our understanding, why should this articulation not suffice as a ground for rational inquiry? In short, why should it not qualify as an explanation of the way things are?

In light of these questions, it is clear that the drama of Simmias and Cebes, the temptation of misology, bears on the misologists of our own time. This drama teaches us to inquire whether Nietzsche's response to the undeniable human perplexities is dictated not by the desire to know but by a disappointed desire for certainty. It teaches us to inquire whether the opposition between wisdom and life exists only if we conceive of wisdom as pure wisdom. In other words, it is possible that what distinguishes Nietzsche from Socrates has as much to do with the response to the object of understanding as with the character of that object itself. In locating the examination of moral and political concerns at the core of philosophic investigation, Socratic rationalism reflects the philosophic need to consider the human response to the object of understanding as well as the object of understanding itself. Such a consideration, I believe, is especially pertinent to an investigation of the conflict between Nietzsche and Socrates.[116]

Appreciating that there is some degree of proximity between Socrates' reflections and those of Nietzsche does help to explain the manner in which Socrates presents his teaching. The manner of Socrates' presentation can be understood, in part, as a response to the danger of absolute skepticism which may follow the perception of the elusiveness of pure wisdom. Thus, Socrates' most manifest presentation is of a mathematicized version of philosophy, a view of philosophy as beginning from agreed-upon premises concerning the ultimate explanatory principles which then proceeds to explain the world in terms of these first things. It is philosophy that is secure in its beliefs and insulated from worldly concerns, a philosophy perfectly suited to the sect.

Socrates begins from the hypothesis of the existence of the comprehensive intelligibles. He then proceeds to "what comes next to those things"—namely, that these intelligibles are the cause of all things (100c3). In response to these vast assertions, Socrates asks only for agreement, encouraging no discussion. Socrates emphasizes the familiarity of what he proposes. It is "nothing new but what I have never stopped saying in our earlier discussion as well as at other times"(100b1–3). He even provides a sort of chant that the young men can use when confronted by the contradictors: "it is by the beautiful that beautiful things are beautiful" (100d7–8).[117]

This portrayal, as we have seen, makes much of both the fear of being contradicted and the corresponding safety of *the* hypothesis. It has the young men shouting loudly and protesting that they know of only one sort of cause, an admittedly simple-minded rather than sophisticated notion of causality. The goal clearly is not truth but agreement. These details obscure, as far as is appropriate, the notion of philosophy as ascent. A portion of Socrates' bequest to those in his cell is the "certainty" of the intelligibles as proof against those men who exploit the truly problematic character of rational explanation which underlies Socrates' perplexities. The young men can hang on to the safety of these intelligibles until that time, if it should ever come, at which they resolve to risk the ascent beyond these.

Socrates' presentation does not fail to point the way towards this ascent. The brief definition of a philosopher, quoted above, has little to do with asceticism recommended to the "genuine philosophers." It has little to do with the adherence to any particular doctrine, whether the doctrine of the Ideas or of the Immortality of the Soul. It is not oriented on pure wisdom. It consists, rather, in the clear recognition of our distance from a comprehensive account of the whole of nature. For many, this recognition acts as a solvent of certain belief and thus causes pain. But for some this awareness can serve as the impetus to self-understanding; it can lead some to treat their lives as a question. Such awareness can begin to satisfy that desire, too easily satisfied in some, to know one's place in the whole of nature. Socrates differs from many others in that he is not willing to be satisfied with unfounded assurances regarding this question. Instead, he desires to know how things truly are. Thus, Socrates' 'second sailing' does not necessarily provide access to The Good, but to the extent that it begins to answer this desire it is good.[118] For this reason, perhaps, Socrates can know that to continue in ignorance would be an evil thing (91b5–6).

Socratic rationalism corrects the self-forgetting inclination of Socrates' predecessors—evident also in Cebes—the inclination to seek an understanding of the whole of nature while neglecting the character of the seeker. Socrates' intellectual autobiography suggests from the beginning the primacy of self-knowledge in our attempt to know the whole as it shows him gazing into himself before relating his personal experiences concerning his search for an account of nature as a whole (95e7–9). The unavailability of a rational and comprehensive account of the whole points to the need to place self-understanding, human wisdom, at the core of this inquiry. It is this self-understanding that yields first the wisdom (*phronesis*) to discern the best way of life. But it is this self-understanding that comprises the wisdom (*sophia*) concerning what we know of ourselves and our world.[119] But in locating such human wisdom at the core of philosophy, Socrates does not recommend a Simmias-like circumscription of view to human concerns alone. The character of human existence itself moves us to seek explanations in that which transcends humanity. As the *Phaedo* makes clear in its focus on death and immortality, human existence is characterized by an awareness of incompleteness, an awareness that confronts us most powerfully when we face our mortality. We cannot explain ourselves to ourselves without reflection on that which might begin to complete our inherent incompleteness, on that which therefore transcends humanity.

Socrates' rationalism, then, rests neither on some certain, possibly anachronistic, cosmology nor on an exclusive focus on human affairs. It rests rather on a clear view of the starting point of reflection, a view that heeds the complexity of both the soul and the beings. Socrates achieved this view through his relentless self-questioning. Unless and until we undertake the same level of self-questioning, we cannot dismiss the possibility that Socratic rationalism remains as available today as it was for Plato's Socrates. Indeed, this possibility becomes more difficult to dismiss when we recognize that it is a possibility best examined through engaging in the characteristic Socratic activity.

Socrates' Final Teaching

Overview

(102a10–118a17)

Commentators usually regard the final proof of immortality as Socrates' most serious attempt to prove this doctrine. Based on the premise that the Ideas exist and are something, the proof directly enlists in this effort the doctrine that is usually taken to be Socrates' most profound.[1] But this final proof of immortality calls into question the explanatory power of the Ideas insofar as the proof is characterized by great ambiguity, not to say obscurity. Thus, while many commentators find the last proof the most serious, few find that it achieves what it sets out to accomplish, especially ending as it does in a bald assertion of the soul's imperishability. David O'Brien is surely correct when, in speaking of this final argument, he states: "Judgments on its value have usually been adverse."[2] Even one so credulous as Hackforth concludes:

> It is only if we allow that the appeal is to faith that we can avoid a feeling of deep disappointment in this matter inasmuch as from the standpoint of logic, the argument has petered out into futility.[3]

The ambiguity of the proof is undeniable. Yet that ambiguity has a discernible source which, upon examination, reveals the intention behind both the unsatisfactory end of the argument and the ambiguity of the argument as a whole. Socrates has previously stated clearly what this final argument sets out to accomplish. He has maintained that an answer to Cebes' objection requires a proof not only of the soul's immortality but also of its imperishability (95b8–c4). Presumably, that one account of why anything comes to be, passes away, or *is,* would answer both requirements. Crucial for understanding this last proof, however, is an appreciation of the difference between these requirements. A proof of the soul's immortality differs from a proof of the soul's never-ending existence—that is, of its imperishability. The soul can be immortal and nevertheless perish: the soul may be immortal—that is, not dead, *whensoever* it exists. But Socrates has no single explanation of causation which pertains both to *what* something is—in this case, alive—and to *that* it is. The structure of the last proof exhibits this lack in that it is really two separate attempted proofs, one of immortality and another of imperishability. What gives rise to the ambiguity of the proof of immortality, then, is precisely that which necessitates that there be two arguments instead of one; the ambiguity derives from Socrates' less-than-explicit shifting between the heterogeneous senses of being.

These heterogeneous senses of being also explain the unsatisfying conclusion of the proof. The proof of immortality ends with a statement of the kind of thing the soul is. But the proof cannot establish that a certain soul always exists; individual existence as such remains in the realm of body and thus of chance. To the extent that this is the case, the 'proof' of imperishability can only be an assertion or a hope.

Given its position in the dialogue, and given its manifest inadequacy, the final proof suggests the unavailability of a single cause of all coming into being and passing away, a cause that could make intelligible the perfect harmony of humanity and nature. Moreover, it shows Socrates distancing himself from the core of his orthodoxy—the doctrine of separate Ideas—in this, the last argument of his life. The final argument then confirms the uncertainty that precipitated Socrates' turn to the speeches of humans. Accordingly, Socrates concludes the final argument of the *Phaedo* with the recommendation that the "initial hypotheses," the existence of the Ideas themselves, be examined. The conclusion of the final proof of immortality directs us back to that ascent characteristic of Socratic rationalism. In this conclusion we see the rationale for the last proof of immortality. It is, at least potentially, a solvent for any sectarianism that might arise on the basis of Socratic orthodoxy.

Following Socrates' last argument, he delivers his last myth. One purpose of myth is to portray a realm in which we have access to satisfactions for which we can only hope in this world. The final myth of the

Phaedo does indeed speak of such a realm, but it also differs in significant ways from the concluding myths of such dialogues as the *Gorgias* and the *Republic*. Socrates speaks less of the posthumous career of the soul in the final myth of the *Phaedo* than he does in those myths. Instead, the myth takes as its theme what he calls the true earth. And in this account of the true earth, the view is expressed that, far from the whole of nature being created with an eye to human good, we are fortunate that life is possible in any manner whatsoever. The myth does speak of human happiness, but it is a distinctly terrestrial matter. The myth is a sort of recantation of the manifest depreciation of sight, beauty, and terrestrial life that preceded it.

Plato often casts the relation between the soul and the cosmos in mythic form, thus enabling the hearers of the myth to reflect on the bearing that this vast issue has on their own lives. The final myth provides support for the life of the one who would see the limits of human existence without abandoning the possibility of happiness, the one who can gaze unblinkingly at our situation without succumbing to the tragic view of life. Finally, in the words and deeds of Socrates as he lives his last moments, Plato presents the exemplar of this nontragic human existence.

Immortality and Imperishability

Phaedo reports that Socrates' argument begins from the agreed-upon premise "that each of the Ideas (*eidōn*) was something and that other things partaking in them took the name of the Ideas themselves" (102b1–2). Socrates thus embarks on a proof of immortality that *begins* from an understanding of what he has asserted to be the cause of all things. Far from an ascent toward first principles, Socrates' aim seems to be agreement based on accepted first premises. Phaedo is more than ready to agree to these premises. His report simply relates that the premises were granted and omits any of the details of their presentation. We must consider what occurs in the course of the last proof that warrants Socrates' conclusion that the premises require further examination.

Having been granted the foregoing premise, Socrates asks:

> If you say that this is so, then whenever you say that Simmias is larger than Socrates but smaller than Phaedo, you mean don't you that both things are in Simmias, largeness and smallness? (102b3–6)

Socrates speaks here of the possession of nonessential or accidental predicates by a continually existing subject. This possibility points to the fact that we can understand Simmias in a variety of ways. Our understanding of Simmias varies depending upon how we wish to regard him—in himself or in relation to others. The qualities on which Socrates chooses to focus emphasize this possibility. The accidental character of the predicates in question allows Socrates to make the point that Simmias remains Simmias as he changes from being larger to being smaller. The relational aspect of the qualities serves this same purpose.[4] In contradistinction to opposing qualities, which are accidental but nonrelational, opposing pairs of accidental relational qualities, such as smallness and largeness, can be possessed simultaneously; Simmias can be both large and small at the same time.[5]

As Jacob Klein has noted, the example given in the present context of Simmias being larger and smaller raises the same issue as that raised by the *Republic*'s example of the relationship between big and small fingers. Klein writes:

> There are perceptions of visible things, says Socrates, which give us enough clarity about the things perceived (the perception of single fingers, for example) so that most of us do not feel compelled to raise any question about them (in particular, not to raise the question, "*what is* finger?"); there are other perceptions which must seem at first perplexing and confusing (a finger appears both big and small, thick and thin, hard and soft) because "opposite" qualities (τ'αναντία) have been somehow "mixed up" (σμγκεΧυμένα) in them—as our reflecting about this "mix-up" *at once*, and with little effort on our part informs us. Indeed, the very fact that we feel perplexed about such perceptions manifests the presence of διάνοια "in" them. For to apprehend "opposition" or "contradiction" is within the province of διάνοια, not of the senses.[6]

As we saw in Socrates' intellectual autobiography, the complexity of the beings entails that they are known through comparison with one another, through the recognition of similarities and differences. Moreover, to explain how Simmias "takes the name of being both small and large" is not yet to have explained how Simmias takes the name of Simmias—that is, to have explained what Simmias is in himself (102c10–11). Nor is it to have explained how Socrates can be both small and "what I am, this same individual" (102e4–5).

We might think that the role of the knower becomes prominent when the beings are susceptible to being known in a variety of ways. But, as Socrates proceeds in the present proof, he attempts to explain this relationship without reference to the knower. In the second proof of immortality, Socrates eroticized the particulars in order to avoid treating the difficult issue of the affect of the character of the knower on that which can be known. In this last proof, he once again relies on the separate Ideas in order to explain our experience of the world. And once again this effort requires that Socrates personify the intelligible:

> Not only is largeness itself never willing to be large and small at the same time, but also . . . the largeness in us never admits the small nor is it willing to be overtopped. Rather, one of two things must happen: either it must retreat and get out of the way, when its opposite, the small, advances toward it; or else, upon that opposite's advance, it must perish. But what it is not willing to do is to abide and admit smallness and thus be other than it was. (102d6–e3)[7]

The question that remains, however, is whether we can understand the connection between the intelligible and the perceivable without reference to the human mind. The question is especially acute given what Socrates has already said concerning his ignorance with respect to the doctrine of participation, the famous Socratic explanation of this connection.

An unnamed interlocutor expresses an objection that goes to the heart of the problem. The anonymous objector wonders at the difference between the opposites discussed in the first and last proofs. In response, Socrates will make explicit the distinction between opposite Ideas—the intelligibles themselves—and opposite particulars in order to indicate the superiority of explanation by opposite intelligibles rather than by opposite things. Socrates insists dogmatically on precisely this distinction. The degree of his dogmatism is perhaps an index of the questionable character of the explanation by separate Ideas. In offering this explanation by opposite intelligibles, Socrates says that he is "talking like a legal document"; his desire is to win his case, to insure that his interlocutors "think as I do" (102d3, d5).[8] Through Socrates' self-characterization, Plato alerts us to the heightened need to challenge Socrates, to follow the advice Socrates gave in the misology section:

> if I seem to you to say anything true, agree with it; but if not, resist it with every argument you can, taking care that in my zeal I don't deceive you and myself alike. (91c2–5)

It is clear from the next stage of the argument that we cannot rely on Cebes and Simmias to undertake this task for us. Rather, we must rely on the unnamed person who interrupts to voice the crucial objection. Though he remembers the names of many others, none of whom speak, Phaedo cannot remember the name of this particular person who raises such an important objection (103a4–5). Perhaps such an objection seems to Phaedo at this late moment to be the product of someone who is hard-headed, ill-mannered, and obstinate in his refusal simply to accept what Socrates says. The sect has as little tolerance for pointed questions as does the political community, and for similar reasons. The objection draws a connection between the last proof and the first, a proof that has little appeal for the group in Socrates' cell. Why bring it up now, in the midst of more familiar and more persuasive doctrines, doctrines that promise to provide a basis for the doctrine that all want to believe in, the immortality of the soul? Perhaps such considerations explain this unusual lapse of Phaedo's otherwise prodigious memory. As for Socrates, he praises the courage of the remark. Philosophic courage seems to consist in a willingness to follow the argument wherever it may lead, no matter what the cost in terms of reputation (103b1 and 90e3).[9]

Socrates knows that the question raised by that disdained first proof concerning the adequacy of explanation by opposites—whether opposite things or opposite intelligibles—has not yet been resolved. The great difference emphasized here between things and the intelligibles themselves causes the unnamed objector to recall the claim made in the first proof that, as he states, "coming-to-be is, for opposites, just this—they come to be from their opposites. Whereas now I think it's being said that this could never happen"(103a5–10). Again, in response, Socrates simply distinguishes opposite things from opposite intelligibles themselves: the former change into their opposites while the latter never do so (103b2–5). Having made this distinction, Socrates secures Cebes' assurance that this point does not trouble him—although, Cebes admits, "many things do" (103c5–6). Socrates does not inquire into Cebes' troubles. Instead, he forcefully asserts: "We have agreed absolutely on this point: an opposite will never be opposite to itself" (103c7–8). In this response, then, Socrates not only reiterates but makes sharper the distinction between opposite things and opposite intelligibles. But Socrates does *not* insist that opposites alone are causal. It is necessary to recognize this in order to appreciate the next step of the argument. For at this point, in the light of this deep distinction between opposite things and opposite intelligibles, Socrates abandons explanation that runs in terms of the separate Ideas alone.

Contrary to what Socrates says in the present context, his line of argument is not "on the lines of what we were saying earlier" (103d6).[10] In important ways, Socrates has abandoned his initial premise. The most obvious of these ways is that Socrates introduces a new causal entity that does not take the name of the intelligible (102b2). This is a sign of a deeper alteration: the nature of these entities is not wholly determined by their partaking in a certain intelligible. Something other than those intelligibles is allowed to be causal.

Why did this movement in the argument prove necessary? The vast separation between opposite things and opposite intelligibles, emphasized by the recent objection, points to the need for an intermediate entity that would include both realms and thus bridge this gap. As such, this intermediate entity must exist on both ontic levels and thus not simply be an opposite. Causation by opposites implies that the causal entity exists on a single ontic level such that the opposites can oppose each other. Accordingly, Socrates introduces entities that are intended not to be *opposite* but *other* than either opposite things or opposite intelligibles themselves.

As prefigured by the distinction between the intelligible itself and the intelligible-in-us, Socrates seems to have distanced himself from a central tenet of what might be called his orthodoxy—namely, the separateness of the intelligibles themselves or the Ideas (103b5). This seems necessarily to be the case insofar as Socrates' explanation of causation now relies on entities which carry the intelligible but are not themselves the intelligible. Socrates' vagueness throughout the *Phaedo* concerning the explanatory range of the Ideas is warranted by the fact that the doctrine of independently existing Ideas does not serve to explain what must be explained here—namely, the being of a living thing. The explanatory range of the independently existing intelligibles is apparently limited.[11]

The next stage of the final proof of immortality is one of the most vexed passages in the Platonic corpus. Several commentators, recalling the story of Theseus at the start of the dialogue, use the image of a labyrinth to describe the passage.[12] Before embarking on the twisting course of the passage, it is useful to be aware of the outline of the argument as well as the difficulties it presents.

Socrates first offers examples of the entity whose purpose it is to bridge the gulf between the intelligible and the perceivable thing. His first examples are fire and snow. Subsequently, in order to make his argument clearer, he adduces the example of the number three. The question thus raised is whether these intermediate entities are more akin to fire and snow or to the number three in their causal activity. The way in which this question is usually approached is to ask whether the intermediate entities are concrete things or whether they are immanent Ideas or Forms. This alternative follows from the obvious concreteness of fire and snow on the one hand, and Socrates' reference to the number three as the idea of three on the other. This question is especially important because soul itself will be said to be one of these intermediate entities. A further complication of the argument stems from Socrates' replication of this same ambiguity *within* the examples of fire and snow on the one hand and three on the other. In other words, each is treated as both particular and intelligible. The argument moves through these complications toward an attempted definition of the intermediate entity. Following this attempt, Socrates announces that, on the basis of what has been said, he now sees yet another kind of causation, a more sophisticated kind. He presents several more examples of this newer kind of causation and then finally applies his reflections on causation to the crucial question of the activity of the soul in relation to life. With this outline in mind, we must now consider the details of this puzzle.

Socrates brings up the examples of fire and snow, and he maintains that these are not themselves opposites but are always characterized by an opposite—cold in the case of snow and hot in the case of fire (103c10–d12). What is it that designates such entities as a kind? An answer to this question is made more complicated by Socrates' first statement concerning the nature of these entities. This statement suggests that they themselves combine heterogeneous senses of being. Socrates states:

> The situation then in some cases of this kind is as follows: not only is the form (*eidos*) itself entitled to its name for all time; but there's something else too which is not the same as it [the Idea] but which *whensoever it exists* always has the character (*morphēn*) of it [the Idea]. (103e2–5, emphasis added)

Socrates does refer here and throughout the passage to what something is essentially, to its unchangeable character. He states that fire cannot admit the cold nor snow the hot and "still be what it was" (103d12). Yet this perpetuity, that which is 'always,' pertains to *what* the entity is in contradistinction to *that* it is: the entity always is such, "*whensoever* it exists." This dual sense of being is one source of the great difficulty in determining with any precision the kind of causal entity that Socrates has in mind: can a single entity explain both senses of being? Perhaps only a cause that could both "order and effect" would suffice. But cosmic teleology has proved elusive.

Without prompting, Socrates recognizes the lack of clarity in his definition and once again offers a 'clearer' mathematical example in order to make his case (103e6). In fact, this new example consists of a series of questions. It is difficult to tell whether or not Cebes follows Socrates' discussion because Socrates allows him to answer only the last of a series of questions. The point suggested by the series of questions is that threeness is "not the same as the odd" yet it is "by nature such that it can never be separated from the odd" (103e9–104a3).

Socrates instructs Cebes to "look closely at what I want to show" (104b6). Socrates wants to show that:

> Apparently it is not only the opposites we spoke of that don't admit each other. This is also true of all things which, although not opposites to each other, always have the opposites. These things too, it seems, don't admit whatever Idea (*idean*) may be opposite to the one that's in them. (104b7–9)

In this way, the new causal entities while existing as particulars behave in the same way as the intelligible itself. Or at least this behavior is one of the two possible responses to the attack of the opposites, for Socrates concludes that they "either perish or they get out of the way" when the opposites attack (104b10–c1). This alternative—"perish or get out of the way"—leaves open the question: are these entities concrete individuals which as such come into being and pass away, or are they more akin to the intelligibles that "get out of the way" but endure as what they are? As with his discussion of fire and snow, Socrates' locution in this passage reflects the heterogeneous senses of being. Consider Socrates' example. He refers to both three and threeness, but we can well imagine a group of three objects coming into being and passing away while threeness—the idea of three—endures.[13] We don't know that it endures eternally, or that it exists if no particular group of three exists, but we can know that it exists in a different way than does any particular group of three.

Having adduced several examples of what he means, Socrates now undertakes to define these entities. He asks Cebes: "Would you like us, if we can, to define what sort of things these are?" (104c11–22). Socrates' qualification—"if we can"—is warranted. He asks Cebes this question at 104c11, but at 105a1 he proposes once again that they attempt to define these entities as a kind. In the intervening passage, a difference emerges between the examples of fire and snow and the example of three:

Socrates: Would they, Cebes be these: things that are
              compelled by whatever occupies them to have

	not only its own Idea (*idean*), but always that
	of some opposite as well?
Cebes:	What do you mean?
Socrates:	As we were saying just now. You recognize, no
	doubt, that whatever the idea (*idea*) of three
	occupies must be not only three but also odd?
Cebes:	Certainly.
Socrates:	Then, we're saying, the Idea (*idea*) opposite
	to the character (*morphēi*) that has that effect
	could never go to a thing of that kind.
	(104d1–10)

Cebes' uncertainty ("What do you mean?") is understandable. The model of causation just presented differs from the model that involves fire and snow. In the latter, it is the intermediate entity—fire or snow—that is always characterized by the opposite and makes a thing hot or cold. Here it is that which is occupied by the intermediate entity that is said always to be three and odd.[14] Which model best describes the causal activity of soul? Is its causal activity best cast in terms that reflect the activity of an efficient cause so that it makes bodies be alive? Or is it an Idea that operates as a formal cause in which things participate in the Idea of soul and life?

Dorter poses the alternative succinctly:

Are we to conceive it (the entity in question) as an immanent form, a 'form in us' and 'the things it occupies' as the individuals characterized by that form . . . ? Or is it a concrete entity and 'the things it occupies' other individuals with which it comes in contact and which it affects . . . ?[15]

Dorter chooses the latter response and rejects the model represented by the number three. Indeed, we have seen the reasons why we should not consider the soul as an Idea. Nor in what follows does Socrates ever refer to the soul as an Idea. But we should be hesitant to simply reject the model represented by the example of the number three. Perhaps it is the case that, as regards its relationship to life, soul is more akin to the former examples than to the latter. But even if one set of examples fits the life-giving function of soul better than the other, there remains the important question of why Socrates sets this maze before his interlocutors. That is: Why does he persist in presenting the heterogeneous meanings of causation?[16] This question becomes more acute as Socrates resolves to try once more to define the intermediate entity. He takes a long run up to his definition:

> So what I was saying we were to define, the kind of things which, while not opposite to a given thing nevertheless don't admit it, the opposite in question—as we've just seen that three-ness while not opposite to the even nevertheless doesn't admit it since it always brings up the opposite of the cold, and so on in a great many cases—well, see whether you would define them thus: it is not only the opposite that does not admit its opposite, there is also that which brings up an opposite into whatever it enters itself and that thing, the very thing that brings it up, never admits the quality opposed to the one that's brought up. (104e7–105a5)

In this passage, Socrates reverts to the model of fire and snow in which the intermediate entity is always characterized by the opposite intelligible. Socrates instructs those present to recall the definition once more because "there's no harm in hearing it several times" (105a5–b3).[17] In the course of setting aside the doctrine of the separate Ideas, Socrates suggests that learning is by repetition and not by recollection of a prenatal vision.

Cebes dutifully responds in the spirit of the passage, saying first that he agrees and subsequently that he follows the argument (105b4). But what would Cebes think if he were later to recall this argument and reflect upon it? He would certainly recall the difficulties of the argument, the tortuous path that it traverses. More important, he might also see that these difficulties do not simply present an opportunity for idle puzzlement. The labyrinthine character of the final proof reflects difficulties or perplexities that inhere in nature itself. Cebes could hardly reflect on causality of any type without recalling the perplexities that he heard in Socrates' last argument. In particular, as becomes clearer in the final step of the proof of immortality, these are the perplexities which engendered in Socrates the doubt, and the wonder, that led him to further investigations. In leading Cebes to these perplexities, the labyrinth of this final proof of immortality might be the source not merely of 'no harm' but rather of a very great good.

On the basis of the foregoing 'definition' of the intermediate entities, Socrates now announces that he sees "a different kind of safeness beyond the answer I gave initially, the old, safe one" (105b6–8). But the old, safe, and also "simple-minded" answers are those derived from the doctrine of Ideas. *Simple-minded* was the word that Socrates used to refer to the mode of explanation expressed in the statement: Something is beautiful for no other reason than that it participates in the beautiful itself (100d4). Yet, Socrates says:

> If you were to ask me what it is, by whose presence in a body, that body will be hot, I won't give you the old, safe, ignorant answer, that it's hotness, but a more sophisticated answer now available, that it's fire. And again, if you ask what it is, by whose presence in a body, that body will ail, I shan't say that it's illness, but fever. And again, if asked what it is by whose presence in a number, that number will be odd, I shan't say oddness but oneness; and so on. (105b8–c2)

Thus, notwithstanding his earlier rejection of "sophistications," Socrates calls his new answers, "more sophisticated" (*kompsoteran*). And with these new answers, it becomes even more clear that Socrates has distanced himself from the orthodox view of the separate Ideas.

These more sophisticated causes again replicate the ambiguity in the argument leading up to them: will the soul be like fire or like fever? Fire conveys heat to bodies and is itself hot. Fever conveys illness but is not itself ill. Will soul itself be thought to be alive? Or will it simply be the vehicle of life and not itself alive? As for the example of oneness, it expresses in itself this ambiguity because it is not clear whether oneness is itself odd or not.[18]

Socrates now applies his new understanding to the case of life and soul. He first elicits from Cebes the notion of soul as efficient cause: "Answer, then, and tell me what it is by whose presence in a body that body will be living" (105c9–10). Cebes obligingly answers: "Soul" (105c11). Soul makes bodies be alive. But a few lines later Socrates implies a different conception of the causality of the soul. He asks: "Now the soul will absolutely never admit the opposite of what it brings up as has been agreed earlier?" (105d10–11). Implicit in this question is the conception of soul as itself alive, as the bearer of the Idea of life. With respect to the status of soul as an intermediate entity, Socrates does not resolve the question of which of the two models best explains the activity of the soul in relation to Life itself.

Related to Socrates' reticence concerning this issue is the question he poses precisely between his alternative presentations of soul. Socrates asks: "Is there an opposite to life, or is there none?" (105d6). What the others long ago accepted remains for Socrates a question. He will not commit himself to the notion that life and death are opposites. If we recall what is involved in the alternative between explanation by opposites as opposed to non-opposites, we can see the bearing of the issue of opposites on the question of the reconcilability of the senses of being.

When the question of opposites arose in the first proof, Socrates suggested that explanation by opposites is not comprehensive. Specifically, such explanation seems inadequate to an understanding of essential change, the coming into being and passing away of a being as such. Thus, the possession of one or the other of two accidental qualities by a subject is capable of being understood as the translation of opposites because the qualities can be thought to exist on the same ontic level and, therefore, as opposing one another. Change of an essential or a substantial kind, however, resists explanation by opposites because it involves alterations which are not on the same ontic level; the elements involved in such change seem not to oppose one another but to be *different* from one another.

In the first proof, the disanalogy between sleeping-waking and dying-living illustrates the difference to which I am referring. The latter pair, unlike the former, cannot be treated as the qualities of an existing subject for that is precisely what is in question. To account for the existence of a being as such, for example a living being, one must account not only for an entity's being in the way that it is, but also for its being at all. In other words, one must account not only for *what* it is but *that* it is. And these are *different* senses of being rather than opposites. In doubting that life and death are opposites then, Socrates suggests that life must be explained by heterogeneous senses of being, traceable to heterogeneous causes the reconcilability of which remains in question.[19]

The asymmetry of life and death is evident in death's lack of a surrogate analogous to soul. Soul is said to bring life but no mention is made of the bearer of death.[20] Introducing the new causal entities, one of which is soul, Socrates had said that their existence obtained "in *some* cases of this kind" (103e2, emphasis added). But death is not one of these cases, for it attacks alone. The asymmetry between life and death becomes most apparent, however, in the structure of the final argument itself. As will soon become evident, this structure shows that the simple negative of death does not capture all that is meant by life.

Socrates goes out of his way in the present context to define things by the privation of their opposites. So, for example, the opposite of just is unjust, and the opposite of musical is unmusical (105d16–e1). But these examples should alert us to the questionableness of this procedure. These pairs of opposites, which Socrates has not mentioned in a very long time, belong to that type of opposite which are precisely *not* necessarily defined by the privation of their opposites. Adding to the questionable character of Socrates' discussion is his coinage of new words for the purpose of maintaining his point regarding the privation of opposites. Most important, of course, is the bearing of this dubious procedure on the crucial opposites—life and death. If life and death were simple opposites, this procedure—defining things by the privation of their opposites—would be adequate. But having defined soul as that which is not-dead, Socrates must nevertheless go on to prove that soul is also imperishable. The implication is that soul could be the kind of thing that, *whensoever it is*, it is not-dead. But clearly this does not prove that it never perishes, that it always is.[21] Soul may not admit death—that is, soul may be deathless or immortal. But deathless soul can perhaps be destroyed. In short, the heterogeneous meaning of a living thing is demonstrated by the need for a proof of imperishability in addition to the proof of immortality.[22]

Socrates begins the proof of the soul's imperishability by canvassing the other causal entities as regards their imperishability. He speaks first of the number three, asking, "If it were necessary for the uneven to be imperishable, three would be imperishable, wouldn't it ?" (105e10–106a1). Concerning snow and fire, he then asks:

> Or again, if the un-hot were necessarily imperishable likewise, then whenever anyone brought hot against snow, the snow would get out of the way, remaining intact and unmelted? Because it couldn't perish, nor again could it abide and admit the hotness. And in the same way, I imagine, if the un-coolable were imperishable, then whenever something cold attacked the fire, it could never be put out nor could it perish, but it would depart and go away intact. (106a3–10)

It is easier to conceive of threeness as imperishable than it is of snow or fire. The idea of threeness survives the demise of any group of three things. But we have experience of snow melting and fires being doused. We know that, in the presence of heat, snow does not "get out of the way, remaining intact and unmelted," and we know that fire can be extinguished. Having adduced these dubious examples, Socrates finally reaches the soul. He states: "*If* the deathless is also imperishable, it's impossible for soul whenever death attacks it, to perish" (106b1–3, emphasis added). Of course, whether the deathless is also imperishable is precisely what is in question. At this point, Socrates himself raises a possible objection to what has been said:

"But," someone might say, "what's to prevent the odd, instead of coming to be even, as we granted it didn't, when the even attacks, from perishing, and there coming to be even in its place?" (106b7–c1)

In response, Socrates makes clear that only if the question of imperishability is granted can he maintain the imperishability of the odd, three, or anything else:

If it's granted us that soul must also be imperishable, then soul, besides being deathless, would also be imperishable; but if not, another argument would be needed. (106c9–d1, emphasis added)

Cebes is willing to grant this, seeing no need for any further argument because "it could hardly be that anything else would not admit destruction if the immortal, being everlasting, is going to admit destruction" (106d2–4).

In order to challenge Socrates, Cebes would have to entertain the possibility, as Socrates has done, that the whole may perish.[23] This Cebes is not now willing to do. In response to Cebes, Socrates offers God and the eidos of Life as entities which "would be agreed by everyone" to be immortals that never perish (106d5–7). This response brings Socrates to ask: "Then given that the immortal is also indestructible, wouldn't soul, if it proves to be immortal, be imperishable as well?" (106e1–3). On the basis of such a question, laden as it is with hypotheticals, we must conclude that, far from being "beyond all doubt," the proof of imperishability is more properly characterized as an assertion or a hope.

In this final proof of immortality, Socrates undertakes to provide the cause of all coming into being, passing away, and existence that he had said is required to meet Cebes' objection. He began from the premise that the Ideas exist and are causal. Yet in the course of the proof Socrates introduces new causal entities in order to remedy the inadequacies of the doctrine of the Ideas. And even on the basis of these new causal entities, Socrates is unable to provide that single account of why anything comes into being, passes away, and exists. As implied by Socrates' refusal to characterize life and death as opposites, the being of beings and of the whole remains heterogeneous, there being no single cause of the whole immediately available. In other words, the kinds of cause represented, on the one hand by God and on the other by the eidos of Life, remain unreconciled; there is not available to Socrates a cause that not only orders but also effects. This being the case, although we might know what something is, we cannot know for certain the fate of any particular example of that thing. Such particulars or individuals—including the individual soul—remain subject to chance. Socrates ends the last argument as he did the first proof of immortality, with an emphatic statement of the desired conclusion: "Beyond all doubt then, Cebes, soul is immortal and imperishable and our souls really will exist in Hades" (106e9–107a1; compare with 72d6–e2). This similarity draws our attention to the fact that, with respect to the question of the cause of the whole of nature, we stand at the end of the final proof precisely where we stood at the end of the first proof. This cause, the principle by which the whole is a whole, remains a hypothetical. If we regard Socratic thought as an advance, it is not because Socrates provided what his predecessors did not—a comprehensive account of the whole of nature.[24]

The doctrine of Ideas has foundered on the difficulty of explaining the connection between the intelligible and the perceivable. Socrates admitted earlier that he is not sure of the mechanism by which the particulars might participate in the Idea. And in this final proof, the failure to define clearly some intermediate entity between the intelligible itself and the particular leaves the connection between the two in the dark. Nor does the attribution of desire or military maneuvering to either the particulars or the intelligibles provide a plausible solution. But these personifications of the beings do serve to point us to that consideration raised by Socrates' first example in the final proof of immortality, the consideration of the role of the human mind in making this connection. It points us back to a consideration of the soul as capable not only of giving life but also of being musical and just, that is, the soul as capable of intelligence.[25] (105d16) It is to this consideration that Socrates points his young interlocutors at the conclusion of this his last argument.

At the argument's conclusion both Cebes and Simmias express their approval of what they have heard. Cebes states:

> Well, Socrates, for my part I've no further objection, nor can I doubt the arguments at any point. But if Simmias here or anyone else has anything to say, he'd better not keep silent; as I know of no future occasion to which anyone wanting to speak or hear about such things could put it off. (107a2–77)

These are the last words we hear from Cebes. He has heard the argument for immortality that is based on the premise of the ever-existing intelligibles. And, although he approves of it, the argument seems not to meet his

personal concern. He remains very much in doubt that the present conversation will be possible in this world after Socrates is gone or, after
death, in the next world; he doubts that there is personal immortality.[26]
Cebes, then, does not seem to know what he is saying; he cannot doubt
the arguments for immortality and imperishability, but he does not think
there is personal immortality. The last words we hear from Cebes express
that tension, evident in the opening scene of the dialogue, between the
arguments and the human concerns of Phaedo and Echecrates. Perhaps
this should not be surprising. It is characteristic of the sectarian to hold
his views for reasons that are not intrinsically related to the truth of these
views. Cebes will not begin to actualize whatever potential he has as a philosopher unless and until he begins to reflect on the relationship between
the arguments and his own life.

Simmias chimes in with his customary doubts, born of his view that
it is difficult for humans to get a handle on such a vast subject. He states:

> "nor have I any further ground for doubt myself, as far as the
> arguments go; though in view of the size of the subject under
> discussion, and having a low regard for human weakness, I'm
> bound to retain some doubt in my mind about what's been
> said." (107a8–b3)

Simmias is aware of the distance between the arguments and his own
deepest views in a way that Cebes is not. But precisely because of this
awareness, Simmias' response raises a serious question about his philosophic potential because this awareness does not trouble him. He is un-
concerned about the lack of rational support for his deepest views.
Simmias' response raises doubt that the philosophic motive, the desire to
know, is present within him. He remains mired in his self-concern.

Socrates responds to these comments in a most striking way. He
states:

> the initial hypotheses, even if they're acceptable to you people
> should still be examined more clearly: if you go through them
> adequately, you will I believe follow the argument to the fur-
> thest point to which man can follow it up; and if you get that
> clear, you will seek nothing further. (107b5–9)

What Socrates finally has to offer to his interlocutors is not an account of
nature as a whole, such as is expressed in the initial hypotheses that the
Ideas exist and are the cause of all things being what they are. Rather, it

is the approach to nature articulated in his intellectual autobiography. Socrates finally recommends the need for continued investigation, the need for continued ascent. And he indicates here what we have seen in the context of his 'second sailing,' that such an investigation leaves in question the ultimate causes of the whole of nature and must therefore proceed in full awareness of the possible limits that human nature places on what we can know. Accordingly, Socrates says that they are to follow the recommended course "to the furthest point to which man can follow it up." This searching skepticism is the potential remedy for philosophic sectarianism, whether born of the dilettantism of Simmias or the self-forgetting abstractness of Cebes.

The labyrinthine argument that begins from Socrates' most famous doctrine culminates in his casting that doctrine in a skeptical light. Socrates' last argument is meant finally as an antidote to Socratism.[27]

The True Earth

Socrates appropriately presents his last reflections on the cosmic situation of the soul in a myth. Myth provids a means by which this vast subject can be presented in the time remaining to Socrates. But the mythic form has a deeper connection to the teaching presented thus far. As Charles Griswold points out, the mythic form "allows the reader to identify with the events narrated in the story in a way that is difficult to do with the logical syntax of an argument."[28] This identification is important as it induces the reader to remain aware of his own circumstances even while considering the vast issue of the soul and the cosmos.

Like the great myths that conclude the *Gorgias* and the *Republic,* the final myth of the *Phaedo* traces the posthumous career of the soul. It differs from these others, however, in dwelling on what Socrates calls "the true earth" (110a1). Socrates expends much of his last imaginative power elaborating an account of the composition and mechanism of the true earth, an account that proves to be a somewhat enhanced view of the earth as we know it. He speaks at great and seemingly inordinate length of the places in and on the earth, providing an intricate rheography of the various substances that flow through these places. Socrates does speak of the reward and punishment of souls, but this reward and punishment takes place in an unusual setting. The character of Socrates' final myth is such that some commentators ask what in the myth is 'scientific,' presenting a view of the physical makeup of the earth, and what in it is mythic, pertaining to the ultimate fate of souls.[29] The distinction cannot ultimately be maintained, but the odd character of Socrates' final myth does suggest such a distinction. A usual task of such myths is to indicate the trans-human support for a certain way of life. The final myth of the *Phaedo* fulfills this task, but it does so in a most unusual manner.

In the preface to the myth, Socrates begins with what is 'just' to keep in mind (107c1). Socrates states that "if a soul is immortal, then it needs care" that it might "become as good and wise as possible" (107c2, d1–2). This view of soul as improvable, and thus alterable, is necessary if humans are to believe that their actions in this life determine their existence in the next. They must believe that "the soul enters Hades taking nothing else but its education and nurture" (107d2–4). Socrates relates the problem for morality if this were not the case:

> If death were a separation from everything it would be a godsend for the evil when they died to be separated at once from the body and from their own evil along with the soul. (107c5–8)

Of course, beginning with Socrates' defense, it was maintained that the separable soul was required for the attainment of perfect wisdom. In that context, I raised the question as to how anything we did as embodied humans, as unities of body and soul, could have anything to do with the perfectly separable soul. Socrates raises this question at the outset of the final myth and, in so doing, presents in brief compass the tension between the requirements of morality and intelligibility. The existence of the tension between these goods points to the conclusion that nature's support of human good is equivocal. At the outset of the myth, then, Socrates reminds us of reasons to think that nature as a whole is not simply constructed as a comfortable home for humanity. This is a fitting preface to Socrates' last myth.

Launching into the myth itself, Socrates' account of the disposition of souls after death begins:

> Now it is said that when each man has died, the daimon allotted to each while he was living proceeds to bring him to a certain place, where those gathered must submit to judgement and then journey to Hades with the guide appointed to conduct those in this world to the next and when they have experienced there the things they must and stayed there for the time required another guide conveys them back here during many long cycles of time. (107d5–e4)

Socrates does not specify either what is experienced in these places nor—as he does in both the *Republic* and the *Phaedrus*—does he specify the time required for the experiences.[30] As for the rewards and punishments meted out to the various souls, Socrates gives a somewhat cursory portrayal. He does say of the wise and well-ordered soul that it follows along and is "not ignorant of its surroundings," whereas the soul desirous of the body offers "much resistance and suffers greatly" (108a6–7, 108b1–2). Remarkably, however, both end up in the same place. And at this place the punishment, should any be required, issues not from gods but from other souls. The punishment consists of being ostracized for "certain periods of time" (108c1–2). Socrates makes little claim to being divinely informed regarding the next world. His knowledge is explicitly an inference from what is observable on earth. Speaking of why he thinks the road to Hades has many forkings and branchings, Socrates says: "I speak from the evidence of the rites and observances followed here" (108a5–6).[31] Socrates' inferences do not stray far from the evidence. In fact, they are nearly indistinguishable from descriptions of terrestrial life.

These details alone, although rather peculiar from the standpoint of mythic accounts, do not by themselves substantiate the strange character of Socrates' myth, but they prepare us for the remarkable turn the myth now takes. Socrates speaks of the places to which various souls are taken, and we are told that these places are places in the earth. Socrates asserts: "There are many wondrous regions in the earth, and the earth itself is of neither the nature nor the size supposed by those who usually describe it" (108c5–8).[32]

Here begins the account of what Socrates calls the *idea* of the earth and its places (108d9). At the end of his life, Socrates dwells on this earth rather than on the glories which await him in the next life. This account is nearly three times as long as the combined length of the accounts of the disposition of souls that surround it. Opposing what is said by those who usually describe the earth, he relates instead that of which "someone has convinced me" (108c7–8). Moreover, he wishes to speak of the idea of the earth even though he is operating under a severe time constraint, a constraint to which he calls attention in this context (108d8–9). This account of the true earth is not forced upon Socrates but rather follows from his own choice.

This last Socratic discussion of what he refers to as an *idea* differs markedly from the incorporeal, unchanging Ideas of Socratic orthodoxy. Socrates does not speak here of what they have always talked about. If we were to define the meaning of an idea on the basis of Socrates' last usage of the term, we would conclude that an idea conveys the nature of something, its form, its matter, and its particular activity.[33]

In discussing this idea, the thing of which Socrates must speak 'first' is the equilibrium of the earth (108e4, 109a6). Not only does Socrates concentrate on this earth, but his discussion of the earth does not focus on the earthly delights for humanity. The places of the earth do not seem wondrous, at least primarily, because of what happens to souls there. Rather, what is primary is the physical composition of the earth. Socrates claims that the earth itself is a system in equilibrium and is placed in a uniform medium. Because a thing in equilibrium will be stable when placed in something uniform, the earth remains at rest and does not incline or fall. Socrates reiterates that this is the first thing about which he must speak (109a6).

Socrates' second point initiates his exaltation of earth. He explains that the earth is far more vast than we realize, and its vastness involves a diminishment in the importance of our existence. In addition to us humans, there are many 'others' living around the multiplicity of hollows in the earth like "ants or frogs around a marsh" (109b2–4). Not only are there more places in the earth akin to our own, there exists a whole region superior to ours in purity and beauty. Our environment is but the dregs of this much-purer medium, aether, which exists above us. Purity as well as beauty are now qualities of body. They do not involve a total abstraction from body.

Socrates describes this more beautiful region by drawing an analogy between its relationship to our region and our relationship to the bottom of the ocean. Just as those existing on the bottom of the ocean mistakenly believe the ocean above them to be the peak of rarefaction, so do we mistakenly take the air as the most rarefied medium (109c3–7). But just as fish, could they stick their heads above the surface of the water, would be astounded at the purity of our region in comparison to theirs, so if a human being could "sprout wings" and "stick his head up into this region" he would be astounded (109e2–5). If his "nature could bear the vision," he would see the "true heaven, the genuine light, and the true earth" (109e6–110a1). In the present myth, unlike in the myth of the *Phaedrus,* it is not the soul which may briefly stick its head over the vault of heaven for a glimpse of the beautiful.[34] Rather, it is an improved human, a superhuman who, possessing the right nature, might stick his head up and view the beautiful things on earth.

Socrates now states that if it is "beautiful to tell a myth," he will describe these things upon earth and beneath heaven (110b1).[35] Throughout the subsequent passage, Socrates uses *idea* and *eidos* in their original significations—that is, in relation to sight. The passage is replete with references to seeing, color, and visible beauty. Socrates describes the multicolor surface of the earth composed of colors "far brighter and purer . . . more numerous and beautiful than any we have seen" (110c1–6). Both the things that grow on the surface and the stones composing the mountains are more pure and beautiful by "the same proportion" as the purity and beauty of the surface of the earth exceeds the purity and beauty of our hollow (110d6).

Socrates also speaks of those who dwell in these lofty, aether-filled regions. He calls them human beings (111a4). But they are humans who are free from sickness and live a far longer time than people here. Socrates attributes this not to their moral rectitude but to their "climate" (111b1–2). Moreover, they surpass us in "sight, hearing, wisdom and all such faculties by the extent to which air surpasses water for its purity, and aether surpasses air" (111b3–6). These improved humans attain that which eludes us normal humans. For them, wisdom and perception are apparently identical. Their understanding is not characterized by the distinction between that which is most knowable for them and that which is most knowable in itself. As Socrates has made clear, we—unlike the aether-dwellers—do not accurately know what supervenes over us: In our perception of our situation, we are as mistaken as those who dwell on the ocean bottom and think that the sea is heaven (109c5). But the situation is different for the aether-dwellers: "The sun and moon and stars are seen by them as they really are, and their happiness in all else follows this" (111c1–3). They need not look at the image of the sun, but rather they see the sun as it is. With this acute sight, these superhumans view the beauty around them, and Socrates says: "Happy, therefore, are they who behold the sight of it"(111a2–3). The world around these beings is made for their happiness. The very atmosphere, the corporeal medium in which they live, supports their happiness (111b1–2). They have but to open their eyes to achieve wisdom.

Having described what is above and on the earth, Socrates now turns to what is below the earth. It is here that Socrates' myth makes the clearest connection between human existence and the nonhuman world. The connection differs significantly from that which characterizes the existence of the aether-dwellers. In this presentation of what is literally the underworld, Socrates never mentions the name *Hades*. Rather, we learn in great detail of the series of passages connecting the various hollows below the ground. Through these passages flow hot and cold water—and mud, lava, and fire. Using the Heracleitean phrase, Socrates says that this flux keeps going "up and down" without end (112b3).[36] It is in this context that Socrates indicates that the kinship of the human and the nonhuman exists most clearly on the plane of body.[37] What keeps everything circulating through the vessels is a "pulsation" within the earth, the result of which Socrates calls "breathing" (111e5, 112b6). And "just as in breathing the current of breath is continuously exhaled and inhaled" (112b6–7). The connection between the human and the nonhuman is made most clearly in the physical processes of our existence.

The moral character of the nonhuman world is more dubious. Socrates maintains that the flowing matter never ceases because it has no "true basis"—that is, no true foundation. Accordingly, Socrates speaks of the "*so-called* downward region" (112c1–2, emphasis added). It appears that even 'up' and 'down' are distinctions appended by humans to the nonhuman.[38] The status of moral distinctions in this world is suggested by Socrates' treatment of divine punishment in the context. In this regard, Socrates quotes a line from Homer concerning what "the poets have called Tartarus" (112a4–5). This is the hole which, according to Socrates, perforates the earth. In Homer's full statement, he refers to Zeus hurling other recalcitrant gods into this pit as punishment for misdeeds.[39] But Socrates makes no mention of Zeus or the connection between Tartarus and divine punishment. Instead, he simply describes rivers of mud and lava. He even cites an actual example of such a river of mud in Sicily (111e1–2). Socrates views the world through the lens of the disinterested investigator rather than through a moralizing lens. This becomes more evident as it emerges that life itself, much less moral life, exists on a tenuous foundation.

Concluding his account of the regions beneath the earth, Socrates pays particular attention to four underground rivers, three of which play a role in the forthcoming description of the soul's travels. Keeping with the character of the myth, the first-mentioned and largest river, Oceanus, plays no part in the transportation of souls. As for the other rivers, Socrates tells of the lands through which they pass, because "each acquires its character from the nature of the earth through which it flows" (112a6–7). Moreover, given the kinship between the human and the earth, it is possible that Socrates means to draw a closer connection between the types of souls and the several rivers than is immediately apparent. Accordingly, Dorter has conjectured that Socrates means to apply what he says concerning a river to the type of souls associated with that river. In other words, Socrates may be presenting here a deterministic account of character.[40] At any rate, Socrates' further description of souls is in keeping with the de-moralized presentation of human existence.

Socrates adds two new classes to the three classes of souls mentioned in the *Gorgias* and *Republic*. There exist not only the incurably evil, the curably evil, and the pious, but also the mediocre and a subgroup of the pious, those who have practiced philosophy. Speaking first of those who have lived mediocre lives, Socrates says that this class consists of those who are neither exceptionally evil nor exceptionally pious (113d4). This class would seem to include the majority of humans, for Socrates has told us in the misology section that "extremely good and bad people are both very few in number and the majority lie in between" (89e7–90a2). Those in this group travel on the Acheron river as it winds through "bereft" regions before emptying into the Acherusian Lake (112e8). There they

> pay the penalty for their wrongdoing and are absolved, if any committed any wrong, and they secure reward for their good deeds each according to his desert. (113d7–e1)

This terse description is Socrates' entire description of the fate of most human beings. It seems that the lives of most humans have no great moral import, whether for good or ill.

Socrates turns next to the incurables, those who have committed "many grave acts of sacrilege or many unjust and illegal killings" or, Socrates adds rather offhandedly, "any other deeds that may be of that sort" (113e1–3, e4). Here Tartarus does come into play. But it is not Zeus who hurls these souls downward. Rather it is the "appropriate destiny" that flings them into Tartarus whence they nevermore emerge" (113e5–6). This is certainly a severe fate, but it is leniency itself compared to the sufferings of the incurables in the Myth of Er.[41] Perhaps this difference stems from the fact that, whereas in the present myth Socrates claims that "a daimon is allotted to each man," in the *Republic*'s Myth of Er he insists that each soul chooses its daimon (107d6–7).[42] The present myth expresses a diminished sense of moral responsibility.

As for the curables, they are divided with respect to their offense between those who have committed murder and those who have assaulted their parents. Both types "fall" into Tartarus and are released after only a year, a blink of the eye in mythic time (114a3). The homicides come out of Tartarus by way of the river Cocytus, a river "terrible and wild," and the parent-beaters come out by way of Pyriphlegethon, a river that intermittently erupts with lava (113b6–7, b5–6). In both cases, the ultimate release of the curables depends not on some divine decree but on their persuading the victims of their crime to allow them to come into the Acherusian Lake (114b2). The administration of justice is a matter which rests largely in the hands of other humans rather than with divinities.

Socrates speaks last of the exceptionally pious. Their reward is to be released from the nether regions of the earth to a place, not in heaven, but rather "to make their dwelling above ground" (114c1–2). These seem to be those who, in Socrates previous mythic presentation, "have practiced demotic and political virtue . . . devoid of philosophy and intelligence" (82a11–b3). Still higher than those who are exceptionally pious without philosophy are those who have practiced philosophy. The latter also attain to dwelling-places above ground, but their dwelling-places are "even more beautiful" than those attained by the pious without philosophy (114c4–5). Remarkably, however, Socrates claims that there is not sufficient time to tell of these more beautiful places. But Socrates' reticence on this subject of the rewards awaiting the philosopher is clearly less a matter of external constraint than of his own volition, because he has yet to spend "a long time" with his family (116b6). And to reiterate, Socrates does find time to detail the mechanism of the earth. He concludes the myth by saying: "It would not be fitting for a man of *nous* to maintain (*diïskhurisasthai*) that things are as I have related them" (114d1–2). He then says that he has offered this myth as an incantation: "so one should repeat such things to oneself like a spell; which is just why I've prolonged the tale" (114d6–7).

But what view of human existence, what view of the place of humanity in the whole of nature, would imbue the one repeating this incantation to himself? The one who would adopt the view of the myth would see that the most evident link between the human and the nonhuman is made on the basis of the body. Such a link provides little substantiation for the notion that the cosmos provides support for the human good understood in moral terms. The other details of the myth point in the same direction. There is a paucity of detail concerning the fate of souls; these fates are portrayed as the result of a judgment by other souls rather than as a judgment passed by willful gods. The de-emphasis of the moral view is also seen vividly in the crucial case of the philosopher. Here, unlike in the rest of the *Phaedo,* Socrates all but passes over the issue of the posthumous rewards awaiting the philosopher. He deems it more urgent to know of the mechanism of the earth than of the places to which the philosopher will journey after death.

One who repeated this myth as an incantation would be less assured of the cosmic significance of our every deed. This consideration is especially important as it bears on the potential philosopher. We have seen that precisely this belief—what I have called the providential view of our existence—is *a,* if not *the,* chief obstacle to philosophy. It leads us to supplant the world as it is with the world as we wish it to be. It encourages exaggerated hope as well as its twin, despair. It is the core of the tragic view of human existence, the view that emerges when the world inevitably fails to support our inflated hopes. Socrates' omission of the discussion of the philosopher's ultimate rewards aims to diminish the possibility that the potential philosophers will conceive of the whole in terms of reward and punishment, as organized with a view to their good. The potential philosophers would then be less susceptible to the distortions that accompany this view.

The potential philosopher would see that the place humanity occupies in the whole is a tenuous one. More specifically, with respect to the activity of understanding, the potential philosopher would see that it is only for the superhuman that wisdom is equivalent to perception; for beings such as we are, understanding comes through trial and error, through the inference from experience used by Socrates in his development of the myth (108a5–6). But the recognition of this truth would be a cause for despair only if one cared more for goods other than the good of knowing how things truly are. Having overcome the source of inflated hopes and fears, the potential philosopher could then appreciate the character of the connection between the human and the nonhuman that *does* exist on the plane of understanding. That connection has been made evident in Socrates' intellectual autobiography, in Socrates' realization of the inadequacy of his previous views that permitted him to progress toward a truer view. It is in recognition of just this possibility that Socrates mentions for the first time in the dialogue *the pleasures of learning* (114e3–4).[43]

For the philosopher, this life is not a tragedy. This is not because the philosopher is assured of his goal, understood as the attainment of pure wisdom. Orientation on this goal derives from a particular conception of the way the world 'must' be and is itself therefore a source for tragedy. Indeed, the only remedy for the tragic view is the clear understanding of the way things are, however problematic that might be. In this understanding lies the possibility of a life without deception, whether that deception comes from others or from oneself. Such a life, lived on the basis of the way things are, would truly be characterized by freedom (*eleutheria*) (115a1). This freedom would consist not in release from the prison of the body but from the prison that we help to construct by indulging the hopes that distort our view. Socrates' final myth can lend support to the one seeking to live without deception and therefore freely rather than tragically. Socrates suggests finally, then, that this life need not be understood as a stoic acceptance of bitter truths. Rather, our nature is such as to derive pleasure from the ascent toward more complete understanding. The fulfillment of this non-tragic, free, and pleasurable existence is evident in Socrates' final words and deeds.

The Death of Socrates

Socrates begins this final portion of his death day expressing the conditions under which "any man should have confidence for his own soul . . . as he awaits the journey he will make to Hades, whenever destiny shall summon him" (114d8–115a3). He tells those in the cell:

> You will make your several journeys at some future time but for myself, 'e'en now' as a tragic hero might say, 'destiny doth summon me'; and it's just about time I made for the bath: it really seems better to take a bath before drinking the poison, and not to give the women the trouble of washing a dead body. (115a4–8)

While the tragic hero thinks of his destiny, Socrates heads for the bath. This concern for destiny belongs in the mouth of the tragic hero. To conceive of one's life in terms of a destiny or fate is to orient oneself on some purpose or goal that one has not chosen. The goal is conceived as the determination of some higher power: "Destiny doth summon me." The link between this view and the tragic view is forged by those experiences that belie the notion that an individual human life is supported by that which is trans-human, that there exists a plan and a goal for each and every individual. The view that such support does in fact exist belongs with—indeed, answers to—the despair that we experience when reflecting on the transiency of our lives. It provides the basis upon which we can deny that transiency and thus free ourselves of this despair. But should that basis be thrown into doubt, the despair returns and the danger arises that human life will be regarded as tragic. As I have stated, the tragic view and what I have called the providential view of nature as a whole are, in fact, twins.

Crito, Phaedo, and those gathered in the cell are, for obvious reasons, more aware than usual of the transiency, the fragility, of human existence. They hope that Socrates will have some special words of advice at this unique moment. In particular, Crito asks Socrates what they should do for him, for his children, or with respect to any other special concerns that Crito expects Socrates to have in his present circumstances (115b1–4) Again, however, Socrates tells them only "what I'm always telling you . . . and nothing very new" (115b5). We should note that, at the end, what Socrates is always telling them concerns the right way of life rather than the Ideas (100b1). He continues:

> If you take care for yourselves, your actions will be of service to me and mine, and to yourselves too whatever they may be,

even if you make no promises now; but if you take no care for yourselves and are unwilling to pursue your lives along the tracks, as it were, marked by our present and earlier discussions, then even if you make many firm promises at this time you'll do no good at all. (115b5–c1)

Socrates does not alter his advice in the face of death. He discourages the thought that the onset of death should be cause for novel activity. He especially discourages the making of solemn vows and heartfelt promises not made in the course of the rest of one's life.

These promises express precisely the providential view of the whole of nature. Such promises are made on the basis of the view that there exists some being greater than ourselves, who we hope, can guarantee the possession of a good we know to be fleeting. It is through making promises and positing duties for ourselves that we seek to convince ourselves that we can know or even control the will of this being. What underlies our vows and our promises then is the concern for our own good. Perhaps to emphasize this point, Crito, *the* embodiment of self-concern, now returns to prominence.[44] But statements by Phaedo, too, in the present context reveal the inseparability of his concern for Socrates from his concern for himself. When Socrates leaves for his final bath, Phaedo says that the others

> waited, talking among ourselves about what had been said and reviewing it, and then again dwelling on how great a misfortune had befallen us, literally thinking of it as if we were deprived of a father and would lead the rest of our life as orphans. (116a4–7)

After Socrates returns and drinks the poison, Phaedo reports: "I covered my face and wept for myself—not for him, no, but for my own misfortune in being deprived of such a man for a companion" (117c8–d1). The concern for our own good, coupled with a sense of the fragility of that good, engenders a dependence that leads those gathered in Socrates' cell to characterize themselves as children deprived of a father and to weep out of self-pity.

In order to overcome the tragic perspective, we would need to orient ourselves by that which we truly know of our good, rather than clinging to those individuals or those beliefs on which we depend to assuage our despair at its elusiveness. As is evident in Socrates' last moments, it is this clear knowledge of his good that guides him. When Socrates asks that the poison be brought to him at once, Crito protests. He reminds Socrates that there's plenty of time remaining before sundown, the point at which Socrates is obliged to drink the poison (116d7–e2). Crito adds:

> And besides, I know of others who've taken the draft long after the order had been given them, and after dining well and drinking plenty, and even in some cases enjoying themselves with those they fancied. (116e2–4)

Socrates replies to Crito in this manner:

> It's reasonable for those you speak of to do those things—because they think they gain by doing them; for myself it's reasonable not to do them; because I think I'll gain nothing by taking the draught a little later: I'll only earn my own ridicule by clinging to life, and being sparing when there's nothing more left. (116e7–117a2)

It was apparent at the conclusion of the misology section that the good consists in doing that which is reasonable for oneself. There is no reason that this notion of one's good or of one's self-interest need be confined to the goods of the body. It can be understood in a lofty manner as Socrates does in this passage. Indeed, as we have seen, if one wishes to *know* that which is truly good rather than to be satisfied with unfounded assurances, one will be led to follow the Socratic path. Socrates knows that his path leads him closer to knowing that which is truly good than does the way of the community. Therefore, to choose to act in accordance with the view of the community would make him ridiculous in his own eyes.[45]

In order to be guided by what we truly know of our good, we must, above all, become aware of the limits of our understanding. These limits are represented most prominently by our lack of certain knowledge of the afterlife. For this reason, Socrates characterized philosophy as a preparation for death. He did so not because the philosopher should expect to reap the reward of pure wisdom after death—this expectation is itself a prescription for tragedy, indistinguishable from any other ungrounded human hope—but because it is only through unblinking awareness of our situation that we can avoid the profound disappointment engendered by misconceiving our place in the whole.[46]

Socrates' human wisdom, however—his knowledge of the human situation—is also the source of great satisfaction. This point emerges from the contrast between the laughter of Socrates and the tears of his interlocutors. When Socrates downs the poison, those assembled in his cell collapse into tears (117c5–8). Even the jailer, as he addresses Socrates for the last time, praises Socrates for not cursing him as others had done. He declares that Socrates is the "most generous and gentlest and best of men who have ever come to this place" (116c4–6). Tearfully taking his leave, he advises Socrates to "bear the necessities as easily as you can" (116d1). But Socrates laughs (115c5, 84d8). His laughter arises from Crito's response to Socrates' recommendation that they care for their souls. Crito asks: "But in what fashion are we to bury you?" (115c2–3). Socrates says:

> Friends, I can't persuade Crito that I am Socrates here, the one who is now conversing and arranging each of the things being discussed; but he imagines I'm that dead body he'll see in a little while, so he goes and asks how he's to bury me! But as for the great case I've been arguing all this time . . . I think I'm putting to him in vain, while comforting you and myself alike. (115c5–d6)

Socrates recognizes that his speeches have failed to penetrate Crito's circle of concerns. They have run up against certain intransigencies in the human soul that are, for the most part, impervious to reason. But why should such intransigencies elicit laughter in Socrates? Socrates' calm lightheartedness does not, I think, derive from some willful outfacing of the fear of death, nor is it an expression of some recently drawn conclusion concerning the absurdity of human existence. Rather, it is "nothing very new," an expression of that true preparation for death—the insight into the complexity of the human soul and all its implications. Having reflected on the human situation throughout his life, Socrates became aware of the precariousness, brought to full consciousness for most only when confronted by death, which always characterizes our existence. This awareness enabled him see in this and other intransigencies confirmation of what he knew of himself and his place in the whole. They provided an occasion not for despair but for enjoyment, as this awareness allowed him to partake of the pleasure of learning, a pleasure that resulted from the satisfaction of the desire to know.

    Socrates is aware of the imposing demands made by this philosophic way of life. It requires that we relinquish our cherished hopes for eternal existence, perfect justice, and much that we long for as individuals. Accordingly, Socrates distinguished the few philosophers from the many others precisely on the basis of the philosopher's stance toward death. When Socrates first made this distinction, Simmias noted that the conduct that the philosopher expects from himself makes him ridiculous to the political community (64a10–b6). In the present context, Socrates makes clear that, again, behavior which is expected by the political community would make him ridiculous to himself.

Athens expects Socrates to follow a Crito-like timetable; when in response to Socrates' wishes, the order is given to bring the poison immediately, the boy fetching the executioner is away a long time (117a5). Athens' expectations accord well with the view of its founder, Theseus, who "fought as few men have with danger and with death."[47] According to this view, death is to be resisted in every case, as if we knew what we do not know—namely, what awaits us after death. The descendants of Theseus cannot abide Socrates' stance toward death; Socrates' fate is properly juxtaposed with Athens' celebration of its founder and what he stood for. Being aware of the source of an inexorable tension between the philosophic stance toward death and the stance of the community, Socrates was more aware than were his predecessors of the need to take steps to ameliorate this tension. These steps become all the more urgent when it is recognized that the core of philosophy involves addressing the questions—*What is good? What is just?*—that are of concern to every human.[48] Yet, aware as he was of the difficulties of the philosophic life, Socrates would not cease philosophizing as long as it remained something "not unpleasant."[49]

In accordance with his standard of behavior, Socrates distances himself from the demands of conventional piety. When he is given the cup of poison, he asks to pour a libation not to a god but to some other person. Only after being told that he must drink the whole thing does he settle for saying a prayer to a god (117b6–c2). The same freedom from conventional piety is evident in Socrates' dying words.[50] When Socrates had drunk the poison, and the resulting coldness was moving up from his feet, he walked around until his legs became numb, at which point he lay on the couch (117e4–5). After remaining in this position with his face covered, Socrates uncovers his face to utter his last words.[51] These words reflect what Socrates *saw* of the human situation: "Crito, we owe a cock to Asclepius: please pay the debt, and don't neglect it" (118a7–8). Socrates' characteristic activity left him no time to perform even the most perfunctory of religious obligations. Instead, Socrates characterizes himself in the *Apology* as "making speeches every day."[52] Socrates dies with his mouth and eyes wide open (118a13–14). At the end, Phaedo calls Socrates "a man, who, among those of his time we knew, was so we should say—the best, the wisest, too, and the most just" (118a15–17). Even for Socrates, these qualities are superlatives and not absolutes. Yet Socrates knew enough to know that this incompleteness pointed to the need for philosophy as an ongoing search, as a way of life.

Contrary to Nietzsche's claim, Socrates' last words do not express the view that life is a sickness of which we must be cured.[53] Socrates does not succumb to a tragic view of life. Indeed, Socrates' opposition to the tragic hero stands in stark contrast with Nietzsche's celebration of the tragic perspective. Nietzsche's life-long contest with Socrates begins with his unfavorable comparison of the optimistic and thus superficial Socratic view with the more profound tragic perspective.[54] This comparison reflects Nietzsche's judgment that profundity lies in facing without self-delusion the wisdom of Silenus that we are an " 'ephemeral race, children of chance and misery.' "[55] We must face, in other words, our need for something beyond our individual existence, something enduring that can give meaning and significance to this otherwise transient individual existence. From the Socratic perspective, however, when Nietzsche orients his thought on this need, he misses the true distinction between the philosopher and the non-philosopher because he adopts the providential view of the whole which is the basis of the tragic perspective. In this light, Nietzsche is not a descendant of the philosopher, Socrates, but of the founder, Theseus who teaches us to seek immortal glory in noble deeds done for the sake of the enduring community. Perhaps because he could only see in the notion of the human good something utilitarian in a low sense, Nietzsche's thought focuses on the need for that which is noble, the need for something beyond human good.[56] But the motivations of Cebes, Simmias, and Phaedo should make us wonder whether the concern for that which transcends the individual is separable from the individual's conception of his good. And the portrayal of the Platonic Socrates make us reconsider whether the human good is *necessarily* something low or something that necessarily leads to self-delusion. In that portrayal, we see a laughing philosopher, moved by his desire for wisdom, appreciative of the pleasure brought by progress in understanding, unconvinced that there exists the need to choose between life and wisdom.

Conclusion

From the start of the *Phaedo,* in the conversation between Phaedo and Echecrates, we see how questions concerning our mortality might act as a solvent of certain belief. The fact of death can make us feel the need to know more accurately just what our situation is and thus compel us to confront directly the question that is of the utmost human concern—how should we live our lives? The recognition of our incompleteness can act as a liberating force and a spur to self-understanding. In this way, philosophy is a practice intrinsically related to the fact of death.

But awareness of the limits of our understanding also raises a particular difficulty for the philosophic life. Unlike other ways of life, the philosophic life cannot itself rest on an arbitrary choice. To do so would be the height of self-forgetting for a way of life that claims to follow the guidance of reason in every respect. Yet this is precisely the charge that Nietzsche levels against philosophy: the philosophic life rests on an act of will and is therefore irrational at its foundation.[1] From the start of his career, Nietzsche's indictment of philosophy focuses on Socrates in an attempt to reveal the dogmatic foundations of all previous philosophy.

In this study of the *Phaedo,* I have attempted to show that, contrary to Nietzsche, Socratic rationalism does not rest on dogmatic foundations; that it is, rather, formulated in full awareness of the uncertainties of human existence; and that this awareness dictated the particular themes that characterized Socrates' career. Socrates' realization of the inadequacy of his predecessors' views and his own early views led him to see the need to defend philosophy as regards its rational ground, its inherent goodness, and its superiority to other ways of life.

In his 'second sailing,' Socrates finds the rational ground of philosophy in the knowledge gained through his inadequate views of nature.

This knowledge is the knowledge of ignorance, the human wisdom that describes the human situation in its articulation of the experience of perplexity. In directing us to begin our inquiry with an examination of speeches, the 'second sailing' precisely reflects this articulation. It reflects what Socrates has learned about himself in relation to the world. It reflects Socrates' self-understanding.

In locating the ground of philosophy in self-understanding, Socrates' 'second sailing' establishes the central importance of the philosophic study of human affairs or of political philosophy insofar as this study leads to human wisdom. Understood in this way, philosophy requires political philosophy for another purpose. Given the tentativeness of our understanding, the danger always exists that inquiry into the matters of concern will be guided by, and answer to, desires other than the desire to know. Only an acute awareness of human desire, an awareness provided by political philosophy, can ensure that inquiry will respond to the desire to know rather than the desires answered in and by political life.

It is true that philosophy required the study of political philosophy most urgently, however, in order to defend itself as a choiceworthy way of life. Socrates was compelled to investigate the related questions opened up by the awareness of the elusiveness of pure wisdom—the questions of the goodness of the philosophic life and its relation to other ways of life. As the dramatic context of the *Phaedo* makes clear, the need to investigate these questions put the philosopher in greater danger from the civic authorities. The theoretical focus on human affairs thus made more urgent the need to study politics with a view to formulating a rhetoric that could protect the philosopher from the inherent dangers of this investigation. It is critical, however, to see that the philosophic study of human affairs—political philosophy—begins not as a practical defense of philosophy but as a theoretical defense, a defense of its rational ground. And insofar as this theoretical defense rests on an interpretation of the human experience of perplexity, it cannot be simply dismissed for its reliance on an anachronistic cosmology. Socratic rationalism may yet hold promise as a response to the contemporary critics of rationalism.

To fulfill this promise, however, we must be willing to consider the classical view free of distorting prejudices. Perhaps the greatest obstacle impeding such a consideration is the persistence of that ancient malady called misology, the hatred of reason. Never is this threat more acute than when we reason about the ultimate disposition of our own lives—when we are, as Socrates says in reference to himself, discussing issues that really concern our lives rather than dealing with airy abstractions (70b10–c2). Yet, in light of the unavailability of pure wisdom, it is inevitable that the desire for certainty about our heartfelt concerns, including those with respect to the afterlife, will come into conflict with the desire to know. At that point, the temptation is great to hate reason when it cannot provide us what we desire. At that point, we are most sorely tempted to replace what we do know with how we wish things to be.

In the present circumstances, perhaps the most important function of political philosophy is to make us aware of those desires that incline us toward misology. Were we to be guided by political philosophy in this respect, we would be more aware of, and thus better able to avoid, the misguided hopes and unwarranted disappointments which, I think, lie at the root of the dogmatisms that impede the rehabilitation of Socratic rationalism. I refer to the twin dogmatisms of absolute certainty and absolute skepticism.

On the basis of my interpretation of the *Phaedo,* I conclude that Socrates shares with Nietzsche doubt concerning the availability of a mathematicized philosophy, a philosophy that is strictly deductive in nature, a philosophy that promises certainty in all respects. Socrates rejects his predecessors for purchasing certain and comprehensive doctrines at the cost of making inexplicable their own experience. Thus, the contemporary Socratic would reject understandings which in the name of certainty would make inexplicable the remarkable latitude we have in understanding our world, a latitude exemplified both by Socrates' varying view of nature and by the diversity of understandings represented in that philosophic convention gathered in Socrates' cell (59b5–c6). The contemporary Socratic would not insist on a mathematicized view of philosophy that distorts or neglects the human experience of the philosopher.

The contemporary Socratic would, however, also reject views that take the unwarranted leap from the existence of such latitude of understanding to the ultimate irreducibility of all understandings. Awareness of the various desires that can color our understanding prevents the contemporary Socratic from succumbing to any form of misology, including the "suicide of reason" of which Nietzsche speaks.[2] The contemporary Socratic would ask whether the suicide of reason is itself rational, whether it is based on a clear view of the way things are, or whether it is a result of the disappointments that inevitably follow the desire for an unachievable standard of intelligibility. Rather than adopting the posture of absolute skepticism, the contemporary Socratic would be aware of the intelligibility that must be presumed even in the most thorough-going critique of the possibility of pure wisdom.[3]

The status of rationalism, then, remains a question because the ground on which it was refuted—the dogmatism of Socratic rationalism—is itself questionable. The characterization of Socratic rationalism as dogmatically rational was itself dogmatically asserted. Socratic rationalism, based as it is on the human experience of perplexity, does not rest on those extravagant claims for the rationality of the whole that inevitably lead to the disappointment expressed in absolute skepticism. Furthermore, precisely because of its basis in this experience of perplexity, Socratic rationalism may provide a mode of rational inquiry that can credibly defend rationalism from the impulse toward absolute skepticism. In light of these conclusions, it is reasonable to suggest that the final verdict in the contemporary trial of Socrates has not yet been rendered. It is also reasonable to suggest that we have available no better way to continue this trial than through the Socratic mode of inquiry.

NOTES

Chapter 1. Introduction

1. Friedrich Nietzsche, *The Birth of Tragedy,* trans. Walter Kaufmann (New York: Vintage Press, 1967), p. 93 (sec. 15).

2. On the Platonic origin of the mistake called metaphysics, see Nietzsche, *Beyond Good and Evil,* trans. with commentary by Walter Kaufmann (New York: Vintage Press, 1966), p. 3 (preface); Martin Heidegger, "The End of Philosophy and the Task of Thinking," Joan Stambaugh, trans. In *Basic Writings,* edited by David Farrell Krell (New York: Harper and Row, 1977), p. 375. For a more recent expression of this view, see Richard Rorty, *Philosophy and the Mirror of Nature,* (Princeton: Princeton University Press, 1980), pp. 156–59; Nietzsche makes a distinction between Socrates and Plato, the complexities of which are explored in Werner J. Dannhauser, *Nietzsche's View of Socrates* (Ithaca: Cornell University Press, 1974), and in Catherine Zuckert, "Nietzsche's Rereading of Plato," *Political Theory* 13 (May 1985): 213–238. For my own purposes, I will regard Socrates as the character in the Platonic dialogues or, when so designated, as the character in the works of Aristophanes or Xenophon. This is not to say that I regard Socrates as simply a mouthpiece for Plato. He may well criticize or at least not fully accept the views of his Socrates.

3. Nietzsche, *Birth of Tragedy,* p. 95 (sec. 15). As the last four words of the quote suggest, although Nietzsche finds the origin of the erroneous character of Western metaphysics in Socrates, it is the modern consequence of this error—modern technology and the society based on it—to which Nietzsche objects.

4. Nietzsche, *Beyond Good and Evil,* p. 3 (preface); Heidegger, *Introduction to Metaphysics,* trans. Ralph Manheim (New Haven: Yale University Press, 1959), p. 184. Rorty, *Philosophy and the Mirror of Nature,* pp. 162–163.

5. Nietzsche, *Beyond Good and Evil,* pp. 10, 11–12, 21–22 (secs. 2, 4, 14); Heidegger, *Introduction to Metaphysics,* p. 106.

6. Nietzsche, *Twilight of the Idols,* trans. Walter Kaufmann, in *The Portable Nietzsche* (New York: Viking Press, 1968), pp. 479–480, 484 ("'Reason' in Philosophy," secs. 1, 6); and pp. 485–6 ("How the 'True World' Finally Became a Fable").

7. It should be noted that Nietzsche too sees a conflict between life and wisdom. Moreover, he seems to think that periodic reconciliations between the two are possible. But he does not conclude that this possibility provides a basis for the Socratic way of life. See "The Dancing Song" in *Thus Spake Zarathustra* in *The Portable Nietzsche,* trans. by Walter Kaufmann (New York: Penguin, 1982), pp. 219–222.

8. Nietzsche, *Twilight of the Idols,* p. 473 ("The Problem of Socrates," sec. 1); See also *The Gay Science,* trans. by Walter Kaufmann (New York: Vintage Books, 1974), p. 272 (sec. 340). The quote reflects the greater degree of self-awareness that Nietzsche, in his later writings, attributed to Socrates. But despite this self-awareness, Nietzsche always maintained the position that Socrates' hyper-rationalism results in a negative judgment on life.

9. Cicero, *Tusculan Disputations,* trans. J. E. King (New York: G. P. Putnam's Sons, 1927), p. 435. In speaking of Socrates' alteration of philosophy, Cicero notes that it occurred after Socrates listened to Archelaus, a pupil of Anaxagoras. In the *Phaedo,* Socrates states that it occurred after he heard someone reading a book by Anaxagoras. John Burnet suggests that the unnamed person was intended to be Archelaus. John Burnet, ed., *Plato's "Phaedo"* (Oxford: Clarendon Press, 1980), pp. 103–4.

10. Nietzsche recognizes the possibility that Plato may not have intended the teaching of immortality to be his ultimate word, but he does not pursue the implications of this possibility. See Nietzsche, *The Will to Power,* trans. Walter Kaufmann and R. J. Hollingdale (New York: Random House), aphorism 428.

11. As will be made explicit in chapter 4, the difference between my interpretation and that of Ronna Burger (*The "Phaedo": A Platonic Labyrinth* [New Haven: Yale University Press, 1984]) is encapsulated in this paragraph.

12. On this point, see Leo Strauss, "What is Political Philosophy?" in *Political Philosophy: Six Essays by Leo Strauss,* ed. Hilail Gildin (Indianapolis: Bobbs-Merrill, 1975), pp. 37–38.

13. Strauss, *The City and Man* (Chicago: University of Chicago Press, 1977), p. 20.

Until recently, the identification of the study of human affairs with political philosophy would have seemed strange because the realm of politics was held to occupy only a limited portion of the scope of human affairs. But those political thinkers who are referred to as communitarians have recently reminded us of the inseparability of moral and political concerns. See, for example, Alasdair MacIntyre, *After Virtue,* 2d. ed. (South Bend, IN: University of Notre Dame Press, 1984), pp. 204–225; and Charles Taylor, "The Nature and Scope of Distributive Justice," in *Philosophy and the Human Sciences: Philosophical Papers* 2 (Cambridge: Cambridge University Press, 1985), pp. 289–317. The limited scope of the political realm is of course a tenet of the liberal understanding of politics. But even within liberal political thinking, this limitation is being questioned. See, for example, William A. Galston, *Liberal Purposes: Goods, Virtues, and Diversity in the Liberal State* (Cambridge: Cambridge University Press, 1991), pp. 79–97, 165–190, 213–237.

14. For extended defenses of this mode of reading the dialogue, see Strauss, *The City and Man,* pp. 50–62; Jacob Klein, *A Commentary on Plato's "Meno,"* (Chapel Hill: University of North Carolina Press, 1965), pp. 3–31; Stanley Rosen, *Plato's "Symposium,"* (New Haven: Yale University Press, 1968), pp. xi–xxxviii; H. G. Gadamer, *Dialogue and Dialectic: Eight Hermeneutical Studies on Plato,* trans. P. Christopher Smith (New Haven: Yale University Press, 1980), pp. 1–6; Drew Hyland, "Why Plato Wrote Dialogues," *Philosophy and Rhetoric* 1 (1968):38–50; Charles L. Griswold, Jr., "Style and Philosophy: The Case of Plato's Dialogues," *Monist* 63 (1980): 530–546.

15. Kenneth Dorter, *Plato's "Phaedo": An Interpretation* (Toronto: University of Toronto Press, 1982); Ronna Burger, *The "Phaedo": A Platonic Labyrinth* (New Haven: Yale University Press, 1984).

I have relied on John Burnet's edition of the *Phaedo* (*Plato's "Phaedo"* [Oxford: Clarendon Press, 1980]). Translations in the text are from David Gallop, *Plato "Phaedo,"* trans. with notes (Oxford: Clarendon Press, 1983), altered occasionally for greater literalness.

16. Burger, p. 219, n. 12.

17. David Bolotin, "The Life of Philosophy and the Immortality of the Soul: An Introduction to Plato's *Phaedo*," *Ancient Philosophy* (1987): 55–56, n.1.

Chapter 2. The Defense of Socrates

1. For brief biographical sketches of Phaedo and Echecrates, see Burnet, pp. 1–2; Dorter, pp. 9–10; Gallop, p. 74.

2. On the Pythagorean character of the dialogue, see Dorter, pp. 9–10; Jacob Klein, *A Commentary on Plato's "Meno"* (Chapel Hill: University of North Carolina Press, 1965), pp. 126–127; H. G. Gadamer, "The Proofs of Immortality in Plato's *Phaedo*," in *Dialogue and Dialectic: Eight Hermeneutical Studies on Plato* (New Haven: Yale University Press, 1980), pp. 30–32; Gallop, pp. 74–75; Burnet, p. 29; A. E. Taylor, *Plato: The Man and His Work* (New York: Dial Press, 1929), p. 175; G. S. Kirk, J. E. Raven, and M. Schofield, *The Pre-Socratic Philosophers* (Cambridge: Cambridge University Press, 1983), pp. 214–215.

3. For biographical sketches of those in attendance, see Burnet, pp. 7–11.

4. This deed of Philolaos is noted by Joseph Cropsey, "The Dramatic End of Plato's Socrates," *Interpretation* 14 (May and September, 1986): 167.

5. Aristotle, *Metaphysics*, 987b9–13; W. D. Ross, *Plato's Theory of Ideas* (Oxford: Clarendon Press, 1951), pp. 13–14, 64, 160–161.

6. Aristotle, *Metaphysics*, 980b26–27.

7. See, for example, R. S. Bluck, *Plato's "Phaedo"* (London: Routledge and Kegan Paul, 1955) p. vii.

8. See R. Archer-Hind, *The "Phaedo" of Plato,"* (London: MacMillan and Co., 1894), p. xiii; R. Hackforth, *Plato's "Phaedo"* (Cambridge: Cambridge University Press, 1972), p. 3; Robert Patterson, *Plato on Immortality* (University Park: Pennsylvania State University Press, 1965), p. 1.

9. As Christopher Colmo has pointed out to me, such orthodox accounts of Socrates are most likely to emerge after Socrates' death, when he is no longer around to question them. This consideration could provide a rationale for writing: to ensure that the questioning "Socrates" is always present.

10. Plato, *Symposium,* 173b10–e3.

11. For different interpretations of Plato's absence, see Burnet, p. 9; Burger, p. 16.

12. Dorter (pp. 4–5,9) follows Klein (*Meno,* pp. 126) in considering the *Phaedo* as a re-enactment and thus a reinterpretation of the Theseus myth. In other words, they see it as a mythological mime with certain details of the dialogue mirroring the details of the myth. For example, the number of people in attendance at Socrates' deathbed is the same number as the seven pairs of youths who sailed with Theseus. I think that the comparison of Socrates and Theseus is important but for reasons other than those offered by Dorter. See pages 30–32 in the present chapter and page 177 in chapter 5. For Dorter, more generally, Socrates relies on myth to induce his interlocutors to believe what they otherwise would not believe had Socrates relied on simply rational grounds. As will become clear in the text, I offer a different interpretation of Socrates' reliance on myth.

13. This includes Socrates' explanation of why he died when he did, which finds the cause in his choice rather than chance.

14. This is not at all to deny that precisely such self-concern may lie behind the desire for a true and certain teaching that obscures the human questions. In order to appreciate this, however, we must first appreciate the distinction between the two, and that is my present concern.

15. See note 2.

16. See, for example, Hackforth, p. 3; Gallop, p. 74; Dorter, p. 4–11; Klein, *Meno,* p. 126 and p. 126 n.49.

17. This is true of Gallop, Dorter, and Klein in the places cited in the previous note. Contrarily, Martha C. Nussbaum holds that it is Plato's intention to downplay the importance of the drama in relation to the arguments. As I will indicate, this view is of a piece with her interpretation

of the *Phaedo* as a whole in that it doesn't sufficiently appreciate the extent to which Plato recognizes the problematic status of the arguments. See, Martha C. Nussbaum, *The Fragility of Goodness* (Cambridge: Cambridge University Press, 1986), p. 131.

18. Plato makes clear in other dialogues that the particular or the individual—including our deeds—has its basis in our corporeality, in our being embodied. Plato, *Republic,* 464d8–9; *Laws,* 739c1–d2.

19. In the *Theaetetus* (155d3–5), Socrates maintains that wonder is the beginning of philosophy.

20. The Greek word is, of course, a pronoun and not a substantive, but the word does serve to emphasize the particularity of one human being as compared to the notion of the incorporeal soul on the basis of which it is difficult to explain human individuation. This point is elaborated in the second proof of immortality, among other places.

21. The importance of this first word is recognized by Strauss, *The Argument and Action of Plato's "Laws"* (Chicago: University of Chicago Press, 1975), p. 75; Burger, p. 15.

22. I owe this point to Gerald Mara.

23. Dorter (p. 10) rejects this explanation of the title but without offering a convincing reason for doing so. He states: "True, Phaedo narrates the dialogue but that is rather an extrinsic function, and none of the other narrated dialogues is named after its narrator." I think that this is precisely a reason to take more seriously the implications of the role of the narrator.

24. There is a repetition in the first few pages of forms of the word, *present*. The notion of presence calls attention to existence in a specific space and time which is as such embodied existence. See 57a1, 58c7, 58c8, 58d1, 59a2, 59a5, 59a7, 59b5, 59b11, 59c3, 59c5, and 59c6.

25. On the issue of whether there is an Idea of the soul, see the material referred to in Charles Griswold, Jr., *Self-Knowledge in Plato's "Phaedrus"* (New Haven: Yale University Press, 1986), p. 260 n.21.

26. Plato, *Crito,* 44b6–50a6. Perhaps to call attention to Crito's concerns, he is first referred to in the *Phaedo* as "father of Critobolus."

27. Socrates' son is called *to paidion*. I do not share the view of Stanley Rosen (*Plato's "Symposium,"* pp. 28, 243, 250–51, 265, 279) that Socrates is puzzled by sexual love and only engages in sexual relations with a view to public relations.

28. These dismissals occur at 63e3, 64c1, 65c7, 82d, 83d, 100d2, 101c8, 114e, and 116d. Burger recognizes the importance of these dismissals (Burger, p. 36).

29. Aristophanes, *Clouds*, 102–4, 185–86, 198–99, 225–34, 503–4, 693–721, 1337–40, 1397–1405, 1467–75. Nietzsche, *Beyond Good and Evil*, p. 3 (preface), pp. 103–4 (sec. 191); *Twilight of the Idols*, pp. 473–79 ("The Problem of Socrates"); *The Gay Science*, p. 272 (sec. 340).

30. Plato, *Crito*, 45b4.

31. See Bolotin (pp. 39–55) for an excellent treatment of the motivations and feelings of both Cebes and Simmias.

32. See Burger pp. 20–21, 29; Dorter, pp. 6–9, 194.

33. Socrates refers here to philosophy as a *pragma*, as a thing or an affair.

34. For a consideration of the various translations of this passage see Dorter, pp. 12–16; Gallop, pp. 79–83.

35. The word, *düskhurisaimēn*, occurs twice more in the dialogue, at 100d5 and at 114d1. The central usage occurs with respect to Socrates' uncertainty concerning the doctrine of participation.

36. Plato, *Phaedrus*, 272d2–273a3.

37. One of the chief issues of the *Phaedo* is the status of the intelligibles. Reflecting the complexity of this issue is the shifting terminology by which Socrates refers to the intelligible. When I refer to the intelligible as the Idea or, to use another of Socrates' locutions, the X-itself, I am referring to the intelligible that is separate from the corporeal world, eternal and unchanging. I will leave until the fifth chapter the terminology of the final proof where the status of the intelligible, and thus the terminology, grows still more complicated.

38. The religious character of the speech is widely recognized. See D. Stewart, "Socrates' Last Bath," *Journal of the History of Philosophy* 10 (1972): 253–259; Hackforth, pp. 15, 38; Burnet, p. 152 (citations to Orphicism in index); W. K. C. Guthrie, *Orpheus and Greek Religion* (London: Methuen and Co., 1952), p. 157; My interpretation begins from a note in Strauss, "The Law of Reason in the *Kuzari*," in *Persecution and the Art of Writing* (Westport, CN: Greenwood Press, 1973), p. 121 n.7.

39. Strauss, "Niccolo Machiavelli," in *History of Political Philosophy*, ed. Leo Strauss and Joseph Cropsey (Chicago: University of Chicago Press, 1987), pp. 296–297.

40. Nietzsche, *The Birth of Tragedy*, pp. 92–93 (sec. 14).

41. See Plato, *Apology*, 20d9–21a10; Homer, *Illiad*, 5.440–2, 21.461–7. On Apollo generally, see Walter Otto, *The Homeric Gods* (New York: Pantheon, 1954), pp. 61–80. In addition to composing hymns to Apollo, Socrates also claims that he is consecrated to Apollo from whom he has received the gift of prophecy that enables him to speak of the next world (85b4–7).

42. Of course, there are many in the reading audience who may not sympathize with Socrates.

43. Plato, *Apology*, 31d5–e1, 32e2–33a1.

44. Aristophanes, *Clouds*, 367.

45. In the *Phaedo*, unlike the *Clouds*, we are permitted to hear Socrates' indoor teaching.

46. Plato, *Apology*, 29a6–b3.

47. "That which transcends humans" includes not only nature but human nature as well to the extent that we do not create our own nature.

48. I do not mean to suggest that these desires are mutually exclusive, only that they are distinguishable and that the former seems more prominent in the character of Simmias, the latter in the character of Cebes.

49. Here again, neither Burger nor Dorter adequately appreciates the extent to which Socrates' defense of philosophy indicates a problem for philosophy itself. Burger (p. 50) writes that its "rhetorical purpose is necessitated by interlocutors who are moved by their own fear of death, together with pity at the imprudence, and anger at the injustice of Socrates' acceptance of his own death." Dorter (p. 20) suggests that although "Socrates is using traditional religious terminology he is not using it in its traditional sense." This again reflects Dorter's view that Socrates' references to the gods reflect the need to persuade through use of nonrational means. Both commentators' views reflect the presumption that Socrates possesses a certain defense of the life of reason in the face of the uncertainties of death. I think that Socrates does ultimately provide a defense of reason, but my account of this defense, given in my treatment of Socrates' 'second sailing,' differs from that of Burger and Dorter because I see the life of reason as more problematic than do Burger and Dorter.

50. See, Strauss, *Persecution and the Art of Writing,* pp. 36–37, with regard to this educative function of an exoteric presentation.

51. An important question in the context of American political thought is whether our community can, in fact, fully abstain from dealing with issues that bear on aspects of human existence that transcend the lives of presently existing individuals. An examination of this question would, perhaps, have to focus on such speeches of Lincoln as the Lyceum Address, the Gettysburg Address, and the Second Inaugural.

52. Hannah Arendt, *On Revolution* (New York: Viking Press, 1965), p. 285.

53. As will be made clear, Socrates does not share the view of the political community as regards death. The latter view, I will argue, does not overcome the tragic character of human existence as the Socratic view does. On the tragic character of the thought expressed in these lines, see Nietzsche, *Birth of Tragedy,* p. 42 (sec. 3).

54. Sophocles, *Oedipus at Colonus,* trans. Robert Fitzgerald, in *Sophocles I,* ed. David Grene (Chicago: University of Chicago Press, 1954), pp. 105 (line 565). See also Plato, *Symposium,* 208c2–209e4, where Diotima addresses the possibilities in the political realm for those who would overcome the transiency of human existence. A critique of this understanding of the political could begin from Aristotle's discussion of the

distinction between true courage and political courage in *Nicomachean Ethics*, 1115a33–1116b3.

55. Plato, *Apology*, 29a4–8

56. Socrates is of more assistance intellectually to those who contradict him than he is to those who agree with him. On this point, see Strauss, *Xenophon's Socrates* (Ithaca: Cornell University Press, 1973), pp. 122–123.

57. See also Plato, *Republic*, 516e8–517a4; *Theaetetus*, 174a3–c9; Aristotle, *Nicomachean Ethics*, 1179a13–16.

58. In the *Phaedo*, the Ideas most often refer to qualities or mathematical concepts. It should be added that the Ideas serve not only as exemplars or paradigms but in some cases as universals. There is also, of course, an understanding of causality based on participation in the Ideas. These and other aspects of the Ideas will be treated as they arise in the dialogue.

59. Burnet, p. 33.

60. In addition, if Socrates truly thought that death was good but that suicide is not permitted, he would certainly praise war as a capital opportunity to die by another's hands.

61. Qualifying phrases appear at 64e1, 64e5–6, 65a1, 65a6–7, 65c2, 65c7, 65c8, 65d7, 66a4, 67a3–4, 67c6, 67c9, and 67d1–2.

62. The existence of this difference is recognized by several commentators. See, for example, Hackforth, p. 16; Burger, pp. 38–50.

63. Plato, *Symposium*, 174a9.

64. Plato, *Apology*, 33c2.

65. On the view that it is the ensouled body that desires, see Plato, *Gorgias*, 492e ff.

66. On the various views of the soul, see T. M. Robinson, *Plato's Psychology* (Toronto: University of Toronto Press, 1970), pp. 70–72. Rob-

inson recognizes the shifting definitions of soul throughout this passage but he does not ascribe these shifts to Plato's intention.

67. Nussbaum (pp. 151–155) takes at face value Socrates' recommendation of asceticism. My reasons for not doing so emerge in the text, but it may be useful to summarize them here. First of all, the recommendation depends on a simplistic body-soul distinction that Socrates himself questions both here and in other dialogues. Second, Socrates also recognizes here and in other dialogues that there are desires of soul as well as body; he speaks repeatedly of the philosopher's love of wisdom in the defense itself. Moreover, the recommendation is replete with qualifications. Finally, Socrates himself does not engage in this practice. The difference between my interpretation of the recommendation of asceticism and that of Nussbaum derives from my view of the importance of the distinction between Socrates and the "genuine philosophers." For an appreciation of a similar distinction in the *Republic,* see Mary P. Nichols, "The *Republic*'s Two Alternatives: Philosopher-Kings and Socrates," *Political Theory,* 12 (May 1984): 252–74.

68. Gallop, p. 91.

69. That mathematical wisdom may not be the whole of wisdom is also suggested by the *Theaetetus* where we see mathematicians holding the opposite of what is maintained here. They hold that knowledge is precisely perception.

70. It is noteworthy that Socrates uses the same word here (65b3)—*thrulousin*—to describe his expression of the doctrine of Ideas at 76d8 and as a participle at 100b5. Simmias himself will, of course, rely on an image later in the dialogue.

71. I follow Gallop's translation rather than Hackforth's or Bluck's.

72. See also 67b1—"through ourselves." This point was suggested to me by David Bolotin.

73. Dorter (p. 28) sees the possibility that our ascent toward greater understanding may be a "process arising out of sensory experience" but he does not seem to appreciate the question this raises for our access to the intelligibles conceived as unchanging and eternal.

74. Dorter (pp. 31–32) does not, I think, sufficiently appreciate this problem. He sees the notion of philosophy as preparation for death as dictating the attempt to subject body to the rule of reason as far as possible. Following this dictate, we are doing "our service to the gods—or the cosmos, in accordance with whose teleological nature we humans have come into existence." In my interpretation, exactly what it is (if anything) that transcends us remains in question, much less any detailed notion of what the gods want from us.

75. Plato, *Republic,* 372c1–374e1; Allan Bloom, *The Republic of Plato* (New York: Basic Books, 1968), pp. 346–348; Aristotle, *Politics,* 1290b20–27.

76. I owe this point to Bolotin, p. 55

77. Nussbaum, p. 389.

78. Contrary to my own interpretation, Nussbaum (pp. 154–155) sees Plato's goal as pure wisdom. She ascribes to Plato the notion that the true view is that of the philosopher who "can stand apart from human needs and limitations" since needs and desires are obstacles to true judgment. In my interpretation, some desires are obstacles, but they are obstacles to the desire to know, a fulfillment of which may lie precisely in a clear view of human needs and limitations. Nussbaum's book fulfills the possibility that Plato's focus on pure wisdom could lead someone to examine closely the obstacles to pure wisdom.

79. The true ground of this distinction concerns how one faces death—whether one can face up to the uncertainties surrounding it and not claim to know what one does not know.

80. Gallop, pp. 98–102; Terence Irwin, *Plato's Moral Theory* (Oxford: Clarendon Press, 1977), p. 162.

81. Hackforth recognizes the presence of the alternative conceptions of wisdom, writing that there is "an identification . . . of intelligence and virtue"; but in the lines that follow he seems to waver between this and the conception of *phronesis* as a *means* or *aid* to virtue. This latter conception prevails in the end but both are present in the difficult words at b1-2 καὶ τούτου μὲν πάντα καὶ μετὰ τούτου ὠνούμενά τε καὶ πιπρασκόμενα, τούτου implying the former and μετὰ τούτου the latter. This

running together of the two ideas is, it seems to me, the chief source of difficulty both in this particular sentence and in the passage as a whole" (Hackforth, p. 193); Paul Gooch also sees the presence of wisdom as both end and means in this passage, but states that "their 'running together' is instead of a puzzling contradiction a consistent statement of the instrumental and contributory value of wisdom in relation to the good life." Paul Gooch, "The Relation Between Wisdom and Virtue in *Phaedo* 69a6–c3," *The Journal of the History of Philosophy* 12 (1974): 159; Irwin likewise sees Plato as using wisdom in what he calls a "moral" and "contemplative" usage, but he thinks that Plato is to some extent confused for he (Plato) does not see that "the moral and the contemplative uses of these terms cannot be identified as readily as Plato suggests." (Irwin, p. 163.)

82. Both Bolotin and Burger see this conflict. (Bolotin, pp. 47–48; Burger, p. 44.)

83. A variety of commentators consider Plato's Socrates as portrayed with a view to responding to the criticism of Socrates and of philosophy in general which is found in Aristophanes' *Clouds*. On this point, see Mary P. Nichols, *Socrates and the Political Community: An Ancient Debate* (Albany: State University of New York Press, 1987), p. 2, and the material cited on p. 190 n. 6. See also Thomas C. Brickhouse and Nicholas D. Smith, *Socrates on Trial* (Princeton: Princeton University Press, 1989), pp. 69–70. I agree with the view that considers the Platonic Socrates as a response to the Aristophanean criticism so long as it is remembered that among the issues raised by this critique is the one with which Socrates deals in the present defense. Given that this is the case, the response to Aristophanes requires not only a defense of philosophy to the political community but also a theoretical defense of the possibility of philosophy itself.

Chapter 3. The Proofs of Immortality

1. See, for example, Michael Davis, "Socrates' Pre-Socratism: Some Remarks on the Structure of Plato's *Phaedo*," *Review of Metaphysics* 33 (March 1980):566. Bluck, p. 20; Gadamer, p. 22. Socrates himself indicates the inadequacy of the proofs at 84c6–7 and 107b4–6.

2. Davis, p. 566–573.

3. Bluck, p. 57.

4. Commentators, likewise, are dismissive of this first proof. Gallop (p. 104) concludes that the first proof "is better construed as an opening dialectical move than as an argument to which Plato was seriously committed." Bluck (p. 57) states that Plato "was almost certainly not convinced himself by this 'proof' and he is probably offering it merely for the benefit of those who do find mechanistic arguments impressive."

5. For a somewhat different view of the reason for the absence of the Ideas, see Burger, p. 54.

6. Burger seems to suggest that the last argument for immortality corrects the first. (Burger, p. 53–54.) My reasons for disagreeing with this position will be apparent in what follows.

7. This phrase—*houtōs ekhei*—reflects the attempt of the first three proofs to consider how the human soul is, beginning from the standpoint of how it is with nature as a whole.

8. Socrates has thus far referred to the "souls of men," "those who have died," "our souls," and "the dead" in referring to the entity that exists in Hades.

9. See Gallop, p. 113; Dorter, p. 40; and Burger, pp. 63–64.

10. Several commentators recognize these different types of opposites. Paul Gooch, "Plato's Antapodosis Argument for the Soul's Immortality: *Phaedo* 70–72," *7th Inter-American Congress of Philosophy, Proceedings* (1967), pp. 239–244; Julian Wolfe, "Plato's 'Cyclical' Argument for Immortality," *7th Inter-American Congress of Philosophy, Proceedings* (1967), pp. 252–254; Gallop, pp. 107–108; Dorter, pp. 37–83; Burger, p. 57.

11. Burger recognizes this ambiguity. (Burger, p. 55.)

12. This begging of the question is recognized by T. M. Robinson, "*Phaedo* 70c: An Error and an Explanation," in *Dialogue* 8 (1969): 124–25; and by Gallop, p. 110.

13. On the types of opposites and their significance, see the sources cited in note 10.

14. Several commentators recognize this point. See, for example, Dorter, p. 39; Burger, p. 60.

15. Gallop, pp. 104–6.

16. Dorter, p. 36.

17. See Burger, p. 61, for a slightly different view of the source of his dissatisfaction.

18. The word Socrates uses here is *antapodōsomen*. The proof is sometimes called the antapodosis argument in recognition that the principle of opposites from opposites operates only if this reciprocal alternation between opposites is posited. See Burnet, p. 48; Gooch, "Plato's Antapodosis Argument," p. 244. There is, however, little discussion of the meaning of this proof's dependence upon the human positing of a view of nature.

19. See T. M. Robinson ("*Phaedo* 70c," p. 125) concerning the way in which the use of the word *coming-to-life-again* helps Socrates beg the question. Robinson, however, sees no alternative to the view that this usage, if witting, accuses "Socrates of a piece of shoddy philosophical sharp-practice," while if unwitting, that Socrates commits an "elementary blunder."

20. Dorter (p. 44) does not adequately appreciate the extent to which the eternality of nature is made hypothetical in this passage. Burger (p. 62) sees this hypothetical character but does not pursue the problem this poses for philosophy.

21. See Dorter (pp. 43, 46) for a different treatment of the mythical aspect of the proof.

22. Aristotle, *Metaphysics*, 984b15–18.

23. Gallop, p. 113.

24. Gallop, p. 114.

25. Compare *Meno*, 81e5–86c8. For a brief account of the difference between the doctrine of recollection as presented in each of these dialogues, see Gallop, p. 115.

26. Early in the dialogue Socrates expresses his pleasure at Cebes' dogged pursuit of argument (62e8–63a3). He gives no such praise to Simmias.

27. The details of this passage are found in 72e3–73b10.

28. A good account of the secondary literature concerning the issue of sense-perception and the doctrine of recollection which is raised here can be found in Michael L. Morgan, "Sense-Perception and Recollection in the *Phaedo*," *Phronesis* 29 (1984): 237–251. The problem raised by the dependence of recollection on sense-perception is that this dependence seems to lead to the paradoxical conclusion that all humans, indeed even infants, apprehend the intelligibles. Morgan states (p. 237, n.1) that the problem is usually "resolved by modifying the role of sense-perception in recollection . . . or by tallying it as a Platonic failure." My resolution of this problem differs from Morgan's. He attributes the existence of the problem to the earlier stage of Plato's development that is expressed in the *Phaedo* as compared to the *Republic*.

29. That such an account precludes error is recognized by Norman Gulley, "Plato's Theory of Recollection," *Classical Quarterly* NS4 (1954): 199.

30. We must also note that Socrates treats all of the senses as equal. Later, in speaking of the access to the intelligibles in the proof proper, Socrates states: "We haven't derived the thought of it, nor could we do so, from anywhere but seeing or touching or some other of the senses—I'm counting all these as the same." Simmias replies: "Yes, they are the same, Socrates, for what the argument seeks to show" (75a5–10). Socrates can consider all the senses the same insofar as, at least in the proof proper, he is presenting a doctrine of knowing which does not involve discourse. If it did, seeing and hearing would be considered more important than touching or tasting or smelling.

31. Simmias and Cebes remember the lyre and the cloak in their later objections.

32. See 73e1–2, "Especially (*malista*), however, whenever it happens to someone in connection with things he's forgotten . . ." Socrates only dwells upon forgetting and learning when he must explain the manifest differences of humans with regard to knowing. At this point, this is an issue that he must ignore.

33. This point is recognized by Burger, p. 72.

34. Burger follows J. L. Ackrill in this regard. See Burger, p. 73; J. L. Ackrill, "Anamnesis in the *Phaedo:* Remarks on 73c–75c," in *Exegesis and Argument, Phronesis,* supplementary vol. 1 (1973): 185. In my view, the ambiguity of the example is intended to raise the question of the precise relation between the perceivable and the intelligible.

35. Gallop, p. 118. One of the most serious considerations of this issue that I have seen, that of J. Gosling, ("Similarity in *Phaedo* 73b seq.," in *Phronesis* 10 [1965]: 151–161) founders also on the failure to appreciate the part played by dissimilars, however implicit, in the proof proper.

36. Gallop does not answer the question.

37. I owe this point to Davis, pp. 570–571.

38. See Plato, *Parmenides,* 132a–132b.

39. This question was suggested to me by David Bolotin.

40. Owing to its subject matter (the intelligibles) and its perplexed language, this passage has engendered a small library of secondary literature. These articles revolve around the several questions presented in the text. One can refer, for example, to M. Wedin, "αὐτὰ τὰ ἴσα and the Argument at *Phaedo,* 74b7–c5," *Phronesis* 22 (1977): 191–205, in order to see where the debate has been. In my view, expressed in the text, the ambiguity is intentional, the intention being to raise the problem of the link between perceivables and intelligibles, rather than to resolve that problem. Judging from the volume and character of the secondary material produced by the passage, one can at least say that this has been its effect.

41. This passage too has perplexed editors leading most nineteenth century editors to bracket it (Dorter, p. 60). Burnet (p. 56) writes that "this step in the argument is not perhaps strictly necessary." Hackforth (p. 68, n.1) writes that here this point is dismissed as unimportant." It is perplexing only if it is not recognized that the relation between intelligible and particular begins to look very much like one of the dissimilars.

42. This is not a thought that is the product of a mind at work. It is, rather, passively received (74e6).

43. Compare 74a6 with 74a9–e2. Dorter (p. 51) recognizes this difference.

44. "*bouletai,*" 74d9; "*oregetai,*" 75a2,b1; "*prothumeitai,*" 75b7. Burnet (p. 58, emphasis in original) writes that *prothumeitai* is "a still more picturesque way of expressing *tendency* than βούλεται or ὀρέγεται above." Another name for this "tendency" is, I think, eroticization.

45. Dorter (pp. 62, 68–69) also points to this question, but he seems less troubled than I think is appropriate by the problem this question raises for our access to the unchanging intelligibles and thus for the orientation of philosophy on pure wisdom.

46. Plato, *Symposium,* 209e5–212a7. It is, of course, Socrates who relates the speech which he attributes to Diotima.

47. The requirement that the soul be complex in order to account for there being good and bad souls, as well as wise and foolish souls, is explored in Socrates' reply to Simmias' objection. See 92e4–95a2.

48. The notion that the philosopher desires wisdom is mentioned in the *doxa,* for example, but the implications of such desire for the character of the soul are not explicitly articulated. See 68a1, a7.

49. Plato, *Symposium,* 210a4, 210e3–4, 211b6.

50. Gallop (p. 130) recognizes this point, writing: "The inference at 75c1–6, that we must have gained knowledge of the equal before we were born, would suffice to prove the soul's pre-natal existence directly. Yet it takes a further page of argument, proving the Recollection doctrine, before prenatal existence is inferred at 76c11–13. What is the role of this further argument?" Dorter (p. 63) also recognizes that what follows "is irrelevant to the question of pre-existence since pre-existence is supposed on both alternatives." Neither, however, adequately answers Gallop's final question.

51. 75d7, 75e2. See Gallop, p. 132.

52. Plato, *Sophist,* 263e3–5.

53. Simmias' reply is that he forgot (*elathon*) he was saying nothing. His language indicates that he is captured by the doctrine of Recollection.

54. That Simmias gives in too easily is recognized by Burger, p. 80; Dorter, p. 64; and Gallop, p. 134.

55. Socrates later takes refuge in speeches, not to forestall doubt but for the sake of better understanding.

56. It will be recalled that in Simmias' view, Socrates' willingness to die seems a personal injury to Simmias so that Socrates regards Simmias' charge as bearing on the justice of Socrates' decision. See 63a4–b2.

57. The ambiguity in the usage of *telos* in this passage perhaps points to the question of how can one achieve a single understanding of this entity called soul which seems to have two ends, one related to life and existence, the other to reason and perfection (77b5 and 77c5).

58. Burger (pp. 85–86) recognizes Cebes' dependence as well as that of Simmias. But she provides a different understanding than my own of what each is seeking from Socrates.

59. See Dorter, p. 75–76; Burger, p. 87–88; Compare Gallop, p. 137.

60. See Gallop, p. 138.

61. To recur to a point made in the context of Socrates' defense, perhaps Socrates' hesitancy with respect to the incomposite is explained by the significant differences which exist among the intelligibles; It is difficult to imagine how what must be incomposite, without parts, could partake of such differences.

62. See note 4, chapter 1.

63. At 103c5–6, Cebes seems to indicate that his doubts go beyond those he expresses.

64. Dorter, p. 72. Though he recognizes this distinction, Dorter does not fully explore its implications. What I consider to be the inadequacy of Dorter's interpretation of this theme is especially evident in the context in which Dorter calls attention to this distinction. Running through his book is a distinction between the rational and nonrational human motives. Dorter sees Socrates as answering to both through arguments and incantations. But Dorter does not question, as I think Socrates

himself questions, whether there *is* a true and certain argument that vindicates the practice of philosophy. See Dorter, p. 76.

65. This phrase is striking because it is seldom used in the *Phaedo*.

66. Burger (p. 89) recognizes this distinction but gives a somewhat different interpretation of its significance.

67. This is not at all to say that this movement occurs unfailingly. Precisely, if we must begin from experience then a question is raised as to whether all that is unseen ("by men") is necessarily invisible. The realm of the unseen, that which we do not see, includes all that we imagine to exist, all the explanations, true and false, that we construct to explain what is seen. The invisible must exist to be invisible, but the unseen may not exist at all. And to use the serious pun that Socrates makes later in this proof, when we attempt to move from the known to the unknown, we might be led to Hades (*Haidou*) rather than to the invisible (*aidē*) (79a4 and 79b11–13).

68. Cebes uses an odd locution here, stating that something is "totally and altogether more similar." The absoluteness of the phrase seems inappropriate to something which is a matter of degree. Burnet points out that, in fact, "the usual phrase is ὅλῳ καὶ παντὶ διαφέρειν, 'to be totally different.'" (Burnet, p. 69.)

69. Burnet, p. 70.

70. See Bolotin, p. 48.

71. Burnet (p. 72) writes: "The protasis is interrupted at e5 and resumed at 81a4."

72. See my comments on Simmias' remarks at the start of Socrates' defense.

73. Bolotin, p. 48.

74. Related to this point is the characterization of Simmias in the *Phaedrus*, 242a7–b3. There, Socrates places Phaedrus as second only to Simmias as a generator of speeches.

75. I leave this word untranslated in order not to exclude beforehand any of the several meanings that emerge in the text. This ambiguity plays an important role in Socrates' response to Simmias' objection. See C. C. W. Taylor, "The Arguments in the *Phaedo* Concerning the Thesis that the Soul is a *Harmonia*," in *Essays in Ancient Greek Philosophy, II,* eds. John P. Anton and Anthony Preus (Albany: State University of New York Press, 1983), pp. 217–231.

76. As Dorter (pp. 86–87) notes, Socrates treats the two objections as parts of a single argument. I differ with Dorter, however, with respect to what constitutes this unity.

Chapter 4. Socrates' 'Second Sailing'

1. Several commentators point to the central location of the misology section. But I am arguing for the centrality of the entire section bounded by Echecrates' interruptions. Perhaps the most important implication of my interpretation in this regard is that I consider the final proof as having less importance than is usually accorded to it.

2. Dorter, p. 86–87. Contrary to his usual procedure, Socrates wished to hear both objections before responding to either (86d8–e4). Moreover, he attributes one to Harmonia and one to Cadmus who, according to mythic accounts, were married (95a4–6). He also refers to the two objections in the singular as "the argument of Simmias and Cebes" (89c3–4).

3. My interpretation differs from Dorter's. See Dorter, pp. 86–87.

4. Bolotin, pp. 48–49.

5. Dorter (p. 83) and Cropsey (p. 169) suggest the possibility that the *Phaedo* is so named because of the importance of Phaedo's exchange with Socrates.

6. Plato, *Euthydemus,* 297b9–d1.

7. Plato, *Seventh Letter,* 342e3.

8. But perhaps equally unsettling is that in the *Euthydemus* Socrates evinces a surprising appreciation of the sophist's art. Perhaps this is explained by the possibility that the character of reason, its weakness, which makes possible eristics, also makes possible dialectics. From this might follow Socrates' otherwise surprising appreciation of the sophists' art.

9. Several commentators maintain the view that Socrates' 'second sailing' provides this art. But, as I indicated in the opening chapter and as I will later discuss, there is much dispute concerning the precise way in which the 'second sailing' accomplishes this task. Moreover, as I will also make clear, I do not think that this art or *techne* is by itself the deepest teaching of the *Phaedo*.

10. See Burnet's note on 90b9 (p. 90).

11. See Gallop (p. 232, n.46) for a discussion of the distinction suggested in the final phrase of the quote between the truth of the beings and knowledge of the beings. I follow Burger (p. 118) in my interpretation of the importance of the distinction.

12. My understanding of this passage, as well as the misology section as a whole, is much indebted to Cropsey (pp. 168–169) and to Bolotin (pp. 54–55).

13. But why does Socrates consider it good to engage in this discussion? First of all, we know that Socrates found pleasure in discussion. Moreover, when he dismisses his family, he indicates that he prefers spending his last day in calm discussion with his acquaintances rather than in the emotionally turbulent atmosphere that would have resulted had his family stayed the whole time. Finally, Socrates' reaction to the questions of Evenus suggest that Socrates is not devoid of concern for how he will be thought of after he dies. Nor is he devoid of concern for the good of the potential philosophers among his acquaintances.

14. Again, I think that Burger (pp. 119–120) assumes too quickly that Socrates is being ironic at this point.

15. This continuation begins at 92e3 and runs to 95a5.

16. 88d3–6. Aristotle also notes this when introducing the soul as *harmonia* thesis in *De Anima*. Aristotle, *De Anima*, 407b26–30.

17. Klein (*Plato's "Meno,"* p. 132, n.71), and Dorter (p. 215, n.2) both see Simmias' error, but neither offers the interpretation offered here.

18. Plato, *Republic,* 443c9–e1.

19. On the different meanings of *harmonia,* see C. C. W. Taylor, "Soul is a *Harmonia,"* pp. 217–218.

20. The boundaries of the arguments are indicated by the phrase, *ti de.* Thus, the first argument begins at 92a3 and runs to 93a10. There, it is interrupted by the "contained" argument which runs from 93a11 to 94b3. From 94b4 until 95a4, we have the completion of the "containing" argument. This structure of the argument is presented by, among others, W. F. Hicken, *"Phaedo* 93a11–94b3," *Classical Quarterly* (1954): 16–22; Gallop, p. 158; Dorter, p. 99; and C. C. W. Taylor, pp. 223–224.

21. Socrates' omission of music is all the more striking given the dominant image of the passage. Perhaps, he omits music because the need for music suggests that the soul too has conflicting aspects which must be ordered.

22. Plato, *Republic,* 441b6.

23. Plato, *Republic,* 431a3–5.

24. C. C. W. Taylor, p. 225; Gallop (p. 162) simply notes that "from the premise that no soul is more or less a soul than any other, conjoined with the hypothesis that soul is an attunement [*harmonia*], it would not follow that no attunement [*harmonia*] whatever is more or less an attunement [*harmonia*] than any other, but only that no soul-attunement is more or less a soul-attunement than any other." Some (for example, Hackforth [p. 115, n.4] and Dorter [pp. 103–5]) would revise the text itself to get around the statement.

25. C. C. W. Taylor, p. 225.

26. *Ibid.*

27. The answers to these questions are also peculiarly controversial. Plato, *Euthyphro,* 7b6–d5; *Phaedrus,* 263a2–b1.

28. This distinction occurs several times in Socrates' reply to Simmias. See 93b1–2, 93b5–6, 93d1–4, and 93d12–e5. Commentators have recognized this distinction but have not dwelled on it. Gallop (p. 159) states that the distinction is "of minor importance" and that "whatever difference may be intended between the two pairs of terms, no use is made of it in the argument. Similarly, Hackforth (p. 115, n.1) states: "I do not believe that any difference of meaning is intended between the two terms." Burnet (p. 95) follows the ancient commentator Olympiodorus in assigning the difference a musical meaning. Dorter (pp. 110–11) sees that the use of the phrase, to a lesser or to a greater extent, introduces the notion of a paradigm. However, he takes this to be Socrates' way of suggesting various meanings of harmony. I would add that it also thereby suggests various meanings of disharmony.

For another treatment of this distinction, see Plato, *Statesman*, 283c11–284e9.

29. Plato, *Apology*, 37e2–38a9; *Laws*, 963a1–966b4; *Republic*, 429a7–430c4; Aristotle, *Nicomachean Ethics*, 1177b30–1178a24; *Politics*, 1252b28–1253a9.

30. Plato, *Apology*, 31d6–32a3, 32e1–33a1.

31. On the issue of whether there is an Idea of soul, see Griswold, pp. 88–92; p. 260 n.21; and p. 261 nn.24–26.

32. Or perhaps he believes that he possesses a ready answer to this question in the doctrine to which he is so attached, the doctrine of Recollection.

33. In this light we can understand why Plato's Socrates refers to the sovereign metaphysical problem with an expression drawn from politics. The metaphysical problem of the one and the many becomes evident in the attempt to understand the relationship between the many individual humans and the idea of human perfection.

34. On the phrase, 'second sailing,' see K. M. W. Shipton, "A Good Second Best: *Phaedo* 96 ff.," *Phronesis* 24 (1979): 50, n.15. Plato also uses the phrase in the *Statesman* and in the *Philebus*. In the *Statesman* it is used to refer to the rule of laws as an alternative to the rule of the wise (*Statesman*, 300c2). In the *Philebus*, Protarchus uses the phrase to distinguish Socratic knowledge of ignorance from divine knowledge (*Philebus*,

19c2–3). See also Aristotle, *Nicomachean Ethics,* 1109a34–35. In each case the phrase refers to an awareness of the limits and thus the character of the human situation.

35. Davis, p. 559. Both Davis and Dorter recognize that the stages of Socrates' intellectual autobiography are philosophically significant.

36. This is, I believe, the only mention of *sophia* in the *Phaedo.* I will argue, however, that Socrates never lost his desire for wisdom; his alteration of philosophy does not involve a circumscription of view. But the wisdom that he seeks is not the pure wisdom that is the desire of the "genuine philosopher."

37. Compare Hackforth, p. 124, n.2.

38. Dorter (p. 119) sees that the inadequacy of Socrates' first view of nature points to the need for formal explanation, contrary to Gallop (p. 172) who maintains that Socrates' claim to be blinded is "ironical."

39. I therefore disagree with Gregory Vlastos, "Reasons and Causes in the *Phaedo,*" in *Plato: A Collection of Critical Essays I,* ed. Gregory Vlastos (Garden City, NY: Doubleday, 1970), p. 151, n.50, who states that the nutritional perplexities and the mathematical perplexities are unrelated. Particularly helpful in shedding light on the perplexities is Davis, pp. 561–562.

40. See, for example, Plato, *Republic,* 524d3–d5; *Theaetetus,* 184e8–185c2; *Sophist,* 250a4–e2; *Hippias Major,* 301d4–303d5.

41. For an example of one who, because of ambition, wished to be learned with regard to nature as a whole, see Aristotle, *Politics,* 1267b22–1269a27.

42. Again, Dorter sees that what Socrates missed was the need for formal cause, but he does not sufficiently appreciate the question that Socrates recognition of this need raises.

43. The word, now (*Nun*), is emphasized by Plato's making it the first word of Cebes' question. Vlastos (pp. 155–156) maintains that the perplexities show a confusion of logical and physical causality, a confusion which is addressed by the doctrine of the Ideas. By relying on the doctrine

of Ideas Plato may, as Vlastos claims, avoid the reduction of physical to logical causality. But as Vlastos also sees, the doctrine of Ideas is peculiarly uninformative (156) and fails to explain the world of our experience (166). My view, presented in the text, is that Plato's Socrates is calling attention to the problem of the heterogeneity of causality and thus of nature so that we can appreciate the concerns that led to his 'second sailing,' an approach to nature which preserves this heterogeneity in a way that the Ideas do not.

44. Dorter treats the teleology section in a rather cursory manner. This, perhaps, permits him to maintain that Socrates presumes there is cosmic teleology (pp. 122, 123, 124). Dorter states that Socrates does not entertain the possibility that the world is absurd (p. 119). But a close examination of the teleology section, with special attention paid to the reason that Socrates does not himself offer a teleological account, shows that, for Socrates, teleology is at best elusive. This claim of Dorter's is an important example of his reluctance to see just how far Socrates' questioning of the life of reason goes.

45. See, for example, Gallop, p. 169. Gallop, like Vlastos (p. 134) translates the word *aitia* as reason instead of as cause. Gallop calls the latter a mistranslation because "it covers at most only part of the field with which Socrates is concerned. Many of the things he will mention are not amenable to what we should call causal explanation." I follow Burger (p. 252, n.2) in thinking that this is a reason to preserve the usual translation since it serves to make more evident the question underlying Socrates' treatment of causality, whether there is a single cause which accounts for all coming into being, passing away, and existence. On the distinction between 'reason' and 'cause' more generally, see Stephen Salkever, *Finding the Mean: Theory and Practice in Aristotelian Political Philosophy* (Princeton, NJ: Princeton University Press, 1990), pp. 46–47.

46. Unlike many of the other subtitles, there is evidence that Plato himself referred to the dialogue in this way. See *Thirteenth Letter,* 363a7.

47. See, for example, Aristotle, *Politics,* 1252b28–31.

48. Plato suggests that the body and its needs impedes complete harmony of the individual and the common. See *Republic,* 464d8–e2; *Laws,* 739c1–d2.

49. Plato, *Apology,* 38a1–7.

50. Plato indicates that, at best, the existence of the best regime is dependent on chance. See *Republic,* 499b2–c3, 540d1–541a8; *Laws,* 709a1–b9. Even this may be too optimistic; the best regime may be possible only in speech. See *Republic,* 473a5–b11, 592a7–b5.

51. On the view that a perfect regime may be possible only if a god rules rather than humans, see *Statesman,* 271d3–272b1; *Laws,* 713c2–714b1; *Theaetetus,* 176a5–b1.

52. This formulation was suggested to me by Joseph Cropsey.

53. C. C. W. Taylor ("Forms as Causes in the *Phaedo,*" *Mind* [January 1969]: 46–47) recognizes the rift between humanity and nature in this passage. He writes that Plato is here "singling out human action as unique" Taylor thinks that Plato finally integrates man and nature through an explanation in terms of the "Form of the Good" although Taylor admits that such explanation is not forthcoming in the present dialogue.

54. Again, this point is evident in Book I of Aristotle's *Politics,* where he says that the city is natural but that the man who first founded the city was the greatest benefactor. *Politics,* 1252b30–a3 and 1253a30–31.

55. On this point, see Christopher Bruell, "Strauss on Xenophon's Socrates," *Political Science Reviewer* (1983): 124.

56. Richard Robinson, *Plato's Earlier Dialectic* (Oxford: Clarendon Press, 1953), p. 143; Vlastos, p. 138, n.15; Hackforth, p. 132; and Burger, p. 254, n.27 contend that the goal of the 'second sailing' is not teleological, that the goals of the two sailings are different. Against this, David Wiggins ("Teleology and the Good in Plato's *Phaedo,*" in *Oxford Studies in Ancient Philosophy,* vol. IV [Oxford: Clarendon Press, 1986], p. 3), Dorter (*Plato's "Phaedo,"* p. 120), Taylor ("Forms as Causes," p. 53), and Shipton ("A Good Second-Best," pp. 33, 40) maintain that the goals are the same. In my view, cosmological teleology has been shown to be unavailable. However, I do think that Socrates continues to strive for knowledge of the whole, but he does so in awareness of the limits of that quest. Indeed, I will argue that awareness of these limits forms the core of the understanding of the whole of nature that he has achieved.

57. This phrase of mine—"arises in the mind"—expresses in what I think is a suitably vague way the mystery concerning how this movement from perceivable to intelligible occurs. One purpose of the doctrine of recollection is to explore this mystery. See Klein, *Plato's "Meno,"* pp. 149–50.

58. Dorter, p. 124.

59. Gallop, p. 78; Klein, p. 120–25.

60. Plato, *Republic,* 504e7–535a1.

61. See, for example, 65d4, 78d1–5, and 74a11–12, where Socrates refers to the intelligibles using the locution *the X-in itself.*

62. I am here and in what follows pursuing a suggestion made by Cropsey (pp. 169–174) concerning Socrates' distancing himself from his own orthodoxy.

63. See, for example, Gallop, p. 179; Dorter, p. 124; Vlastos, pp. 139, 143; Shipton, pp. 42–43; Dorothea Frede, "The Final Proof of Immortality of the Soul in Plato's *Phaedo* 102a–107a," *Phronesis* 23 (1978): 28. Burger's interpretation is superior to the foregoing interpretations in its rejection of this understanding. As I indicate in the notes below, however, I do not think that Burger adequately appreciates the implications of this rejection of the separate ideas.

64. Aristotle, *Aristotle's De Generatione et Corruptione,* trans. C. J. F. Williams (Oxford: Clarendon Press, 1982), pp. 52–3 (335b18–20).

65. Gallop, p. 183. Hackforth (144–46) thinks that Aristotle's criticism is relevant. He offers an interpretation different from my own of why Plato argued in this questionable fashion, but he does recognize the unitary character of Socrates' explanation of causality in this passage. Hackforth writes:

> It is well that we should be reminded that the doctrine of Forms as causes is put forward by Socrates as a second-best doctrine relatively to that which he had hoped to build on the principle suggested by Anaxagoras. Nevertheless Plato seems in our present section, and indeed throughout the rest of the argument which gives his final proof of immortality, to

have forgotten this; for again and again Socrates asserts that γένεσις and φθορά, in the restricted sense in which he is using these terms, viz. the acquisition and loss of attributes by particular sensible things, are due *solely* to things coming or ceasing to participate in Forms. (p. 146, emphasis in original)

66. Aristotle, *De Generatione et Corruptione,* pp. 52–4 (335b7ff).

67. In *De Generatione et Corruptione,* 335b8–23. Aristotle critiques the view presented here of the Ideas as being the sole kind of cause.

68. On Socrates' uncertainty concerning participation, see Vlastos, pp. 141–42.

69. Burnet, p. 111.

70. Vlastos, p. 157–8, n.64.

71. On the safety of the ideas, see 101d1–2 and 100d8–e1. On the fear engendered by the sophists' arguments, see 101a5, 101b2, 101b5, 101b7, and 101c9–d1.

72. See Vlastos, p. 156.

73. The most complete expression of the difficulty can be found in Robinson, *Plato's Earlier Dialectic,* pp. 126–9.

74. Gallop, p. 180.

75. Bluck, pp. 13–14, 164–66. See also Gallop's comments (pp. 178–179) on Bluck.

76. Robinson (*Plato's Earlier Dialectic,* pp. 143–144) and Gulley (pp. 40–41), for example, maintain that there is no connection. I disagree, but I think that their conclusion points to the incompatibility of the hypothetical method with the intelligibles understood as the separate Ideas as opposed to the intelligible understood as a speech, a logos which is tentative and capable of being revised.

77. Socrates begins this passage in a particularly perplexed manner using the same verb, *ekhō,* in precisely opposite meanings at 101d1 and 101d3. This leads some commentators to amend the text although there

seems no reason, aside from the perplexity, to do so (101c7–d2). The word, *kompseias*, is important for the final proof. (See 105c2.)

78. Robinson, *Plato's Earlier Dialectic*, p. 130. For a brief discussion of the problem, see also Gallop's note on this passage. (Gallop, p. 235, n.67.)

79. Plato, *Republic*, 510b4–7.

80. Plato, *Republic*, 510c2–d3.

81. Plato, *Republic*, 511b5–7.

82. Gallop, p. 190.

83. Dorter (pp. 127, 128, 132, and 133) recognizes the issues that make questionable that Socrates means us to understand the Ideas or the Forms as the initial object of our understanding. He sees the problem of the doctrine of participation and the question raised by the hypothetical method in its emphasis on ascent from the initial hypotheses. But Dorter apparently thinks that Socrates does not treat the problem raised by these issues. In this context, he quotes Simmias' expression of skepticism and says that it prefigures Socrates' own skepticism. But I see a difference between the two. Simmias is not all that concerned whether that which is aloft is accessible to reason or is some divine doctrine. But Socrates is well aware of the difference between the two and the questionability of philosophy in the light of uncertainty about this issue. The 'second sailing' is precisely Socrates' response to the way in which philosophy can be justified in the face of this doubt.

84. See, for example, Robinson, *Plato's Earlier Dialectic* (p. 142–45) and Julius Stenzel, *Plato's Method of Dialectic* (Oxford: Clarendon Press, 1940), pp. 10–12.

85. Dorter seems to waffle on this point. At times he suggests that Socrates totally abandoned physical causes (p. 128–129). But other times he indicates that Socrates sees the need for several kinds of causation although formal cause is more important (p. 131). I think it is important to see both that Socrates recognizes the need for both kinds of causation and the difficulty that this heterogeneous causation engenders with respect to explaining the whole of nature.

86. Burger appreciates the various reasons to doubt that the separate Ideas qualify as the object of Socrates' 'second sailing' (pp. 144–160). But I do not think that she adequately treats the uncertainties that remain if the object of knowledge is the truth of the beings or, in other words, speeches. Specifically, she sees Socrates' goal as instilling in Cebes a confidence in reason as a safe refuge against the sophists (pp. 153–160). But what remains unclear is why Socrates thinks one should have confidence in reason in light of the recognized uncertainties, why one should *not* abandon it (p. 153). In my view, Socrates shows the ground of his confidence in reason through his articulation of the experience of perplexity in his reply to Simmias and his intellectual autobiography.

87. On this point, see Gadamer (pp. 37–40) and Frede (p. 39).

88. See also *Apology*, 20d6–e2, 21d2–10, 29b3–7. Burger (p. 136) does refer to Socrates' acquisition of the knowledge of ignorance. She states, "Socrates was compelled by the perplexities of the logos to investigate the presuppositions of his own reasoning"(139). My view is that these perplexities themselves, in constituting the relation between humanity and nature, articulate the presuppositions of Socrates' reasoning.

89. Helpful for understanding Socrates' knowledge of ignorance is Bruell, pp. 141–143.

90. In the last chapter of her book, Burger writes: "Socrates/Theseus has been victorious over that monster [the fear of death] thanks to his discovery of the safety of taking refuge in logoi"(p. 213). See also Burger, p. 159. But if the 'second sailing' is equivalent to the *techne* of logos, then it is difficult to see how it can be an alternative to teleology. Moreover, this would leave open the question of the basis of *Socrates'* confidence in recommending this mode of investigation. As I have attempted to show, the uncertainties concerning the philosophic life, evident most vividly in light of the fact of death, pertain equally to Socrates. The question of Socrates' confidence in reason is one that he too must face. I think that he does face this question and that he responds by providing the self-understanding that I have presented.

91. Plato, *Apology*, 20d8.

92. In fact, Kant's view seems closer to Cebes insofar as it is a response to the desire for certainty. See Immanuel Kant, *The Critique of*

Pure Reason trans. N. K. Smith (New York: St. Martin's Press, 1965), pp. 21–22 (B, xvi).

93. Perhaps in order to emphasize the importance of the path rather than the destination, Plato entrusts the elaboration of the view of the whole that follows from Socrates' approach not to Socrates but to the Eleatic Stranger. In the *Sophist*, the issue of Being is investigated with a view to how it must be conceived given the existence in the world of such undeniable aspects of our experience as error, falsehood and, more fundamentally, mind.

94. Gallop, p. 90.

95. Also in support of this point is the suggestion that life has some relation to heat and it can be extinguished by the cooling action of the poison. See Cropsey (pp. 173–174) on the relation of heat and life in the dialogue.

96. Gallop, p. 88.

97. Gallop, p. 90.

98. We should recall that Socrates' first words addressed to the crowd in his cell referred to the wondrous character of an aspect of human existence.

99. Plato, *Sophist*, 237d2–4.

100. Aristotle, *Nicomachean Ethics*, 1095a31–1095b4.

101. See Burger, p. 147.

102. Plato, *Republic*, 523b9–525a2; *Theaetetus*. 154c1–155c5.

103. Dorter (p. 119) sees that Socrates' statement about Atlas is meant to convey the idea that the explanations of the Pre-Socratics "differ only in subtlety and form, not in essence from those of mythology. . . ."

104. The treatment of Being in the *Sophist*, focusing as it does on error and falsehood is an example of an investigation that does not neglect this lesson.

105. Davis, pp. 565–66.

106. At the end of the first proof of immortality, as well as at the end of the last proof, Socrates suggests that *the* premise of intelligibility, that nothing can come from or pass away into nothing, or that everything has a cause, is a matter of assertion rather than demonstration (72a11 and 106c9d8). Contrary to Wiggins (p. 11), Plato does question this fundamental principle of intelligibility.

107. On the importance of this distinction, see Aristotle, *Ethics,* 1095a31–1095b4.

108. So fervent is the concern for these issues that we even fall into conflict over them. Speaking of these issues in the *Euthyphro,* Socrates says:

> Isn't it because we differ about these things and can't come to a sufficient decision about them that we become enemies to each other, whenever we do, both you and I and all other human beings? (*Euthyphro,* 7d2–5)

109. Burnet, p. 4 (note to 58a10).

110. *Ibid.*

111. It might be asked whether such conversations presuppose an answer to precisely that which is in question—whether reason can guide life. But it might be asked in response whether the proponents of faith can maintain their belief through silence, that is, whether a conversation examining belief is not inevitable even if that conversation remains an internal one.

112. See, for example, Nietzsche, *Beyond Good and Evil,* pp. 9–13 (secs. 1–5).

113. This aspect of the *Phaedo* is, however, characteristic of the dialogue form in its portrayal of active cross-questioning and scrutiny of various views, a scrutiny that often ends aporetically. In this light, the dialogue form is inseparable from the teaching it conveys.

114. Nietzsche, *Beyond Good and Evil,* p. 224 (sec. 281).

115. Part One of *Beyond Good and Evil* is entitled "On the Prejudices of Philosophers."

116. In Nietzsche's terms, the issue between Socrates and Nietzsche is which of the two thinkers is the more adept psychologist. Nietzsche, *Beyond Good and Evil*, pp. 31–32 (sec. 23).

117. Its chant-like character is more pronounced in the Greek.

118. Dorter says that Plato nowhere discusses thematically the connection between the intelligibles and purposiveness or good (p. 124). I would say that the teleology section is a discussion of precisely this issue. It is seen that the purpose of the whole, cosmic teleology, is elusive. The subsequent discussion of Socrates' 'second sailing' treats the issue of how philosophy can be justified, how it can be known as a good when The Good is not available. Burger (p. 149) seems to suggest that an investigation of good is required but that Socrates does not undertake this investigation in the *Phaedo*. I think that Socrates does address the issue of good in the way mentioned above, but also he addresses it to the extent that he lays the ground upon which the philosophical life can be thought to be good.

119. References to *phronesis* occur at 65a9, 66a6, 66c5, 66e3, 68a2, 68a7, 68b4, 69a4, 69b3, 69b6, 69c2, 70b4, 79d6, 80d7, 81a5, 94b5, and 118a17. Socrates speaks of *sophia* at 96a7. The relative paucity of references to *sophia* should not obscure that Socrates remains desirous of *sophia*. But the meaning of *sophia* is such that it can appear as *phronesis:* the object of Socratic wisdom is the human situation as it has been defined above. Thus wisdom can seem to be only what can be put to use in order to guide one's life rather than the object of reflection for its own sake. This appearance can be beneficial with respect to Socrates' relations both with the political community and with potential philosophers. First of all, it makes less clear that Socrates was in fact devoted to understanding the nature of all things, to the extent that this is possible. Such devotion puts him in direct opposition to the teachings of the political community that concern the whole. Second, for reasons discussed in the text, preparation is necessary before the potential philosopher can appreciate that the wisdom that is the object of his or her love may consist in those perplexities that Socrates has detailed in the *Phaedo*. Finally, however, by referring to the object of philosophy as *phronesis* in his discussion with these sectarians,

Socrates can move them to apply their philosophic doctrines to their own lives. This is the first step out of the dogma of the sect. On the issues dealt with here, see Bruell, pp. 149–153.

Chapter 5. The End of Socrates

1. It is particularly important to understand the terminology by which Socrates refers to the intelligibles in this final proof. But this is made particularly difficult by the complications (I think, deliberate) in this terminology. I will continue to use the terms *Idea* and *intelligible itself* to refer to the unchanging, incorporeal intelligible. There are at least three entities that we need to keep track of: the concrete thing, the intelligible itself, and an intermediate entity which 'carries' the intelligible itself, and which is either itself a concrete entity or a different sort of intelligible. As I said, Socrates will be ambiguous in his referents and will alter the referent from passage to passage.

2. D. O'Brien, "The Last Argument of Plato's *Phaedo*," *Classical Quarterly* 17–18 (1967, 1968): 199. I found O'Brien's article useful especially as he points out the ongoing ambiguity of essence and existence in the proof. He does not, however, pursue this ambiguity to discern the intention behind it. He ultimately finds the proof valuable insofar as the arguments therein "anticipate to a certain very limited extent Anselm's ontological argument for the existence of God." (O'Brien, p. 199.)

3. Hackforth, p. 164.

4. Burnet (p. 115) recognizes that Socrates here intends a distinction between essential and accidental predication. There is some debate however, as to whether this distinction or the relational aspect of the qualities under consideration is the crucial feature of the passage. O'Brien (p. 200, n.1) holds that the relational aspect is merely incidental with the crucial feature being the distinction between essential and accidental predication. Gallop (p. 193) thinks the relational aspect is most important in allowing for the compresence of opposites. My position is that the distinction between essential and accidental predication is ultimately most important but that the relational aspect of the qualities under consideration contributes to the sharpening of the distinction between thing and the intelligibles themselves, which makes explanation by opposites untenable in explaining essential predication.

5. A useful examination of the meaning of this possibility may be found in F. C. White, "The Compresence of Opposites in *Phaedo* 102," *Classical Quarterly* 27 (1977): 300–311.

6. Klein, *Plato's "Meno,"* p. 116 (emphasis in original).

7. Dorter (p. 219, n.4) does not see the importance of this anthropomorphism, and thus he rejects the translations of Burnet, Hackforth, and Gallop, all of whom preserve the military metaphor.

8. This translation differs from Gallop but agrees with that of Archer-Hind. See also Burnet, p. 116.

9. Plato, *Apology,* 29d1–5. *Meno.* 86b7–c2. *Republic.* 503e1–504a1.

10. The phrase is intended to raise the question of whether what is now being said is in fact simply an extension of the previous argument. See Hackforth, p. 149, n.3

11. The vagueness is evident, for example, at 65d13, 75c9, 76d8–9, 77a4, and 100b6–7.

12. See Klein, *Plato's "Meno,"* p. 126; Dorter, p. 141; and, of course, the title of Burger's book.

13. Dorter (p. 220, n.10) and Gallop (p. 201) reject the notion that the distinction between three and threeness is applied systematically. Gallop writes: "The casual shifting from 'threeness' and 'fiveness' to 'two' and 'four' in parallel contexts suggests that no systematic distinction is intended between the two types of terms." O'Brien and Burger disagree. O'Brien explains the anomalous 'two' by saying that "it is natural enough for Plato's language to become firmer with *elaboration* of his example.'" (P. 218 emphasis in original.)
I think that the problem which 'two' poses for this distinction is answered by Klein, who writes that "only oddness is characteristic of that which is countable as such, while evenness represents something within the realm of numbers, and of everything countable, which goes, as it were, beyond it—something 'other' namely the possibility of unlimited divisibility. . . ." Further on, Klein writes of "the priority of the odd over the even . . . which is based on the fact that the odd imposes a limit on un-

limited divisibility in the form of an indivisible unit." I take this to mean that as between odd and even there exists that difference between what something is and that it is, the odd pertaining to what something is, the limit, and even to that it is, to its being unlimited, unformed as is matter. Thus, Socrates uses 'two' where he also uses threeness as exemplifying this crucial distinction. See Klein, *Greek Mathematical Thought and the Origin of Algebra* (Cambridge: MIT Press, 1968), pp. 57–58, n. 63.

14. See Gallop (pp. 202–205, 235–236) for this change in the argument and the various interpretations and translations of this passage.

15. Dorter, p. 146. O'Brien (p. 201–203) and Gallop (p. 202) agree with Dorter. See also Burnet, p. 119. Hackforth (p. 161–166) considers the entities as immanent forms and translates or mistranslates the passage as if the entities were unambiguously such immanent forms. But Hackforth has trouble fitting the soul into his understanding and finally finds Plato guilty of waffling on the status of the soul. For an account of the proponents and problems of the contending views, see Michael Morris, "Socrates' Last Argument," *Phronesis* 46 (1985): 226–227.

16. It is this further question that Dorter does not adequately address. I should also note that Dorter refers to the Idea as a 'form.'

17. The distinction between numbers considered as multiplicities versus as cognitive wholes which we have already seen in the problem of two can also be seen in the examples Socrates gives just prior to formulating his more sophisticated explanation of causality. See 105a6–b3.

18. See Gallop, p. 209–213; Burger, p. 173.

19. We have seen Socrates reach this conclusion before on a more general level. The heterogeneous senses of being requires the heterogeneous causation which underlies those perplexities that helped to engender Socrates' alteration of philosophy. And the necessity of ontic heterogeneity in the present context is evident in Socrates' abandonment of explanation by opposites, relying instead on causal entities which, combining somehow the intelligible and corporeal, resist being captured by a single definition.

20. See, for example, Gallop, p. 218, and Cropsey, p. 171. Several commentators relate this absence to Socrates' use of the example of snow

in his initial set of examples of the intermediate causal entities. The more obvious example would have been ice. But this unusual example of snow as that which engenders coldness can lead to a consideration of other cold-inducing entities such as the poison that Socrates will soon drink. If life is considered to be a function of heat, then the bearer of death is that which induces coldness. See Cropsey, p. 173–174 and Burger, p. 166. C. Gill ("The Death Of Socrates," *Classical Quarterly* 22 [1973]: 25–28) establishes that, in focusing on the cooling aspect of the poison, Plato was being very selective among the several affects of the poison.

21. As several commentators note, there is a shift in the definition of death from the original separation of body from soul to the perishing of the soul as described in Cebes' objection. The last proof of immortality concludes that "soul does not admit death." Since this conclusion occurs prior to Socrates' 'proof' of the soul's imperishability, death in this instance cannot mean to perish. But the only other definition of death is that it is separation from the body. In saying that soul does not admit death, Socrates could therefore be taken to mean that soul is not separable from body. But this would be to know more about the soul than in fact Socrates claims to know. On the issue of the definitions of death, see Gallop, p. 216, and O'Brien, pp. 229–231.

22. This point is recognized by several commentators. See Gallop, p. 216; Dorter, pp. 151–152; Burger, p. 177; David Keyt, "The Fallacies in *Phaedo* 102a–107b," *Phronesis* 8 (1963): 170–171; Frede, p. 31.

23. Dorter (pp. 154–157) adduces several reasons why he thinks Cebes does not challenge Socrates. He does not offer the reason that I offer in the text. This points to a significant difference between our interpretations. Dorter does not seem to think that Socrates raises as a serious possibility the perishing of the whole. Dorter finds that it is an implicit conclusion (p. 157) of the conjunction of the first and last proofs that the whole is eternal. But insofar as Socrates indicates that cosmological teleology is unavailable, he leaves open the question of the ultimate being of the whole. Dorter does not then appreciate the depth of Socratic questioning and thus misses the problem that the 'second sailing' is intended to confront. I believe that Burger (pp. 184–86) does recognize here the depth of Socratic questioning but her treatment of the issue remains somewhat implicit.

24. Contrary to Dorter (pp. 157–61) and Wiggins (p. 11), Socrates does question the fundamental principle of intelligibility.

25. Dorter (p. 151) says that Socrates' mention of these opposites reminds us of other dimensions of the soul but he does not make clear the importance of this reminder. For a quite different interpretation of Socrates' motives for mentioning these particular opposites, see Burger, p. 176.

26. Given that this is the case, it could be said that Cebes tacitly recognizes the distinction between immortality and imperishability. Compare Burger (p. 176–177) and Dorter (pp. 154–157).

Burger and Dorter recognize that Socrates does not demonstrate personal immortality of the soul. But Burger (pp. 219–220, n.12) writes of Dorter that he thinks "Socrates does demonstrate . . . a meaningful sense of immortality, whose subject is the 'world-soul' of which all individual souls are portions" (pp. 44, 157). I share Burger's view that such a demonstration would not escape the problems that attend the proof of the immortality of an individual soul. Either demonstration is more than Socrates claims to know.

27. Dorter (pp. 159–161) gives a very different explanation of the obscurities of the passage, as well as of the argument as a whole. He claims that Socrates' purpose in presenting the proofs of immortality is to convince the interlocutors not to fear death since this lack of fear is somehow a basis for "moral behaviour." In saying this, Dorter seems to assume that the only remedy for the fear of death is a proof of immortality. Moreover, if Socrates' goal is merely to "convince," he ought to have stopped the argument at the point at which Cebes agreed that the soul is immortal. Dorter is not clear concerning the specific moral behavior to which the lack of the fear of death would contribute. Nor is he clear as to why we should think that Socrates is motivated by this goal.

28. Griswold, p. 141.

29. Aristotle begins this scientific consideration of the myth in his *Meteorology,* 355b3–356a34. See also Paul Friedlaender, *Plato* vol. I, trans. Hans Meyerhoff (Princeton: Princeton University Press, 1969), pp. 261–273; J. S. Morrison, "The Shape of the Earth in Plato's *Phaedo,*" *Phronesis* 4 (1959): 101–119; T. G. Rosenmeyer, "The Shape of the Earth in the

Phaedo: A Rejoinder," *Phronesis* 4 (1959): 71–72. Compare Hackforth, pp. 172–173, and Dorter, pp. 164–165.

30. Plato, *Phaedrus,* 248e5–b3; *Republic,* 615a5–b2.

31. See Burnet (p. 126) on the possible reference here to the sacrifices to Hecate.

32. On Socrates' reference to Glaucus in this passage, see Burnet, p. 150. For a more recent treatment, see Diskin Clay, "The Art of Glaukus (Plato's *Phaedo* 108d4–9)," *American Journal of Philology* (Summer 1985): 230–236. Clay's interesting interpretation concludes that Glaucus is the figure who threw himself into the sea and became a god. Glaucus, according to Clay, serves as an image of the transcendence of the mortal. In my interpretation, this Glaucus who is always represented as encumbered by all sorts of accretions (*Republic,* 611d) would be an image of the human soul for which transcendence does not lie in the purity desired by the genuine philosophers. Along these same lines, I would see the importance of the similar phrases—'the true or genuine earth' and the 'genuine philosophers'—as lying in the different focus of the two phrases. An alteration of focus has occurred in the course of the discussion on Socrates' last day such that Socrates speaks now of the earth in an exalted manner rather than of the genuine philosopher whose aspiration is to abandon the earth.

33. On this point, see Griswold, p. 262, n.26.

34. Plato, *Phaedrus,* 249c1–7, 47e8–248a3.

35. Several commentators see a kinship between the levels of existence in the present myth and the *Republic*'s allegory of the cave. For a concise statement of this view, see Clay, p. 230–236. I share Dorter's view (p. 221, n.4) in thinking that the differences between the two presentations are what is important.

36. Socrates also uses the phrase at 90c5 and 96b1 with reference to the uncertainty of understanding, first with reference to the controversialists and next with reference to his own confusion. Perhaps nature lends more support to these notions of flux than Socrates explicitly indicates.

37. See Burnet, p. 135; Dorter, p. 166; Burger, p. 194.

38. Cropsey, p. 172–173.

39. Homer, *Illiad*, viii, 14–16.

40. Dorter, p. 170–174.

41. Plato, *Republic*, 615d2–616a6.

42. Plato, *Republic*, 617e1.

43. Socrates refers to these pleasures after having made the relatively moderate statement (in the context of the *Phaedo*) that the pleasures of the body do more harm than good (114e1–3).

44. Several elements of the dialogue to which Socrates had bidden farewell now return. These concerns, related to the body, cannot be resisted or ignored forever.

45. On Socrates' self-regard, see *Apology*, 34d1–35b10.

46. Thus, I agree with Nussbaum's statement that "the *Phaedo* . . . is a clear case of Platonic anti-tragedy," but for different reasons than the ones she offers. (Nussbaum, p. 385.)

47. Sophocles, *Oedipus at Colonus*, 565.

48. Again, this points to the practical impetus for the philosophic consideration of human affairs. In light of the character of Socratic philosophy, it becomes necessary for the philosopher to take seriously political matters for his or her own protection. The core of philosophic activity will involve examination of the same urgent concerns that animate the life of the political community. But as the life and death of Socrates testify, the purpose of the philosopher's examination runs athwart the purpose of the political community. It is clearly in the philosopher's interest to find a way to ameliorate this conflict, to understand the way in which his or her good might, as far as possible, be made compatible with the good of the political community. The classic attempts in this regard are Plato's *Laws* and Aristotle's *Nicomachean Ethics*. In these documents, it is evident that the philosopher can become a true friend to the political community in protecting its central understanding of nobility from intellectual subversion.

It is important to see, however, that the need for philosophy to become politic arises, or at least becomes acute, when it is seen that philosophy, for the sake of its *theoretical* defense, must engage in the study of human affairs.

49. Plato, *Apology,* 29c6–d6, 33c4.

50. In the fact that Plato entrusts to the Athenian Stranger rather than to Socrates the task of articulating a practicable regime in which the philosopher could flourish, there is perhaps an implicit critique of Socrates for being too contemptuous of conventional piety.

51. Socrates utters his last words as the coldness reaches "the region beneath his abdomen"—that is, his groin (118a5). Plato did not have to associate Socrates' last words with this area of the body because it is "when the coldness reached his *heart* [that] he would be gone" (118a3–4, emphasis added). Moreover, there was a "brief time" between the time that he last spoke and when he died (118a11–12). By having Socrates speak for the last time at just this moment, perhaps Plato intends to connect desire or eros and speech. Lending some support to this conjecture is that Plato describes Socrates as uncovering his face before uttering his last words (118a6). This same movement of Socrates covering and uncovering his face occurs in the *Phaedrus,* where Socrates covers his face while delivering a speech depreciating eros. He uncovers it only when recanting his speech, thus associating the movement of uncovering his face with the praise of eros. In the present passage, then, there is a suggestion of what Socrates left unsaid in his consideration of Anaxagoras—namely, his true reason for speaking (98c2–99b2). The connection lies, perhaps, in the relation between eros and speaking.

52. Plato, *Apology,* 38a2–3.

53. Burnet (p. 147) and Bluck (p. 143, n.1) hold that, with his last words, Socrates is thanking the god for his release from the "sickness" that is life. See Nietzsche, *Twilight of the Idols,* "The Problem of Socrates," p. 473 (sec. 1) and *The Gay Science,* p. 272 (sec. 340). Cropsey (pp. 173–74) suggests that Socrates' last words are "a mark of his gratitude to the great druggist for a painless death through cooling numbness."

54. Nietzsche, *Birth of Tragedy,* pp. 81–93 (secs. 12–14).

55. Nietzsche, *Birth of Tragedy*, p. 42 (sec. 3).

56. See Nietzsche's depreciation of happiness in, for example, *Beyond Good and Evil*, pp. 109, 136 (secs. 198, 212). This work, which begins with Nietzsche's explicit opposition to Plato, culminates in an examination of what is noble.

Chapter 6. Conclusion

1. Nietzsche, *Beyond Good and Evil*, pp. 12–14 (secs. 5 and 6).

2. Nietzsche, *Beyond Good and Evil*, p. 60 (sec. 46).

3. Consider all that Richard Rorty, a contemporary Nietzschean, claims to know. He knows both that it is "self-deception" to think "that we possess a deep, hidden, metaphysically significant nature which makes us 'irreducibly' different from inkwells or atoms." He knows also that we cannot understand the essence of knowledge. Rorty, *Philosophy and the Mirror of Nature*, pp. 373, 392. Elsewhere, Rorty asserts that "there is no natural order of justification of beliefs, no predestined outline for argument to trace." Rorty, "The Priority of Democracy to Philosophy" in *The Virginia Statute for Religious Freedom: Its Evolution and Its Consequences in American History*, ed. M. Peterson and R. Vaughen (Cambridge: Cambridge University Press, 1988), p. 271. Rorty's knowledge is not only negative. He does not hesitate to speak dehumanization. *Philosophy and the Mirror of Nature*, p. 377.

BIBLIOGRAPHY

Archer-Hind, R. (ed.). *The "Phaedo" of Plato*. London: Macmillan, 1894.

Aristotle. *De Generatione et Corruptione*. Translated with notes by C. J. F. Williams. (Clarendon Aristotle Series). Oxford: Clarendon Press, 1982.

———. *Metaphysics*. Translated with commentaries and glossary by Hippocrates G. Apostle. Grinnell, Iowa: The Peripatetic Press, 1979.

———. *Nicomachean Ethics*. Translated by H. Rackham. (Loeb Classical Library Series). Cambridge: Harvard University Press, 1968.

———. *Physics*. Translated with commentaries and glossary by Hippocrates G. Apostle. Grinnell, Iowa: The Peripatetic Press, 1980.

———. *Politics*. Translated by H. Rackham. (Loeb Classical Library Series). Cambridge: Harvard University Press, 1967.

Ackrill, J. L. "Anamnesis in the *Phaedo:* Remarks on 73c–75c," in *Exegesis and Argument, Phronesis*. Supplementary volume I (1973): 175–195.

Arendt, Hannah. *On Revolution*. New York: Viking Press, 1965.

Benardete, Seth. *The Being of the Beautiful: Plato's "Theaetetus," "Sophist," and "Statesman"*. Translated with commentary. Chicago: University of Chicago Press, 1984.

Bernstein, Richard. "One Step Forward, Two Steps Backward: Richard Rorty on Liberal Democracy and Philosophy," *Political Theory* 15 (November 1987): 538–563.

Bloom, Allan. *The Republic of Plato*. Translated with interpretive essay. New York: Basic Books, 1968.

Bluck, R. S. *Plato's "Phaedo"*. Translated with notes. Indianapolis: Library of Liberal Arts, 1982.

Bolotin, David. "The Life of Philosophy and the Immortality of the Soul: An Introduction to Plato's *Phaedo*," *Ancient Philosophy*. (1987): 39–56.

Brandwood, Leonard. *A Word Index Guide to Plato*. Leeds: W. S. Maney and Son, Ltd., 1976.

Brentlinger, John. "Incomplete Predicates and the Two-World Theory of the *Phaedo*," *Phronesis* (1972): 61–79.

Brickhouse, Thomas C., and Nicholas D. Smith. *Socrates on Trial*. Princeton: Princeton University Press, 1989.

Bruell, Christopher. "Strauss on Xenophon's Socrates," *Political Science Reviewer* 13 (Fall 1983): 99–153.

Burger, Ronna. *The "Phaedo": A Platonic Labyrinth*. New Haven: Yale University Press, 1984.

Burkert, Walter. *Greek Religion*. Translated by John Raffan. Cambridge: Harvard University Press, 1985.

Burnet, John. *Plato's "Phaedo"*. Edited with notes. Oxford: Clarendon Press, 1980.

Castaneda, Hector-Neri. "Plato's *Phaedo* Theory of Relations," *Journal of Philosophic Logic* i (1972): 467–480.

———. "Plato's Relations, Not Essences or Accidents, at *Phaedo* 102b2–d2," *Canadian Journal of Philosophy* (1978): 39–55.

Cicero. *Tusculan Disputations*. Translated by J. E. King. New York: J. P. Putnam's Sons, 1927.

Clay, Diskin. "The Art of Glaukus (Plato's *Phaedo* 108d4–9)," *American Journal of Philology* (Summer 1985): 230–236.

Crombie, I. M. *An Examination of Plato's Doctrines*. London: Routledge and Kegan Paul, 1962.

Cropsey, Joseph. *Political Philosophy and the Issues of Politics*. Chicago: University of Chicago Press, 1977.

———."The Dramatic End of Plato's Socrates," *Interpretation* 14 (May and September, 1986): 155–175.

Dannhauser, Werner J. *Nietzsche's View of Socrates*. Ithaca: Cornell University Press, 1974.

Davis, Michael. "Socrates' Pre-Socratism: Some Remarks on the Structure of Plato's *Phaedo*," *Review of Metaphysics* 33 (March 1980): 559–577.

———. "Plato and Nietzsche on Death: An Introduction to Plato's *Phaedo*," *Ancient Philosophy* (1980): 69–80.

Dorter, Kenneth. *Plato's "Phaedo": An Interpretation*. Toronto: University of Toronto Press, 1982.

Frede, Dorothea. "The Final Proof of Immortality of the Soul in Plato's *Phaedo* 102a–107a," *Phronesis* 23 (1978): 27–41.

Friedlaender, Paul. *Plato*. 3 volumes translated by Hans Meyerhoff. Princeton: Princeton University Press, 1958–1969.

Gadamer, H. G. *Dialogue and Dialectic: Eight Hermeneutical Studies on Plato*. Translated by P. Christopher Smith. New Haven: Yale University Press, 1980.

Gallop, David. *"Phaedo."* Translated with notes. Oxford: Clarendon Press, 1983.

Gill, C. "The Death of Socrates," *Classical Quarterly* 22 (1973): 25–28.

Gooch, Paul William. "Plato's Antapodosis Argument for the Soul's Immortality: *Phaedo* 70–72," *Seventh Inter-American Congress of Philosophy Proceedings* 7 (1967): 239–244.

———. "The Relation between Wisdom and Virtue in *Phaedo* 69a6–c3," *The Journal of the History of Philosophy* 12 (1974): 153–159.

Gorman, Peter. *Pythagoras: A Life*. London: Routledge and Kegan Paul, 1979.

Gosling, J. B. "Similarity in *Phaedo* 73b seq.," *Phronesis* 10 (1965): 151–161.

Griswold, Charles, Jr. *Self-Knowledge in Plato's "Phaedrus."* New Haven: Yale University Press, 1986.

———. "Style and Philosophy: The Case of Plato's Dialogues," *Monist* 63 (1980): 530–546.

Gulley, Norman. "Plato's Theory of Recollection," *Classical Quarterly* 54 (1954): 194–213.

Guthrie, W. K. C. *Orpheus and Greek Religion*. London: Metheun and Co., 1952.

Hackforth, R. *Plato's "Phaedo."* Translated with commentary. Cambridge: Cambridge University Press, 1972.

Heidegger, Martin. *Basic Writings*. Edited by David Farrell Krell. New York: Harper and Row, 1977.

———. *Introduction to Metaphysics*. Translated by Ralph Manheim. New Haven: Yale University Press, 1959.

———. *Nietzsche*. Vol. IV. Translated by Frank Capuzzi. Edited by David Farrell Krell. San Francisco: Harper and Row, 1983.

Hicken, W. F. "*Phaedo* 93a11–94b3," *Classical Quarterly* NS4 (1954): 16–22.

Hyland, Drew. "Why Plato Wrote Dialogues," *Philosophy and Rhetoric*. 1 (1968): 38–50

Irwin, Terence. *Plato's Moral Theory*. Oxford: Clarendon Press, 1982.

Jonas, Hans. *The Phenomenon of Life: Toward a Philosophical Biology*. Chicago: University of Chicago Press, 1982.

Keyt, David. "The Fallacies in *Phaedo* 102a–107b," *Phronesis* 8 (1963): 167–172.

Kirk, G. S., J. E. Raven, and M. Schofield. *The Presocratic Philosophers.* Cambridge: Cambridge University Press, 1983.

Kirwan, Christopher. "Plato and Relativity," *Phronesis* (1974): 112–129.

Klein, Jacob. *A Commentary on Plato's "Meno."* Chapel Hill: University of North Carolina Press, 1965.

————. *Greek Mathematical Thought and the Origin of Algebra.* Translated by Eva Brann. Cambridge: MIT Press, 1968.

Morgan, Michael L. "Sense-Perception and Recollection in the *Phaedo*," *Phronesis* 29 (1984): 237–251.

Morris, Michael. "Socrates' Last Argument," *Phronesis* 30 (1985): 223–248.

Morrison, J. S. "The Shape of the Earth in Plato's *Phaedo*," *Phronesis* (1959): 101–119

Nehamas, Alexander. "Predication and Forms of Opposites in the *Phaedo*," *Review of Metaphysics* 26 (1973): 461–491.

Nietzsche, Friedrich. *Beyond Good and Evil.* Translated by Walter Kaufmann. New York: Vintage Books, 1966.

————. *The Birth of Tragedy.* Translated by Walter Kaufmann. New York: Vintage Books, 1967.

————. *Twilight of the Idols.* Translated by Walter Kaufmann. In *The Portable Nietzsche.* New York: Viking Press, 1968.

Nichols, Mary P. *Socrates and the Political Community: An Ancient Debate.* Albany: State University of New York Press, 1987.

Nussbaum, Martha C. *The Fragility of Goodness.* Cambridge: Cambridge University Press, 1986.

O'Brien, David. "The Last Argument of Plato's *Phaedo*," *Classical Quarterly* NS 17 (1967): 198–231, and 18 (1968): 95–106.

Otto, Walter. *The Homeric Gods*. New York: Pantheon, 1954.

Owen, G. E. L. "A Proof in the 'Peri Ideon' ," in *Studies in Plato's Metaphysics*. Edited by R. E. Allen. London: Routledge and Kegan Paul, 1965.

Pangle, Thomas. *The Laws of Plato*. Translated with interpretive essay. New York: Basic Books, 1980.

Patterson, Robert. *Plato on Immortality*. University Park, PA: Pennsylvania State University Press, 1965.

Plass, Paul. "Socrates' Method of Hypothesis in the *Phaedo*," *Phronesis* (1960): 103–114.

Plato. *Platonis Opera*. 5 vols. Edited by John Burnet. Oxford: Clarendon Press, 1979.

Rist, J. M. "Equals and Intermediaries in Plato," *Phronesis* (1964): 27–37.

Robinson, Richard. *Plato's Earlier Dialectic*. Oxford: Clarendon Press, 1953.

Robinson, T. M. "*Phaedo* 70c: An Error and an Explanation," *Dialogue* 8 (June 1969): 124–125.

———. *Plato's Psychology*. Toronto: University of Toronto Press, 1970.

Rorty, Richard. *Philosophy and the Mirror of Nature*. Princeton: Princeton University Press, 1979.

———. "Pragmatism, Relativism, Irrationalism." In *Consequences of Pragmatism*. Minneapolis: University of Minneapolis Press, 1982.

———. "Solidarity or Objectivity." In *Post-Analytic Philosophy*. Edited by John Rajchman and Cornel West. New York: Columbia University Press, 1985.

————. "The Priority of Democracy to Philosophy." In *The Virginia Statute for Religious Freedom: Its Evolution and Consequences in American History*. Edited by M. Peterson and R. Vaughan. Cambridge: Cambridge University Press, 1988.

Rosen, Stanley. *Plato's "Symposium."* New Haven: Yale University Press, 1968.

Rosenmayer, T. G. "The Shape of the Earth in the *Phaedo:* A Rejoinder," *Phronesis* 4 (1959): 71–72.

Salkever, Stephen G. *Finding the Mean: Theory and Practice in Aristotelian Political Philosophy*. Princeton, NJ: Princeton University Press, 1990.

Sallis, John. *Being and Logos: The Way of the Platonic Dialogue*. Second Edition. Atlantic Highlands, NJ: Humanities Press, 1986.

Shipton, K. M. W. "A Good Second-Best: *Phaedo* 96ff.," *Phronesis* 24 (1979): 33–54.

Sophocles. *Oedipus at Colonus*. Translated by Robert Fitzgerald. Chicago: University of Chicago Press, 1954.

Stenzel, Julius. *Plato's Method of Dialectic*. Oxford: Clarendon Press, 1940.

Stewart, D. "Socrates' Last Bath," *Journal of the History of Philosophy* 10 (July 1972): 253–259.

Strauss, Leo. *The City and Man*. Chicago: University of Chicago Press, 1977.

————. *Persecution and the Art of Writing*. Westport, CT: Greenwood Press, 1973.

————. *On Tyranny*. Ithaca: Cornell University Press, 1968.

————. *Socrates and Aristophanes*. Chicago: University of Chicago Press, 1980.

————. *Xenophon's Socratic Discourse*. Ithaca: Cornell University Press, 1970.

———. *Xenophon's Socrates*. Ithaca: Cornell University Press, 1972.

———. *The Argument and Action of Plato's "Laws."* Chicago: University of Chicago Press, 1975.

———. *Political Philosophy: Six Essays by Leo Strauss*. Edited by Hilail Gildin. Indianapolis: Bobbs-Merrill, 1975.

———. *Philosophy and Law*. Translated by Fred Baumann. Philadelphia: Jewish Publication Society, 1987.

Taylor, A. E. *Plato: The Man and His Work*. New York: Dial Press, 1929.

Taylor, C. C. W. "The Arguments in the *Phaedo* Concerning the Thesis that the Soul is a *Harmonia*." In *Essays in Ancient Greek Philosophy*, vol. II. Edited by John P. Anton and Anthony Preus. Albany, NY: State University of New York Press, 1983.

———. "Forms as Causes in the *Phaedo*," *Mind* 73 (1969): 45–59.

Vlastos, Gregory. "Reasons and Causes in the *Phaedo*." In *Plato: A Collection of Critical Essays I*. Edited by Gregory Vlastos. Garden City, NY: Doubleday, 1970.

Wedin, Michael. "αὐτὰ τὰ ἴσα and the Argument at *Phaedo* 74b7–c5," *Phronesis* (1977): 191–205.

Weiss, Roslyn. "The Right Exchange: *Phaedo* 69a6–c3," *Ancient Philosophy* (1987): 57–66.

West, Thomas. *Plato's "Apology" of Socrates*. Translated with interpretive essay. Ithaca: Cornell University Press, 1979.

White, F. C. "The Compresence of Opposites in *Phaedo* 102," *Classical Quarterly* 27, No. 1 (1977): 303–311.

Wiggins, David. "Teleology and the Good in Plato's *Phaedo*." In *Oxford Studies in Ancient Philosophy*, vol. IV. Oxford: Clarendon Press, 1986.

INDEX

Theseus, 13, 25, 30–32, 139, 153,
177, 187n.12
Thing, 119–120; as generated by opposites, 53–55
Truth, 26, 58, 61, 134, 142
Tragic character of human life, 26, 31,
149, 171–172, 173–178

Unnamed interlocutor, 151–153

Virtue, 106; demotic and political,
83; genuine versus sham, 45–46;
Vlastos, Gregory, 207nn.39, 43,
208n.45, 209n.56, 211nn.68

War, 36–37, 41
Wedin, M., 199n.40

White, F. C., 218n.5
Wiggins, David, 209n.56, 215n.106
Wisdom, 45, 46, 109, 207n.36; human, 31–32, 40, 92, 130–131,
135–145 passim, 175, 180; pure,
3–4, 9, 10, 28, 29, 34, 36, 40, 68,
72, 131, 139, 175, 194n.78; *sophia*
versus *phronesis*, 5, 144–145,
216–217n.119
Wolfe, Julian, 196n.10
Wonder, 16, 19, 108, 112, 131, 133,
188n.19, 214n.98

Xanthippe, 18, 19
Xenophon, 183n.2

Zeus, 19, 35, 112, 169, 170
Zuckert, Catherine, 183n.2